ADJACENCIES

MINORITY WRITING IN CANADA

ESSAY SERIES 49

Guernica Editions Inc. acknowledges the support of
The Canada Council for the Arts.
Guernica Editions Inc. acknowledges the support of
the Ontario Arts Council.
Guernica Editions Inc. acknowledges the Government of Ontario through
the Ontario Media Development Corporation's Ontario Book Initiative.
Guernica Editions Inc. acknowledges the financial support
of the Government of Canada through the Book Publishing Industry
Development Program (BPIDP).
Guernica Editions Inc. acknowledges the support of Université de Montréal
for this publication.

ADJACENCIES

MINORITY WRITING IN CANADA

EDITED BY DOMENIC A. BENEVENTI,
LICIA CANTON AND LIANNE MOYES

WITH AN INTRODUCTION BY SHERRY SIMON

GUERNICA

TORONTO · BUFFALO · CHICAGO · LANCASTER (U.K.)

2004

Lianne Moyes, Licia Canton, Domenic Beneventi, Guest editors
Guernica Editions Inc.
P.O. Box 117, Station P, Toronto (ON), Canada M5S 2S6
2250 Military Road, Tonawanda, N.Y. 14150-6000 U.S.A.

Distributors:
University of Toronto Press Distribution,
5201 Dufferin Street, Toronto, (ON), Canada M3H 5T8
Gazelle Book Services, White Cross Mills, High Town,
Lancaster LA1 1XS U.K.
Independent Publishers Group,
814 N. Franklin Street, Chicago, Il. 60610 U.S.A.

First edition.
Printed in Canada.

Legal Deposit — Fourth Quarter
National Library of Canada
Library of Congress Catalog Card Number: 2002114650

National Library of Canada Cataloguing in Publication
Adjacencies : minority writing in Canada
Lianne Moyes, Licia Canton,
Domenic A. Bevenenti, editors
(Essay series : 49)
ISBN 1-55071-167-9
1. Canadian literature — Minority authors –
History and criticism.
I. Canton, Licia. II. Moyes, Lianne.
III. Beneventi, Domenic.
IV. Series: Essays series (Toronto, Ont.) ; 49.
PS8089.5.M55A35 2002   C810.9'8   C2002-905353-6
PR9188.2.M55A35 2002

Contents

Acknowledgements

We would like to thank Amaryll Chanady, Joseph Pivato and Pasquale Verdicchio for writing letters in support of the conference which led to this publication, as well as Antonio D'Alfonso for bringing this publication to fruition. We would also like to acknowledge the contribution of the following people in the Département d'études anglaises at the Université de Montréal: Robert Martin, Michelle Hamelin Braun and other members of the office staff, and the English Graduate Students' Society.

We wish to thank the participants of "The Third Solitude: Canadian Minority Writing" Conference, and in particular the contributors to this collection. Special thanks go to Austin Cooke (Canadian Heritage), Domenic Cusmano (Cusmano Communication), Angelo Soares, Nancy Roussy and Nabeela Sheikh.

We gratefully acknowledge the Canada Council, Canadian Heritage, the Social Sciences and Humanities Research Council of Canada, the Association of Canadian Studies, and the Université de Montréal for their financial assistance.

We could not have completed this project without the unconditional support and encouragement of our families.

Preface

The essays collected in this volume provide engaging and thought-provoking responses to questions we posed in establishing the thematic and theoretical framework for "The Third Solitude: Canadian Minority Writing," a conference held at Université de Montréal in March 1998. The conference brought together established and new scholars who discussed writing from a range of cultural communities and intellectual positions, as well as several authors who read from their work, including Jeannette Armstrong, Benet Davetian, Marisa De Francheschi, Hiromi Goto, Makeda Silvera and Pasquale Verdicchio. This collection, which elaborates on some of the heated discussions at the conference, provides a forum in which academics working in both English and French address the intersections between ethnicity and literature from a range of critical and interdisciplinary perspectives including feminist criticism, comparative literature, psychoanalysis, cinema, cultural studies, history, philosophy, gender studies, native studies, and post-colonial studies.

If it is generally recognized that minority/ethnic writing has enjoyed more visibility in recent years, to some extent shifting the focus of literary debate from the "centre" of Canadian letters to its "peripheries" – indeed, unsettling the very distinction "centre" – "periphery" – what does such recognition mean for the ethnic writer working today? What role do critics, small presses, readings, conferences, and critical volumes such as this one play in constructing a cohesive category of "Canadian minority writing" or "Canadian ethnic literature" or, for that matter, "Icelandic-Canadian writing," "Italian-Canadian writing," or any number of other hyphenated literatures which help constitute our patchwork national identity? What issues emerge when a writer labels herself or himself an "ethnic writer" rather than a "Canadian one?" Must such a writer necessarily speak to and of the experiences of his or her community? How does s/he do justice to the complexity of her/his history and identity prior to hyphenation? And is it possible to speak of an "ethnic literature" when that literature is increasingly being produced by an acculturated third or fourth generation that no longer speaks the heritage language, one whose ties to the country of origin are often ambiguous, tenuous, and markedly self-conscious?

The construction of a community of writers who explore different styles, histories, and thematic concerns into a cohesive category – into something that might be called "minority writing in Canada" – is a daunting and problematic proposition. However, as this volume attests, such an effort offers a glimpse of the productive tensions which emerge in the interface between cultures, in the relations of adjacency.

Domenic A. Beneventi
Licia Canton
Lianne Moyes

Introduction

"Land to Light On?"

Sherry Simon

There comes a moment when gradual changes take a decisive turn and suddenly become pieces of a new reality. Such a turn occurred for me – and I suspect for many observers of Canadian literature – with the publication in 1996 of the anthology *Making a Difference*. The 500-odd pages of this volume, edited by Smaro Kamboureli and subtitled "Canadian Multicultural Literature" made a strong statement. They showed that much of the most innovative and energetic writing in Canada is today by minority writers.

The very force of the demonstration made the anthology into something of a paradox. The variety and energy of the writing in *Making a Difference* suggested that there was perhaps no particular need to showcase "multiculturalism," that the work could well have been presented quite simply as "new Canadian writing" or, in many cases, "writing concerned with issues of identity." There is a kind of discomfort which comes in attaching writers to their biographical origins. And, as Smaro Kamboureli made clear in her sensitive introduction, writers "from" a particular community are not necessarily "of" that community.

The essays in this volume can be seen as taking up from the paradoxes of *Making a Difference*. They engage with many of the tensions which Kamboureli so deftly sketched out in her introduction and which she allowed to run openly throughout the volume. The no-

tion of "multicultural" or "minority" writing allows
Kamboureli to produce a volume which has a monu-
mental function. It provides a vigorous display of rich
and innovative writing. On the other hand, Kamboureli
struggles to keep "minority writing" unstable and open
to difference. She emphasizes the separate histories which
have minoritized cultural groups in Canada, reminding
us of shifting economies of difference: the racism which
made publishing initially difficult for Dionne Brand or
Lee Maracle, the runaway international success of
Michael Ondaatje.

In short, Kamboureli confirms the strength of "minority writing," at the same time as she maintains the
openness of the notion itself. This is a critical stance
that refuses easy categorizations, both literary and sociopolitical. It includes the assumption that minority writing is no longer to be automatically equated with
marginality. In fact, as the anthology itself demonstrates,
"the writing of difference" is moving closer to the centre
of the literary landscape. These shifts emphasize the need
to re-explore the tensions pulsing through conceptions
of literary difference, to re-examine the minor.

Many of the contributions to this volume begin with
a recognition of these ongoing shifts and the need to
revise simple ideas of difference. As they confront and
complexify issues of minority writing, they open into
new zones of critical investigation. Many of them con-
verge in highlighting what is surely the most vivid aspect of contemporary writing: the ways in which identity
issues are stimulating the invention of new forms.

Certainly this is one of the strongest impressions one
gets from reading the work of authors like Fred Wah,
Daphne Marlatt, Kristjana Gunnars, Di Brandt, Daniel
David Moses, Evelyn Lau, Hiromi Goto, Antonio
D'Alfonso, Robert Majzels, Aritha van Herk, Michael
Ondaatje or Dionne Brand, many of whom were an-

thologized by Kamboureli. They are among the Canadian writers who have most effectively experimented with literary form and challenged the constraints of language.

The work of Dionne Brand is immensely rich in this regard. Using all the resources of language – rhythm, accent, line, vocabulary – Brand continually forces the boundaries of meaning. Consider for a moment the title of her recent book of poetry, *Land to Light On*. "To light," the dictionary says, means "to fall and settle on a surface, as a bird or snowflake" or "to have a particular place of incidence or arrival." The title could then be read as a wish ("I want . . ."), an invitation ("Would you like?"), perhaps even a promise ("You shall have . . . a land to light on.") But inside the book, Brand spins a different cast on the phrase. "I'm giving up on land to light on," she says, and indeed the poems are heavy with loss: of political ideals, of roads un-taken.

But what is this land? It's not really land, says Brand, "it is the same as fog and mist and figures and lines and erasable thoughts, it is buildings and governments and toilets and front door mats and typewriter shops . . . It's paper, paper, maps. Maps that get wet and rinse out" (47). It is "foolish borders" that she's giving up on (48), what land becomes when it is transformed into territory. And so Brand's title stands as a complex play of meanings, where the brightly illuminated natural landscape meets the grey fog of the city, where the misery of the migrant meets the well-ordered metropolis, where movement and stasis clash like waves. Her poems move through the paradoxes of identity, from the blazing certainties of revolution to the melancholy of snowy solitude.

Brand's writing is an especially powerful example of the ways in which language and literary forms are made to tremble, to receive the shock of difference and the hesitations of doubt. Her title, in troubling the relationship between language and land, introduces us to the double themes of language and of space that run throughout this volume. By pushing literary forms to their limits, the language of minority writing reshapes our relationship to home. It emphasizes the ambiguous nature of contiguity: the power of space (and of language) to both join and to separate. The overriding force of "adjacencies" is to emphasize the spatial dimension of minor writing, the vocabularies which write and rewrite migrant communities into the spaces of the city and the landscape of the country, the words of minority writers which position them with, against, or simply beside their own communities. Spatial relationships tend to be interpreted as affective ones. "Against," for instance, has a neutral spatial sense but also a meaning of antagonism. *Contre* in French carries an even wider range of meanings: to hold someone "against" you is to hold them "close." Spatial relations enter into shifting dynamics, and differences become woven into fabrics of history and belonging.

The conjunction of writing and space is made particularly evident in the contributions by Domenic Beneventi and by Lianne Moyes. Beneventi identifies the dimension of space as crucial to the rewriting of urban experience from a minority perspective. He uses the example of Italo-Canadian writers to show how there is no "single national territory," no "spatial immanence" onto which one can map a homogeneous idea of culture. The ongoing reorganization of urban space which is a corollary of immigration, the testing of spatial boundaries that runs through Italian-Canadian writing, defines immigrant spaces as "heterotopias," spaces whose meanings are ambiguous and contradictory.

Robert Mazjels' novel, *City of Forgetting*, discussed by Lianne Moyes, stands as a signal project of spatial reconfiguration, where the city is transformed into a tangle of trajectories along which characters wander and occasionally meet. Mazjels' city is an anxious space where the trope of cultural migrancy is literally translated into the idiom of homelessness. Majzels' Montreal is not one made up of recognizable communities, but of solitary exiles erring through a hyper-defined urban space and through the past, dramatizing the failure of modernity's ideals. Juxtaposing fragments of texts drawn from different discursive fields, the novel uses intertextuality as another form of homelessness. All the characters are strangers, all battle with exclusion and marginalization. Their battlefield stretches far into the many seedbeds of cultural identity: Hollywood cinema and popular music (through Rudy Valentino and Suzy Creamcheez), architectural form (the high modernism of Le Corbusier), revolutionary ideals (Che Guevara), myth (Clytæmnestra and Lady Macbeth), and epic history (de Maisonneuve).

Majzels' novel raises provocative questions about the definition and intent of minor/minority writing. His is "minor" writing, according to Moyes, which is not "minority writing" belonging to any "third" culture symmetrical with the first two. Preoccupied with questions of identity, the novel "stages intertextual encounters which de-idealize modernity's tropes of homelessness and otherness, foreground processes of colonization and hybridization, expose the lie of universals . . . and map the intersections between cultural, sexual and gender differences." The complex architecture of the book, its deliberate fragmentation, means that there is no centre to the novel. There is no home identity, unless it is the public space of Mount Royal, which the characters occupy as squatters. In other words, there is no central cultural subject in Majzels' novel against which the "others" define themselves.

Mazjels' novel is to be read in the context of his

efforts to reframe English as a vehicle of "minor" writing in Quebec. Like Gail Scott and Erin Mouré, writers who also choose to live in francophone Montreal and write in English, who want to feel the grain of language bristling against otherness, feel their script in dissonance with the street, Majzels uses the distance between languages as a means of questioning the very structure of meaning. Allying themselves with the avant-garde strategies of modernism, their writing engages in a spiral of productive interactions which gives the strongest sense to translation as an activity through which one puts the words of another to creative use. They challenge the common sense communities of English, arguing that English writing in Quebec can only be minor if it is connected to a strong francophone culture and is marked by an intense self-consciousness, by a suspicion of form.

Language issues also figure prominently in the discussion of Aritha van Herk by Christl Verduyn, of Marguerite A. Primeau by Pamela Sing, and of Italian-Canadian novels by Licia Canton. Verduyn's discussion of Aritha van Herk's "lost" and "frozen" tongue opens onto the troubled territory of loss. The discovery and mastery of English for van Herk was gained at the cost of Dutch, but these two experiences were melded into a "pact with fiction." The place of Dutch in van Herk's writing remains "irrevocably lost and eternally present," just as the Dutch language "had rested in my head somewhere like a still pod, waiting to blossom, waiting for the opportunity" (cited by Verduyn). With her characteristic flair, van Herk retrieves Dutchness from its place as a forgettable, easily assimilated cultural difference, restoring its rich accents of difference. But, taken out of the impressionistic vocabulary of biography, what is the import of this difference? Verduyn is eager to keep this discussion open, reluctant to close off the discussion by pronouncing ethnicity. To refer van Herk back to her Dutchness is not the final grounds of an explanation, but one source of a vast network of writerly connections.

Pamela Sing puts a rather unfamiliar spin on the notion of minor writing when she situates it among francophones outside Quebec. The situation she describes is a bleak one: in the Canadian "Far West," the francophone writer has neither institutional support nor a reading public. This particular literary "no man's land" does not even enjoy the privilege of recognition. Dismissed by Quebec nationalists, ignored by her anglophone neighbours, the writer "practices her art in a situation of extreme socio-cultural, geographico-physical and linguistic solitude" (137). If Marguerite-A. Primeau is a faithful exemplar of her species, she will see her work heavily rewritten (if it is published) and known to a very limited readership.

Licia Canton's discussion of language as a representation of hyphenated identity focuses on the tension created when Italian appears in the Italian-Canadian text. Italian surfaces as a "translated or untranslated word; as a literal translation of a phrase or sentence given in English; and as an English sentence having a Latinate structure." Through close readings of novels by Frank Paci, Caterina Edwards, Mary Melfi, Nino Ricci, and Antonio D'Alfonso, Canton argues that the presence of the "heritage" language is a device used by the writer to illustrate the negotiation at work in a bicultural identity.

One of the most striking elements of the essays in this collection is the range of situations to which the notion of "minority writing" is applied. The juxtaposition of these different cases, their confrontation as "adjacencies," is revealing. There is a sense in which these cases literally "stand beside" one another, imposing their

individual differences. The very different nature and status of the texts forces us to acknowledge that the
minoritization of cultural identities comes about through
historical developments which are neither symmetrical
nor commensurate. The conjunction in the volume of
discussions of Doukhobor prison diaries, of the representation of Native realities in Sheila Watson's writing
and of the filmic translation of Michael Ondaatje's *The
English Patient*, for example, is an indication of the increasingly broad regions of exploration undertaken under the banner of minority writing. It also draws attention
to the very different critical modes engaged in this exploration.

The articles by Samara Walbohm and Don Randall
are concerned with the ways in which critical interpretations mask or pervert literary identities. Both papers
reread a classic literary text on the basis of new circumstances: in the first case, the recent publication (1992)
of *Deep Hollow Creek* by Sheila Watson and, in the second, the cinematic adaptation of *The English Patient*.
They read narrative and critical discourse against their
own concern for resistant identities. And so Don Randall,
for example, notes the transformation in the character
of Kip as he is moved from book to screen. Samara
Walbohm shows how Watson's novel, written before *The
Double Hook* but unpublished until recently, gives explicit representation to a tension between First Nations
and white settlers – a tension which becomes abstract
and figurative in *The Double Hook*. Revisiting this now
classic novel in the light of the earlier text opens *The
Double Hook* to more politicized readings and reveals
contradictions and ambiguities which were less visible
before the lens of cultural history was provided. Both of
these texts also foreground a problem of transposition:
what happens when a first text, which carries an explicit problematic of minoritization, is reshaped for a

second public? What happens, in particular, when the second text is apparently crafted in view of a larger and perhaps more heterogeneous public? Through their critical discussions, Walbohm and Randall both show how the major and the minor enter into dialogue as relational terms.

Julie Rak's reading of the prison diary written by Freedomite Doukhobor protestors has a different goal. Her concern is to read the "literary" identity of the Freedomites as a function of the diary form which has created it. Rak examines the point at which the diary form, this "technology of alternative subjectivities," encounters subjects who have been recalcitrant to conventions of selfhood and citizenship and use the form in order to refashion themselves as public voices, to gain visibility for Freedomites – but in opposition to the trope of the Canadian multiculturalist mosaic. These subjects "refuse to stay in the places prescribed for them within that trope." They use the diary not as a means of communication of identity issues, "telling the self to the self or healing the split between the lonely points of enunciation and utterance," but rather to deploy a "performance field" of surfaces, straddling several life narrative forms. The conjunction between the constraints of national juridical forms of interpellation and the counter-writing of the diary is particularly compelling. Narrative and political subjectivities engage in a conflictual dialogue which brings about a continual reshaping of borders.

Heike Harting's discussion of "performative metaphor" is salient in this context. Like Rak for the diary form, Harting undertakes to re-examine the force of metaphor when it is deployed by emergent subjectivities. She critiques Deleuze and Guattari for excluding metaphor from the "intensive" writing practices that they define as constitutive of minor literature and shows the performative force of metaphor in the writing of Austin Clarke. The conch-shell and the inner tube in Clarke's *The Origin of Waves* are not simply markers in the text but figures which "reiterate, disidentify and resignify" the historically sedimented effects of their prior circulation. The rich spatial and historical meanings activated by the metaphors in the text work against normative constructions of cultural Otherness. They are agents of liminality, setting into play new versions of diasporic life.

As we have seen, many of the essays in this volume approach the notions of ethnic or minority writing from oblique angles, using these notions as operative terms as they turn their attention to redefining genres and figures. The three introductory essays by Amaryll Chanady, Lucie Lequin and Daisy Neijmann are frontal. They engage directly with the ambiguities and difficulties associated with the term "minority writing." Neijmann uses the term "Icelandic-Canadian writing" both to affirm and critique its very possibility. Her aim is to explore the variety of aesthetic positions it embraces (from popular novels to postmodernist experimentation) and the different meanings it has been given by Canadian critics and readers. Like Kamboureli, she underlines the different vocabularies which Icelandic writers have used to define their own feelings of belonging/exclusion. In the manner that Amaryll Chanady points to as crucial to contemporary discussions of difference, Neijmann negotiates between rigid and outwardly imposed categories of difference and more "fluid" conceptions of identity.

Chanady's broad overview reminds us that there has been an uneasy relationship between critical frameworks relying on ethnicity and multiculturalism on the one hand, and postcolonialism and the diaspora on the other. Ironically, the same authors find themselves analyzed under the rubric of one or the other categories. The last twenty years have seen increasing complexity in the terms used to describe and analyze literary identities. Homi Bhabha speaks of "the prodigious production of discourses of 'othering'" during the "decade of difference and diversity – the mid80s to mid90s" (431). Critics have struggled with sometimes contradictory mandates: the desire to document the diversity of voices in Canadian literature, to investigate the realities of racism and discrimination which give rise to the very notion of diversity, but also the need to explore the individuality of writers and to understand their often difficult relationship to their communities. Increasingly, a broad range of critical perspectives has been brought to bear on minority writing, especially as it is drawn into a wider critical field recognizing the tensions of postmodernism and postcolonialism.

Lucie Lequin shifts the discussion towards the ethical realm and wonders why we valorize notions of difference, displacement, dissonance. Her answer relies on Iain Chambers' phrase "the ethics of the intellect" to insist on the capacity of difference to inspire innovative thought, to use uncertainty as a lever to provide new understandings. She reads the work of three migrant writers, Nadine Ltaif, Monique Bosco and Régine Robin, as writing which attacks the "truths" proclaimed by oppressive regimes and promotes a reconceptualization of reality through innovative narrative, an escape from the constraints of system.

Lequin and Chanady propose characterizations of minority writing which recall the "anxiety" which Homi Bhabha has defined as the dominant affect associated with minority writing. Anxiety is a "borderline affect," arising out of the "disjunctive relationships" which come with ongoing processes of translation (442). The tentative regions of the in-between, the experience of "being-

in-difference" carry an emotional charge. Writing in translation is always fraught with anxiety about the adequacy
of language to provide a home for meaning, a place
where images will exhaust the force of emotion.

What Bhabha describes in the vocabulary of affect
can apply to the many zones of engagement to which
we are led in reading the essays in this collection. Minority writing is revealed as a site of tension, where literary form moves through and across histories. We are
reminded that language remains that space of conten-
tion through which the anxious subjectivities of today
grapple with community. The central force of anxiety is
its unendingness, its constant pulsing between opposites.
Though writing can never claim a home, the certainty
of "land to light on," it continues to be fueled by the
task of describing this impossibility.

My thanks to the editors of this volume, Lianne Moyes, Licia Canton
and Domenic Beneventi, for their helpful discussion.

WORKS CITED

Bhabha, Homi. "Editor's Introduction: Minority Maneuvers and Unsettled
    Negotiations." Special issue: "Front Lines/Border Posts." *Critical Inquiry* 23
    (Spring 1997): 431—59.

Brand, Dionne. *Land to Light On*. Toronto: McClelland & Stewart, 1997.

Kamboureli, Smaro, ed. *Making a Difference: Canadian Multicultural Literature*.
    Toronto/New York/Oxford: Oxford UP, 1996.

The Construction of Minority Subjectivities at the End of the Twentieth Century

Amaryll Chanady

The study of minority writing, which has become an increasingly popular area of research in Canada, can be situated with respect to a number of important issues, such as the institutionalization of literature, the emergence of new literary forms and the construction of identity in a multicultural nation. In my essay, I will focus on the latter, since this is a particularly complex issue that deserves a more detailed examination not only in the Canadian context, but in that of the Americas in general. On the one hand, some of the criticisms directed at national ideology have subsequently been redirected at minority "identity politics" for being just as exclusive and restrictive as the former, albeit at a different level. On the other, the theoretical deconstruction of identity has been attacked for counteracting the emergence of strategies of empowerment within marginalized groups. Furthermore, racial and ethnic stereotypes often make the construction of positive ethnic identities very difficult, while the mere emphasis on difference within the nation can sometimes be seen as furthering the exclusion of ethnic groups. Since these points have been widely debated outside Canada, and since it is important to locate the Canadian situation within a larger context, I will refer briefly throughout my essay to a few significant contributions to the debate on minority subjectivities in the United States, Latin America and the French Caribbean. However, I will concentrate mainly on two Canadian immigrant writers from the Caribbean, Neil Bissoondath and Austin Clarke, who both raise crucial questions concerning the construction of minority subjectivities within Canada.

In an article on minority discourse in Latin America, Josaphat Bekunuru Kubayanda criticizes the monological and restrictive conceptions of identity in the newly independent Latin American nations in the nineteenth century. In their efforts to construct an imaginary community that would rally the population against the ex-colonial and neocolonial powers, the ruling élites created a unifying and totalizing ideology, thus relegating to silence or marginality the expression of an Afro-Hispano-American consciousness. Kubayanda's critique can be applied not only to those intellectuals and politicians who invoked the Spanish heritage to the exclusion of any other in their discourses of identity, but also to those who appropriated the motif of the Indian in a symbolic filiation and identification with the internal Other. This collective self-representation rarely incorporated the "voices" of the Amerindians or even attempted to represent their perspective. Paradigms of hybridity (the melting-pot, the mestizo nation) did not necessarily entail the valorization of different subjectivities, since the hybrid nation was symbolized as a collectivity in which the various components collaborated in the same project of nation-building and shared the same values. When native Americans, or other marginalized groups, were explicitly included in the symbolic construction of the nation as internal Others, they often became a marker of specificity and difference in opposition to an external Other (Europe or the United States; an example is the Cuban poet José Martí's concept of "our mestizo America" as opposed to the more European America in the North).

In the Americas in general, minorities were expected

to participate in the construction of the nation, albeit in different ways, by embracing the dominant values. The very question of minority subjectivities was irrelevant except as a problem, inasmuch as they might be considered as an impediment to the harmonious functioning of society, especially in the case of persons of African or Amerindian origin. A significant change occurred at the beginning of the twentieth century, when anti-colonial movements in the Caribbean emphasized the African-American culture of the islands. However, the resulting discourses of identity generally privileged the nation, the region or the race as a whole, and not intranational Others as distinct components of a heterogeneous collectivity. Aimé Césaire's notion of negritude has also been widely criticized for essentialist, racialist and monolithic conceptions of blackness. But even the manifesto in "praise of Creoleness" by Jean Bernabé, Patrick Chamoiseau and Raphaël Confiant adopts an essentialist and unifying discourse based on the centrality of oral culture, in spite of the numerous references to hybridity. It invokes not only resistance and the rejection of metropolitan paradigms, but also the celebration of supposedly essential traits of the "authentic" Creolized black culture that should be at the center of a new national (or regional) identity as a whole. Until quite recently, Latin American and Caribbean intellectuals did not stress the issue of minority subjectivities within the nation or region but advocated a totalizing identity that was identified either with a particular group (European, or black, in the case of Césaire and the authors of the manifesto on Creoleness), or with a new, unified hybridity (the melting-pot, the mestizo nation) resulting from the gradual transformation of heterogeneity.

The past three decades have brought about considerable transformations in the conceptualization of the nation and its culture throughout the Americas. Not only

have intellectuals and politicians become increasingly
aware of cultural heterogeneity, but they also frequently
consider this as a value rather than a problem (that of
the "unmeltable ethnic," or the clashing interests of various pressure groups that lead to an ever greater fragmentation of the nation, for example). The fairly recent
interest in minorities and their cultural productions in
North America has led to the creation of academic
programmes, special issues of learned journals, collective volumes and conferences on ethnicity, as well as a
better understanding of the effects of discrimination and
a greater general visibility of literature by authors perceived as ethnic, that is, as not belonging to the dominant ethnic group. Canadian multiculturalism has also
led to an increased emphasis on ethnicity through official discourses, public celebrations of the country's diversity, and funding for ethnic artistic productions.

But although the increased visibility given to
marginalized groups in North America by the creation
of new academic programmes (Black and Chicano studies, for example) has been widely praised and considered as long overdue (I am not referring to canon revision
in literature departments, which has been virulently attacked by traditionalists), the affirmation of and emphasis on ethnicity outside academia has aroused
considerable debate. The best-known recent expression
of scepticism about multicultural ideology in Canada is
perhaps Neil Bissoondath's book *Selling Illusions,* which
goes far beyond the debate on official multiculturalism
in its problematization of the construction of ethnic categories and minority subjectivities in general – in Canada
and abroad. Toward the beginning of the essay,
Bissoondath deconstructs the notion of a monolithic
Trinidadian identity when he describes the country of
his birth as characterized by "multiculturalism without
the name" (10) and presents his childhood friends in

the following terms: "We were a varied group, both racially (black, white, Chinese, Indian, mulatto) and religiously (Presbyterian, Roman Catholic, Hindu, Moslem)" (11).

This heterogeneity, however (of Trinidad, and even more so of the Caribbean and the Third World in general), is homogenized in Canada by the creation of a category of immigrant visible minorities in which racial and cultural differences disappear. Bissoondath is enrolled at a college reserved mainly for Third-World and non-white students in which he is supposed to feel more comfortable (20). The new immigrant is immediately relegated to a category that is considered by the author as artificial and marginalizing. The problem consists not only in symbolically excluding a certain arbitrarily defined group of students from the general student body by housing them in a college specifically set aside for them, but also in refusing to recognize differences between individuals that they themselves consider as important.

The symbolic construction of groups considered as Other has frequently been criticized not only by opponents of official multiculturalism in Canada who argue that ethnic labelling contributes to ghettoization, but also by cultural critics such as Mireille Rosello, who denounces all forms of classification (especially those based on ethnicity or race) as exclusionary, and prefers the notion of strategic alliances and solidarity that can be freely established and abolished. Alliances, however, are intimately interconnected with the social imaginary, and especially with collective self-representations, and these often involve an interiorization of categories created by dominant groups. When Bissoondath criticizes the apparently spontaneous ghettoization in the student cafeteria, he explicitly refers to the role of the general student body in this segregation, explaining that the "idea of 'sticking with your own' was reinforced by various student organizations" (21).

Categorization, whether imposed from without or within the group itself, is the guiding principle behind the seating arrangements in the cafeteria described by Bissoondath, in which "Chinese students congregated behind a wall of Cantonese," and certain tables are "protected by the raucous enthusiasm of West Indian accents," while others are reserved for Jewish students:

> To approach any of these tables was to intrude on a clannish exclusivity. It was to challenge the unofficially designated territory of tables parceled out so that each group, whether racially, culturally or religiously defined, could enjoy its little enclave, its own little "homeland," so to speak, protected by unspoken prerogatives. (21)

Exclusivity, designated territory and prerogatives are far removed from Rosello's free association. Bissoondath rejects this segregation precisely because it reduces him to a representative of a category and thus precludes not only sustained interaction with members of other groups, but also the expression of differences with respect to the dominant traits of his ghetto:

> I learned instead to keep my distance from the tables that would have welcomed me not as an individual but as an individual of a certain skin colour, with a certain accent, with a certain assumed cultural outlook – the tables that would have welcomed me not for who I was and for what I could do but for what I was and for what they presumed I represented. I had not come here, I decided, in order to join a ghetto. (23)

Seen as a traitor by other West Indians, he feels alienated by them rather than by society at large (25). Without rejecting his heritage, Bissoondath expresses the desire to associate with people of any ethnic origin, and to interact with them as an individual on the basis of personal affinity rather than ethnicity. His criticism of racial and ethnic divisions is not limited to Canada, but also applies to his country of origin, characterized by "little pockets of homogeneity, blacks with blacks, Indians with Indians, whites with whites" (14).

In more theoretical discussions of the construction of ethnicity, the latter has been faulted for the same reasons as the construction of the imaginary nation: homogenization and exclusion. Paradigms of hybridity are increasingly applied not only to the nation, but also to intranational groups. Homi Bhabha, for example, has analyzed not only the "appropriation" of Christianity in India and the resulting hybridization of East Indian evangelical discourse, but also the unstable and hybridized constitution of ethnic minority subjectivities in the southern United States. Other critics have also questioned traditional notions of ethnic identity based on simplistic views on race, culture and religion. In the same special issue of *Cultural Critique* on minority discourse in which Kubayanda criticizes the silencing of African-American subjectivity in Latin America, R. Radhakrishnan problematizes the monologism of ethnic identity, which entails a binary, exclusionary, repressive and hegemonic ideology. The critic explains that the "ideologization, in the name of an affirmative programmatic, of heterological, heteroglossic, and heterogeneous realities into a single/identical blueprint is just not in touch with lived reality." The "general hegemony of Identity" should therefore be overthrown, with the result that the "essentialization/hypostasis and the fetishization of 'difference'" will be prevented and a new conception of "heterogeneous difference" made possible (210-11).

There are obvious parallels between the problematization of ethnic identity and the deconstruction of the nation as a homogeneous whole, since both are closely related. In both cases, purity is a symbolic construct.

Furthermore, individuals cannot be considered simply as embodiments of an imaginary group identity, either that of the nation, or that of an ethnic group. In the case of a settler society, each minority is comprised of individuals who originally came from countries with significant internal differences. The category "Italian Canadian," for example, is a construction in which Italy's immense linguistic and cultural diversity is ignored. Can one really talk about a single ethnic identity that subsumes immigrants from both Venice and Naples? It is true that national institutions (schooling, print culture, television) have effected a significant linguistic unification in Italy through the increasing use of the official national language. This contrasts significantly with the situation at the beginning of the century when large numbers of people from various parts of the country could not communicate in the same language since they did not speak standardized Italian. However, heterogeneity has certainly not disappeared and thus warrants a radical deconstruction of "Italianness."

The usefulness of the concept of ethnic identity can also be questioned if we take into account the significant divergences within a particular ethnic group between the class affiliation, education, cultural affinity, ideology and lifestyle of its members. This concerns every ethnic minority, even those immigrating from relatively homogeneous societies. Is ethnic identity at all operative in a group composed of virtually illiterate individuals and highly trained professionals? Which category takes precedence? If we consider identity in terms of identification, or Rosello's more general concept of affiliation and free association, then professional affinity will frequently be much stronger than a supposed ethnic identity. Werner Sollors has made some very interesting observations on the constitution of collective identities in ethnically heterogeneous groups of artists, for example (14). In his introduction to *Beyond Ethnicity*, he also points out that the major cultural transformations that affect immigrant groups as they adapt to life in their country of adoption lead to the emergence of a new, American identity, with the result that the various groups have more in common with each other than with their country of origin. The symbolic construction of discrete ethnic identities thus obfuscates the existence of major cultural resemblances between them, including the need to redefine themselves as ethnic groups.

Ethnic categorization involves not only the practical problem of applying a homogenizing label to groups of people who may have virtually nothing in common except their status as ethnic outsiders. It is also theoretical. How can we subscribe to the widespread problematization of monolithic national ideologies and exclusionary constructions of the (national) imagined community and, at the same time, perpetuate a monolithic and exclusionary conceptualization of ethnic minorities? If we deconstruct the idea of the nation, it is logical that we also deconstruct that of the ethnic group, since both are heterogeneous. In order to avoid contradiction, we need to develop a less essentialist and more complex symbolization of the collectivity at any level, whether national, regional or ethnic. This involves an additional consideration – not only are collectivities heterogeneous, but the boundaries between collectivities are never absolute or stable. A more accurate symbolization of ethnic minorities and nations thus entails a recognition of the presence of internal Others as well as an awareness of the transformations brought about by the inevitable interactions between a group and its external Others, especially in a context of globalization and mass communication. Boundaries between cultures have never been absolute, and are even less so today. Sherry Simon applies the notion of "spaces between cultures" to the increasingly hybrid culture of children of mixed marriages in Montreal who not only have heterogeneous immigrant backgrounds, but also adapt to local anglophone and francophone groups; furthermore, these children often have the means to travel and consume imported cultural products, which leads to complex hybridization through interaction with both internal and external Others (15-16).

A significant number of Canadian immigrants in the last two decades of the twentieth century have made observations on the complexity of identity construction today. Fernando de Toro, for example, invokes the concept of "nomadic subjectivity" and links its emergence to the postmodern questioning of essentialist notions of the collective and individual subject:

> Today, with the blurring of boundaries that once surrounded totalizing discourses, with the bankruptcy of the Hegelian trans-historical subject, we can only position ourselves with regard to a nomadic subjectivity, in a nonhierarchical space, where discourses are being constantly territorialized, deterritorialized, and reterritorialized, and where the only certainty is that nothing is certain. (39)

Robert Berrouët-Oriol and Robert Fournier refer to the new "migrant and mestizo writing" ("écritures migrantes et métisses") in Quebec today, as it is practiced by Anne-Marie Alonzo, Fulvio Caccia, Marco Micone, Naïm Kattan, Régine Robin and Caribbean authors such as Émile Ollivier. They also point out that hybridization has not occurred in one direction only, since the "transcultural dynamic" also affects writers of English and French origin, such as Jacques Poulin, Yolande Villemaire and Pierre Nepveu (12-13). The Haitian novelist Émile Ollivier prefers the term "migrant culture" to "immigrant culture," because of its "emergent character" and complexity (83). He also points to the specific problem of immigrants from different regions within the same country of origin whose culture is transformed by contact with other immigrants from the same country, so that it is both heterogeneous and constantly changing (84).

The title of Ollivier's article includes the term "transculturation" (the term is also used by Berrouët-Oriol and Fournier), which leads me to the critical and theoretical discourse developed within the past fifteen years by Italian-Canadian intellectuals, mainly in Quebec, as well as by an increasing number of critics of French origin. Frank Caucci, for example, applies the paradigm to a number of well-known Italian-Canadian writers such as Fulvio Caccia, Antonio D'Alfonso, Marco Micone, Nino Ricci and Filippo Salvatore. Lamberto Tassinari, commenting on the importance of the magazine *Vice Versa*, discusses the advantages of the term "transcultural" which, unlike "intercultural" or "multicultural," refers to no strictly defined cultural space, but a crossing through and a going beyond a particular culture, displacement, nomadism and rejection of the notion of a strictly circumscribed territory (298-301). He points out that the "Italianness" of Italian Canadians in Quebec has not remained static, and attributes the possibility of creating a genuine transculture to the presence of three languages in Quebec (298). There is no doubt that the bilingual context of Italian writers in Quebec has contributed to their criticism of monolithic notions of ethnicity. Recent problematizations of monolithic ethnic identity can perhaps also be partly attributed to the influence of francophone Caribbean writers such as Édouard Glissant. As for the term "transculture," it is an import from Latin America, since it was developed by Fernando Ortiz in the nineteen forties to account for the hybridity of Cuban society (Ortiz 97-103).

The deconstruction of ethnicity, however, poses certain problems, just as the deconstruction of the nation or gender does. In both cases, there is a fear of fragmentation and loss of identity as well as agency. Feminist critics such as Nancy Hartsock have not only questioned the relevance of postmodern theory to feminist studies, but have also pointed to its deleterious effects on the construction of alternate subjectivities that could challenge dominant paradigms and cultural practices. "Guiding fictions," to use Nicolas Shumway's expression, or "strategic essentialism" (see Spivak), are considered necessary for the constitution, self-representation and self-affirmation of subjugated groups as well as dominant sectors of society engaged in nation-building. Even Édouard Glissant, who uses concepts from deconstruction and chaos theory to criticize traditional notions of identity based on filiation and territory, and who describes culture as a general "magma" of relations (the title of his essay is *The Poetics of the Relation* [*Poétique de la Relation*]), demonstrates an awareness of the insufficiency of the radical deconstructionist model when he proposes an "aesthetics of the earth, free of folkloric naïvetés, but spreading like a rhizome in the knowledge of our cultures" (164), a "literal utilitarianism" and the creation of ideals (187). In a somewhat contradictory proclamation that uneasily juxtaposes deconstructionist discourse with a call for collective paradigms, Glissant advocates new forms of collective identity formation that lead to the emergence of "dynamic structures" situated between the chaos of infinite interaction and the dogmatism of ideology (187).

Italian-Canadian critics such as Antonio D'Alfonso have also tried to develop complex subject-positions that involve the recognition of intra-ethnic differences and fluctuating identifications without falling into "ethnic effacement" (125), melting-pot ideology or the deconstructionist celebration of generalized difference. In his essay *In Italics: In Defense of Ethnicity*, D'Alfonso stresses the importance of "conscious identities" (15) based on "free choice" (125) and a "pluricultural ethos" (143) and defines himself as a "composite": an "Abruzzese/Molisano/Canadian/Quebecois/Italian/ European/North American" (187). Two important issues are raised here: the necessity of free choice and the possibility of cumulative as opposed to dissociative identity. The latter notion, cumulative identity, involves the deconstruction of the binary and exclusionary mechanism of opposing the Self to the Other as well as a general questioning of the "discontinuist" classification of cultures. The former, free choice, implies the construction of personal and collective identity through identification and alliances as opposed to stereotyped and often pejorative labelling of the ethnic Other.

It would be utopian to believe that a freely constructed minority subjectivity is possible, since there can be no society in which every form of classification and labelling will disappear. Establishing distinctions is essential to any cognitive activity, including everyday mechanisms of making sense of the world. Furthermore, the interiorization of dominant paradigms by marginalized groups and the ubiquitous problems of racism and other forms of discrimination will probably always remain. The "free choice" in constructing multiple identities is severely limited by existing power structures and deeply entrenched attitudes toward certain ethnic/racial groups. D'Alfonso's positive multiple identity may not be accessible to everyone, especially to those belonging to a visible minority.

A particularly interesting example of negative minority identity construction can be found in Austin Clarke's short story "Canadian Experience." In this tragic account of the difficulties encountered by a Caribbean immigrant, Clarke (originally from Barbados) describes the unsuccessful eight-year struggle of a man of colour against social and economic exclusion in Toronto before he decides to commit suicide. It is significant that the protagonist has no name. In fact, he represents the immigrant of colour, in general, who is relegated to degrading and poorly remunerated menial jobs, such as distributing handbills and working as a janitor or cleaner in department stores and office buildings at night. He lives in a shabby rented room, sharing bathroom facilities with other impecunious and marginalized boarders. His refrigerator is virtually empty, containing only water in an old juice container, a carton of spoilt milk, three sausages of inferior quality, dry bread and domestic beer. In short, the narrator describes him as one of the "debris of the country's unemployed" (Clarke 52).

The story begins with the description of the protagonist's preparations for a job interview, his first in five years. Very self-conscious about his physical appearance, he perceives himself with contempt and disgust, since his looks contrast markedly with the physical ideal projected by society. The pictures surrounding him daily are those of blond, good-looking Canadians, like the child who smiles at him from the plastic bread wrapper. The initial scene of the story, where the immigrant contemplates himself in the mirror, illustrates the negative image he has of himself: "The knot of his tie was shiny with grease. He did not like himself. He was not dressed the way he had hoped to appear, and his image was incorrect. This made him stop laughing" (49). He becomes increasingly dissatisfied with his appearance: "He wished the pink shirt was cleaner. He wished the dark brown suit was a black one. He should not wear a yellow tie, but no other ties he had would match the clothes on his back" (53). He finally smears Vaseline on his hair, thus conforming to a very negative physical stereotype of the immigrant who does not know how to dress.

On his way to the interview, he is constantly reminded of his own filthy and neglected appearance by
the cleanliness that surrounds him. Even the stairs leading to the subway are spotless, while the handrails, polished like chrome, squeak with cleanliness when hands
slide over them. When he arrives at the financial hub of
the city, with its glass and steel skyscrapers, he stops in
front of the shiny office building in which his interview
is supposed to take place. Its glass walls, shimmering
like gold, confront him with an image of himself that is
even crueller than that of his mirror at home: "Its reflection of his body tears him into strides and splatters his
suit against four glass panels, and makes him disjointed"
(57).

His fragmented image is reflected by a building that
symbolizes wealth, progress and the peak of success in
Western capitalist society, as well as the economic dis-
parities of its inhabitants through its contrastive juxtaposition with the marginalized immigrant of colour. But
it is also a striking metaphor for the problematic identity
of members of visible minorities, who perceive themselves
in opposition to more privileged groups. Furthermore,
they inevitably interiorize the multiple, fragmented and
often contradictory images created by dominant sectors
of society. The resulting negative self-representation de-
stroys any positive image they may have had of themselves initially. In the building's elevator, Clarke's
protagonist is paralyzed by his incongruous presence in
a place of economic power and success: "Five men and
women are beside and behind him. Facing him is glass
and chrome and fresh flowers and Persian rugs and
women dressed expensively and stylishly in black, with
necklaces of pearls" (57). When the elevator comes to a
stop, the glass and chrome of the bank, the black dresses
and pearls of the women, and the blue eyes of the bank
employee coming towards him represent everything that

he is not. The scene concludes with the closing of the two elevator doors, described like threatening hands that throw him into a state of panic and expel him from the building so that he does not show up at the interview. Psychologically destroyed by his repeated failures, Clarke's protagonist dreams of his country of origin before throwing himself under the wheels of the subway on its way south to the lake, full of dead fish and motor oil.

The negative self-representation of the black immigrant in Clarke's story can be read as a particularly effective illustration of Frantz Fanon's discussion of the predicament of the person of colour arriving in Europe. In *Black Skin, White Masks* (*Peau noire, masques blancs*), the black critic from Martinique describes his experiences in France, where he realizes that instead of being "at the origin of the world," he is merely an "object among other objects"[1] (Fanon 88) in the eyes of the white inhabitants. He rapidly discovers the stereotypes applied to people of colour as he views himself with an "objective gaze": these stereotypes concern blackness, particular ethnic traits, cannibalism, mental backwardness, fetishism, racial defects and slavery (90). No longer a genuine subject who elaborates a particular conception of the world and of himself, the person of colour in a white society exists first of all in the contemptuous gaze of the white Other.

The black man is thus no longer simply black, but black for the white person. Since the gaze and behaviour of the white Europeans constantly remind him of his black identity, he has great difficulty elaborating what Fanon calls his "corporal schema" (*"schéma corporel"*; 89). In the case of a person of colour, this schema is not based, as it normally is, on sensations and perceptions related to the various sensory faculties (such as touch and vision), but on the racial categorization and narratives created by white Europeans (90), according to which "the negro is an animal, the negro is bad, the negro is mean, the negro is ugly" (91-92).[2] Henceforth a slave of his appearance, since he is "overdetermined from the outside" (*"sur-déterminé de l'extérieur"*; 93), the black man sees his body as disjointed and fragmented (91-92).[3] This inevitably produces feelings of shame and self-contempt. Clarke's description of the fragmented reflection of the black protagonist in the windows of the office building corresponds exactly to Fanon's portrait of the disjointed black subject/object in the gaze of the European.

The practical difficulties of constructing positive minority subjectivities cannot be ignored, and many Canadian writers belonging to visible minorities emphasize the obstacles they face not only in their elaboration of a positive identity as Other, but even in their attempts to become integrated in society. While the conceptualization of minority identities as plural, constantly changing and cumulative constitutes an appropriate theoretical paradigm for understanding the complex development of subject-positions, it is important to address the problems of labelling, negative categorization and social boundaries in the case of certain minorities. Radhakrishnan's concept of poststructuralist ethnic identity may seem very utopian in the context of Clarke's depiction of discrimination and negative self-representation. However, the construction of fluid and hybridized minority subjectivities constitutes an important ideal, according to which the multiple determinations of our subjectivity – ethnicity, race, class, gender and lifestyle – are considered as both positive and liable to transformation from within.

NOTES

I wish to thank the Social Sciences and Humanities Research Council of Canada for providing funding to carry out research for this paper as part of a three-year project on the symbolic construction of hybridity in the Americas.
1. "À l'origine du monde"; "objet au milieu d'autres objets."
2. "Le nègre est une bête, le nègre est mauvais, le nègre est méchant, le nègre est laid."
3. "Étalé, disjoint."

WORKS CITED

Bernabé, Jean, Patrick Chamoiseau, and Raphaël Confiant. *Éloge de la créolité*. Paris: Gallimard, 1989.

Berrouët-Oriol, Robert, and Robert Fournier. "L'Émergence des écritures migrantes et métisses au Québec." *Québec Studies* 14 (1992): 7-22.

Bhabha, Homi. *The Location of Culture*. London/New York: Routledge, 1994.

Bissoondath, Neil. *Selling Illusions: The Cult of Multiculturalism in Canada*. Harmondsworth: Penguin, 1994.

Caucci, Frank. "Topoi de la transculture dans l'imaginaire italo-québécois." *Québec Studies* 15 (Fall 1992/Winter 1993): 41-50.

Césaire, Aimé. *Cahier d'un retour au pays natal*. Montréal: Guérin, 1990.

Clarke, Austin. "Canadian Experience." *Other Solitudes: Canadian Multicultural Fictions*. Ed. Linda Hutcheon and Marion Richmond. Toronto: Oxford UP, 1990. 49-63.

D'Alfonso, Antonio. *In Italics: In Defense of Ethnicity*. Toronto/New York/Lancaster: Guernica, 1996.

De Toro, Fernando. "From Where to Speak? Latin American Postmodern/Postcolonial Positionalities." *World Literature Today* 69.1 (Winter 1995): 35-40.

Fanon, Frantz. *Peau noire, masques blancs*. Paris: Seuil, 1952.

Glissant, Édouard. *Poétique de la Relation*. Paris: Gallimard, 1990.

Kubayanda, Josaphat Bekunuru. "Minority Discourse and the African Collective: Some Examples from Latin American and Caribbean Literature." *Cultural Critique* 6 (Spring 1987): 113-130.

Mukherjee, Arun. *Towards an Aesthetics of Opposition: Essays on Literature, Criticism and Cultural Imperialism*. Stratford, ON: Williams-Wallace, 1988.

Ollivier, Émile. "Quatre thèses sur la transculturation." *Cahiers de recherche sociologique* 2.2 (Sept. 1984): 75-90.

Ortiz, Fernando. *Cuban Counterpoint: Tobacco and Sugar*. Trans. Harriet de Onís. Durham/London: Duke UP, 1995.

Radhakrishnan, R. "Ethnic Identity and Post-Structuralist Difference." *Cultural Critique* 6 (Spring 1987): 199-220.

Rosello, Mireille. *Littérature et identité créole aux Antilles*. Paris: Karthala, 1992.

Shumway, Nicolas. *The Invention of Argentina*. Berkeley/Los Angeles/London: U of California P, 1991.

Simon, Sherry, et al. *Fictions de l'identitaire au Québec*. Montréal: XYZ, 1991.

Sollors, Werner. *Beyond Ethnicity: Consent and Descent in American Culture*. New York/Oxford: Oxford UP, 1986.

Spivak, Gayatri Chakravorty. *In Other Worlds*. New York: Routledge, 1987.

Tassinari, Lamberto. "Le projet transculturel." *Sous le signe du Phénix: Entretiens avec quinze créateurs italo-québécois*. Ed. Fulvio Caccia. Montréal: Guernica, 1985. 293-305.

Ethics and the Imaginary

Lucie Lequin

Displacement, dissolution, interstices, interludes, inter-
vals, palimpsests, strata, diversity . . . a host of words
informing one particular area of contemporary literary
discourse, the writing of migration. Of course, such a
constellation of words emerges from postmodern thought
and has links to the vocabulary of postcolonial reflection. I mention them here because of their power to
gradually evoke a system-free process of thought capable
of looking at the world and at itself differently, in a spirit
of renewal. Édouard Glissant speaks of this process as
*"une approche qui passe par une recomposition du paysage
mental [des] humanités d'aujourd'hui"* (16). According
to Alain Médam, it is a playing field, a space composed
of rules and randomness: *"Les deux sont indispensables.
S'il n'y a pas de règles, à quoi jouer? S'il n'y a plus
d'incertitudes, pourquoi jouer?"* (55). A playing field
where, between these two forces, shifts of meaning can
occur capable of both stimulating and bringing about
change. For Iain Chambers, this state of mind is:

> a state of knowledge, an ethics of the intellect, an aperture in
> politics, able to acknowledge more than itself; a state of
> knowledge that is prepared to suffer modification and inter-
> rogation by what it neither possesses nor can claim as its
> own. (50)

Here again the notion of opening, change and uncertainty dominates. Glissant, Médam and Chambers also
intersect in their insistence on movement: perception of

the world or of the self can only occur in a context of movement, far from the voices of omniscient authority. All three position themselves on the side of voices that are marginal, different, less audible, attempting nevertheless to hear them and eventually gain insight into their *"paysage mental."* Iain Chambers also calls this state of mind an "ethics of the intellect." The term "ethics" has an important place in the writing of these three thinkers, and indeed, in complex variant forms, it partially underlies post-colonial thought and contemporary writing.

In the more circumscribed area of Quebec writing, the idea of an ethics has currency and bears multiple definitions. On the critical side, the word ethics may sometimes be read as ideology (Pelletier) or as the responsibility of the critic (Simon). Elsewhere it has a closer relationship to spirituality (Charron) and describes a vision of the world and of the role that each person plays before the mystery of the other. It may also be a meditative or inquiring vision of the world, philosophical in nature, that attempts to comprehend the social dimension and to write of the interval. In the work of Robin, ethical preoccupations are sometimes in the foreground, but more often it is in the folds of the text, in the gaps "between" or even "in the margins" that an ethics resides (in *Le Roman mémoriel*, for example), where it is related to the quest for identity and the heterogeneous. I cannot enumerate here the numerous instances of an ethics in literature, but within the writing of migration in Quebec, besides Régine Robin, one may include Joël Des Rosiers, Pan Bouyoucas, Abla Farhoud, Nadine Ltaif and Monique Bosco, to name just a few. But in literature or in literary criticism, as in other areas of social discourse, what do we mean when we talk about an ethics?

I have chosen to examine three authors – Nadine Ltaif, Monique Bosco and Régine Robin – in an effort to grasp the fragments of this vague notion, as well as to broaden the problematics of the writing of migration, in which I believe the narration of identity overlies the watermark of an ethics-in-progress. I have brought together these authors of different origins and generations because their concerns intersect and complement each other. I have selected three volumes of Nadine Ltaif's poetry – *Les Métamorphoses d'Ishtar, Entre les fleuves* and *Élégies du levan* – while for each of the others I have selected a single text – Monique Bosco's *Babel-opéra* and Régine Robin's "Sortir de l'ethnicité." A reading of other works by these authors would reveal additional ethical paths different from those analyzed here, but the prolific nature of their respective works makes it necessary to limit my choice in the present context.

Moreover, the texts I have selected highlight ethical positions held in common by these three authors in the face of the funerary din of the contemporary world. Their ethical reflections are born out of movement and are based on a shared suspicion of all rigidly set and reassuring thought, sometimes referred to as the patriarchal meta-narrative. I will therefore attempt to trace a few ethical threads by organizing my reading of these works around two central ideas: opposition to the erection of thought into systems, and participation in the development of an ethics of the uncertain.

Before considering the writing of these authors, it would be appropriate to present a brief, provisional, open definition of an ethics. According to the philosopher Monique Carlo-Sperber, an ethics is a place for questioning – moral philosophy being the place for argumentation (Ewald 20). This laconic definition captures something of the theories of Glissant, Médam and Chambers referred to above, theories which will guide me in exploring the ethical pathways in Bosco,[1] Robin[2] and Ltaif.[3] Far from affirming their own truths, these writers scrutinize uncertainty and movement, using various metaphors related to the image of the *hors lieu* / out-of-context. Their works are, in effect, places for raising questions – questions of culture, identity and ethics. It is important, however, to remember that theories do not imply an ethical position. They only serve to make more explicit the process of reflection already underway and in the process of constructing itself. The word ethics, in this analysis, allows the selected works to speak for themselves as places for questioning, where new configurations of the self and the world play themselves out in and through the narrative. It is a matter of tracing the pattern of an ethical watermark outlined beneath the words and not of imposing an already very precise and rigid theory on them.

System Story

A system of thought based on the very specific,[4] be it cultural, historical, national or sexual, is reassuring. It defines, organizes, classifies, includes and excludes; data are standardized and foster not only normal/abnormal classifications, but more seriously, conflict, discrimination, distrust and even war. The horizon of this circumscribed thinking narrows, becoming heavier and more threatening. The questioning of these prescriptions, followed by their denunciation, constitutes the primary place of questioning and the narrative construction of ethical thought.

In "Histoire de chameau," the poet Nadine Ltaif recounts, through the voice of the camel, the lamentable ravages of this systematic thinking as it wounds, tortures and often kills for no reason other than a code, a voice of authority, a taste for power. In the absence of a horizon line and a life line, she says, there is nothing but *"le soleil indétrônable qui dessèche et déracine des régions entières"* (*Les Métamorphoses* 23). Real life has turned aside: *"Et les gens de continuer à vivre . . . totalement gouvernés par la mort, absolument paralysés . . . avec ce sourire . . . de ceux qui n'ont plus rien à perdre, qui vivent encore, qui préfèrent être déjà morts"* (26). This camel's voice carries within it the traces of many other voices who have also been victims of the *"règne de l'Homme sur terre"* (22). *"Homme"* here refers to the Man of power who, for the sake of ruling, refuses to share the space he dominates, whether this space be tangible (monetary, for example), or intangible, as in the realm of schemes and reputation. This explains the exclusion of women: *"Aucune femme n'a la place qu'elle mérite dans les pays arabes d'où je viens"* (*Entre les fleuves* 45). For Ltaif, this restriction of space, of women or peoples, arises from the inability to ask questions and, simultaneously, the easy acceptance of the voices of authority, voices she considers death-dealing.

For Monique Bosco, in *Babel-opéra,* thought-as-system is

> Damnation. Plus personne ne prend la parole, en aucune langue. Silence sur Babel. Chacun a oublié les mots d'enfance. Il n'y a plus de langue. Juste des cris, des ordres, des mots d'ordre. (40)

For this poet-narrator such a system is an agonizing, negative silence that brings fear, violence and sometimes death. The rule, still so logical and well organized in spite of Babel's disorder, no longer allows either the impulsiveness and freshness of childhood or creativity. If a creative gesture is ventured at all, it will be discreet, hidden, underground, possibly censored, and the voices of authority will conspire to limit its scope and neutralize it. Questions, like independent thought, have been banished. Thought-as-system demands strict obedience to its orders; in so doing it shares the qualities of a drought in which fertilization of hearts and minds rarely occurs.

Monique Bosco also sees Man as the source of this oppressive system which passes for thought and life: *"Ensevelir le passé / les vieilles lois mauvaises / l'héritage maudit des pères. / Patries. / Inventées par eux"* (48). This is the questioning, not of territory, but of the concept of fatherland – an overdetermined, patrilineal concept that through centuries or over years has developed a whole system of laws to protect itself, to entrench a definition of itself, its dogma, linearity, genetic history, and sometimes, to authorize or refuse affiliation. This concept is linked with others:

Trêve de grands mots
Pièges millénaires
Travail-Famille-Patrie
Égalité-Fraternité. (52)

For Bosco, in *Babel-opéra*, it must be understood that behind these words lurk infamy, lies, authority, and even real or potential violence. World War II is a classic example, as it derives from the "thousand-year pitfalls" of "grand words." Bosco attacks contemporary societies at their very base, a base mired in memorialization, incapable of stimulating movement or any unprecedented gesture.

Régine Robin is also distrustful of thought that has been built into a system and become ossified. In discussing the problematics of the writing of migration, she sees the emergence of a new confinement, *"celui de l'ethnicité, de culture au sens botanique du terme (les racines, les souches, les arbres, les branches, les rameaux)"* ("Sortir de l'ethnicité" 26). A movement of ethnic isolationism developing in competition with the cultural globalization movement. This movement of defense and reaction demonstrates a certain tendency, *"comme tendance: l'absence d'écart, de jeu, de décentrement qui ne peut penser l'identité comme 'devenir autre,' véritable mouvement d'arrêt, arrêt sur une image de l'identité"* (28). Thus, images of overabundance tend to dominate, Robin continues: *"plein de social, plein de déterminé à l'avance, plein de causalité, plein de normé, plein de stéréotype, plein de sens, de certitude"* (29).

There is no place in such representations or images for dissent, contrasts, the ill-assorted, transgressions or dialogue. This is a centralizing mentality satisfied with the status quo of repetition. In speaking of a centralizing mentality, I invoke the definition of Trinh T. Minh-ha: "the indulgence in a unitary self, in a locus of authority, or in words and concepts whose formulation comes to govern the textual (and extratextual) space" (6). For Régine Robin, the political project of Québec has locked itself into such an indulgence. This is why *"il est immanquablement pris dans une épaisseur culturelle, une glu historique qui exclut pour le moment tous ceux qui ne peuvent porter ce poids de mémoire, d'accablement, d'humiliation, de joies du roman mémoriel québécois"* ("Sortir de l'ethnicité" 28).

Though they speak from different contexts – Nadine Ltaif from that of war in Lebanon and her immigration to Quebec, Monique Bosco from the recurrence of biblical tragedies in the contemporary world, Régine Robin from the excessive emphasis on ethnic origins and the exclusion thus entailed – all of these authors stand on the side of questioning. The three images they present of entrenched modes of thought – in fact, three brief histories of rigid systems – speak of exclusivity, homogeneity, consolidation, authority, mirrors without depth, heavy silences, one-dimensional images, and cloistered, monotonous spaces. All three authors denounce the uniformity imposed by thought-as-system.

Their questioning is also deeply related to politics,

especially concerning social hierarchies based on race,
religion or sex, the concept of fatherland and the indulgence in an exclusive political project. The geographical
and historical context is simultaneously important and
unimportant. Monique Bosco, for example, takes the
Bible as her starting point for an exposition of games of
power and discrimination; her narrator sets her short
story of wandering and suffering in a millennial continuum since, in spite of the progress of civilizations,
abuses of power seem to be immutable. The humanitar-
ian and ethical concerns of Nadine Ltaif have their origins in the political situation in Lebanon, but they take
on a universal dimension. Both authors juxtapose time
and space, long-term and short-term history, in an effort to grasp the scope of rigid thought. History also
underlies the writing of Régine Robin. In the text exam-
ined here, she considers the present, and confronted with
certain cultural movements, refuses both assimilation and
the isolationism of ethnicity. She ponders the *"fatigue
culturelle"* of Quebec ("Sortir de l'ethnicité 26"), but
considers the concepts of ethnicity and assimilation in
both their local (Quebec) context and their world context. She then turns to history – the formal discipline of
history, as well as her own history – to illustrate the
consequences of a closed ethnicity. In fact, in this theory-
oriented text, the personal side of her thought reveals,
among other things, the importance of her Jewish, secular, French origins. She expressly renounces any claim to
objectivity as she is aware that her theoretical position –
like all theoretical positions – is connected to the autobiographical.

In this respect, her text shares certain qualities with
the poetic writings of Ltaif and Bosco, who also allow
autobiographical elements to seep into their creative texts
– in particular, allusions to their respective birthplaces
and family culture – Lebanese for Ltaif; Jewish, Aus-

trian and French for Bosco. Robin, however, discussing her own writing in a recent text, reminds us not to confuse these few elements of fact with true autobiography. If the writing does contain any autobiography, it is primarily *"intellectuelle, spirituelle"* ("L'écriture" 34). I believe this explanation of Robin also sheds light on the work of Ltaif and Bosco.

Nevertheless, the presence of autobiographical elements reserves a place, however small, for the personal and underlines the fact that all writing originates with the individual. Such a mixture of reality and fiction, or reality and theory, underlies in its very form, the opposition to thought-as-system. Genres, like ideas, engender each other. What is more, speaking as women, these authors bring a feminist scope to the ethics under construction, albeit different from the discourse of protest associated with the late 1970's. Their experiments with structure include many examples of the complexity of forms, voices, and all types of statement. For all three writers, their cultural references are not nearly as clear as their legal identities might indicate. For example, Ltaif's narrators draw on both western and eastern cultures, weaving them together. Bosco's narrator indicates that she is also Austrian and that her first language is German. As for Robin, she recalls that her parents bequeathed to her, however intangibly, a part of their own family culture through memories of their Polish childhoods. Even autobiographical elements appear as strata, accumulating over years or even centuries. The image of the palimpsest may be seen in both individual and cultural identity.

Toward a History of Uncertainty

As a corollary to their denunciation of entrenched

thought, all three authors call for a new ethics, a new way of approaching the world, along with a renewed sense of responsibility and accountability. Of course, none of them is naïve enough to believe that cultural, ethnic or religious wounds can be healed instantly; the scars will remain:

> Dans la terre il y a une mémoire
> cruelle qui nous met
> dans l'impossibilité d'échapper à l'oubli.
> Cette vivance-là terrifiante
> l'impossibilité de fuir. (Ltaif, *Élégies du levant* 24)

Nevertheless, recognizing the indelible marks of pain in no way implies adopting a position of authority. On the contrary, each author tries to imagine a space of renewal where doubt is continually voiced.

The poet Ltaif, in particular, writes of her increasing hesitation:

> De savoir vivre
> avec les autres
> de ne plus savoir vivre.
> Qui pose la question de l'indifférence
> ou de différence d'éthique.
> Je ne sais plus. J'avoue. Plus j'écris moins
> je sais. (*Entre les fleuves* 28)

Her need to mark out the terrain of a new ethics derives from feelings that are, for the most part, ambivalent – *"savoir vivre"* or *"ne plus savoir vivre."* Rather than flee this tension, and the obligation it imposes to doubt and question, the poet plunges directly into it, writing and nourishing her desire to re-evaluate knowledge and cultures in order to push back frontiers, be they linguistic, political, racial or cultural. The language of power, of *"ceux qui croient tout connaître"* (*Élégies du levant* 42) seems to her wholly inadequate, because it does not penetrate *"le secret"* (42). This language, too limited and too codified, touches people and the world at a merely superficial level. Nadine Ltaif wishes for a creolized language that would allow her to hold on to her own words while switching languages (*Les Métamorphoses* 45). This exercise in linguistic métissage – Arabic and French in the case of Ltaif – goes beyond the phenomenon of cultural blending to assume a political dimension, for she also intends to find a language that will be *"ni la langue du pouvoir. Ni celle des soumis"* (*Entre les fleuves* 45). In the same vein, she also questions the notions of race:

> Rien n'est plus meurtrier
> que le concept de race.
> Ni les Noirs ni les Blancs
> ne sont noirs ou blancs. (*Élégies du levant* 35)

Here also, we are dealing with entrenched words; this concept of race is related to others involving religions and the sexes – concepts that she seeks to defuse and elude, fearing the ravages of a forced or overdetermined identity tied to race, birthplace or sex.

But where does it lead, this writing that erodes boundaries, this paradoxical site of ethical questioning? The literary procedure of Nadine Ltaif leads to the unknown, somewhere to a place *between,* as the title of her second book of poetry, *Entre les fleuves*, indicates. Certainly, Ltaif explores exile – her own exile – her intertwined cultures reflecting the Levant and the West, her geographies – Lebanon, Cairo, Montreal – the difficulties of adaptation, the pain of incomprehension and displacement. Yet, more significantly, she chooses not to confine herself, not to belong to either one place or another: *"Ne me réclamant plus d'aucune tribu. / Mourir libre et déracinée"* (*Entre les fleuves* 32) The poet chooses willingly to *"prendre racine aux racines du déracinement"* (28).

She wishes to remain in the movement of the uncertain, the out-of-context, in order to save her writing from the thought-as-system that necessarily belongs to one place, one vision, one group. In spite of her search for meaning, or more likely because of it, she wants no answers to any of her questions about well-ordered concepts because any answer would be reminiscent of entrenched meaning. This rejection of static meaning derives from an ethics in progress, but also from a specific ordeal: the narrator has lived through war, has witnessed death and discrimination, and has seen in the eyes of many others scars similar to her own, and perhaps worse. From one book to another, she tends to stand among the questioners and to constantly be a *"bâtisseuse(s) de rêves et d'impossible"* (*Élégies du levant* 33).

Like Nadine Ltaif, Monique Bosco also talks about detachment rather than belonging. In *Babel-opéra* the narrator, a young Jewish woman who has taken refuge in France during World War II, comes to Québec. She leaves France with almost nothing: *"Quelques mots d'amour / Mince Bagage / Mains vides / Ne rien emporter qui pèse / Et enchaîne"* (51). She believes she is going to the Promised Land, but soon discovers, to her dismay, that *"Tout est toujours semblable . . . Chacun replié sur sa différence"* (77). All through this poetic narrative for multiple voices (as suggested by the word "opéra") the voice of the narrator mingles with those of the chorus of women who are also trying to shatter the power of entrenched beliefs promulgated by ideologues, from biblical times to the present. These women's voices aggressively challenge phenomena such as past and present holy wars, the segregation of races, the mismanagement of nature, the contempt for pain, the hunger of children, and hatred.

Having consciously chosen denunciation and risk,

"Il vaut mieux blasphémer / que de se taire / Un autre jour encore" (9), says the narrator. In the finale, she turns away from everything that risks hindering her quest for wisdom: *"Moi, j'ai choisi de ne plus idolâtrer dieu ou homme, langue et patrie"* (90). She then aligns herself with a vague, yet-to-be-defined counterforce and opts for a historically oriented scepticism, a *"lamentation ancienne, millénaire"* (9), a scepticism that she hopes will genuinely disturb and whose indignation, turned rebellious, may fuel her quest for harmony. Bosco's narrator wants to act against the history of humanity, a history she sums up as: *"Vengeance. À force de se venger, la vie passe dans d'éternelles vendettas . . . Chacun est saoul de haine"* (91).

Because of her distrust of the restrictive definitions of totalizing thought, she calls for an undefined zone of reflection where the unprecedented can flourish, allowing her to see god, man, language and fatherland in a new light:

> Alors, on ouvre les portes. Il est temps de briqueter des briques. D'ouvrir encore plus largement les portes de l'arche. D'édifier une Babel enfin fraternelle où chacun a le droit de vivre selon les lois de son coeur, toutes origines confondues. (93)

In the end, *Babel-opéra* questions the past and the present to risk a dream of impossible harmony in a fraternal Babel. While realizing that this vision, intimately woven of an ethical conception of the self and the world, is hardly feasible, the narrator does not know how to, or does not want to, avoid the narration. She must ask questions and render them in narrativity. This ethical texture, utopian certainly, arises directly from the multiformed and multivocal narrative of the wanderings, exoduses and metamorphoses related to emigration. It is no longer a matter of denouncing a specific oppression (for example, the pain of having lived through the Shoah) but of passing from indignation to dream, and possibly to ethical and benevolent action. In *Babel-opéra*, the solitude of the immigrant, both man and woman, in the Quebec context, is certainly an issue. However, by placing it in a world-historical context, the author transcends the simple or complex local issue, ensuring that her narrative is not itself hemmed in by official borders. She is aware of an ultimate objective: *"que la langue d'amour se fasse entendre"* (95), but the way to that destination must be mapped out day by day and the arrival point is ever more distant.

In a more theoretical vein, Régine Robin has no solution to offer, *"pas même une esquisse de solution,"* in *"Sortir de l'ethnicité"* (25). She also places herself in a territory of questions and perplexity. As she says, *"C'est . . . dans une problématique de la non-coïncidence qu'il faut peser le tissu social, son dynamisme, son évolution"* (29). A single reality, even a single word, is made up of many layers of sense, sometimes contradictory, sometimes slightly out of phase, whose complexity can only be apprehended through the barely perceptible oscillation of the clairvoyant gaze. When a society or sector of society puts too much emphasis on differences, it risks entrenching them as absolutes. When it misunderstands them it risks subjecting different groups to exclusion. Robin believes that, on the contrary, culture must participate in movement. Culture is at once heritage, transmission and putting into perspective. For her, the only identity possible lies somewhere in between the fragmentation and the ossification of identity, *"un espace où il y a du jeu, du va et vient entre une origine assumée dont on arrive à se déprendre et le devenir-autre, le changement qui ne mène pas à la pulvérisation"* (35). She insists on this *"espace de jeu, avec du jeu qui interroge et déplace"* (38), an *"espace nomade"* (25).

Like Ltaif and Bosco, Robin welcomes the unknown and cultivates it because she believes that it carries the potential for new social, political and cultural experiences. She wants neither to conform nor to fall into line, but rather to move about in a fertile, out-of-context location and experience the passage towards a cultural métissage. For Robin, the worst of humanity is not behind us, but "à l'horizon" (39), whence the importance of constantly asking questions and encouraging the "tremblé de l'identité" (38).

These three authors have experienced the solitude of the immigrant, put it in writing, and gone beyond it. Their visions of the world are attached to one place (sometimes Quebec), culture, or language, while at the same time moving easily between continents, cultures, periods and languages. Coloured by their belief in the power of words as bearers of a better understanding of the world and the self, their visions are still being written; they are in a never ending movement. All three stand under the sign of cultural movement, calling simultaneously for a pluralist sense of belonging, for detachment and the fertile possibilities of deracination. This entails a rejection of sealed borders and staunch declarations of allegiance. In distancing themselves from postures of authority, they demand of their readers a mobile gaze, somewhat like that required by holographic art where the eye must move in a slow, oscillating motion to grasp the scope and multiplicity of what is nevertheless a single work.

Should we still speak of what is referred to in Quebec as the writing of migration? Yes and no. Yes, to ensure that the corpus of Quebec writing continues to be actively read, and does not sink into the rut of cut-and-dried reading habits. No, because the danger of entrenching a body of migrant literature in a separate category is always present and is denounced by migrant writers themselves.[5] Taking their cue from the interstitial writing represented here by Ltaif, Bosco and Robin, critics themselves should no doubt attempt, in a similar but different way, to move between two poles and practise a holographic criticism. In the words of Robin, we need to stand

> Ni dedans ni dehors, à l'affût du renouveau de la pensée critique qui couve sous cendre, à l'écoute, dans l'attente d'autre chose, du nouvel imaginaire propre à exprimer la complexité du devenir diasporique du monde. ("L'écriture" 37)

NOTES

1. Monique Bosco was born in Austria in 1927 and emigrated to Québec in 1948. Poet and novelist, she is the author of several works, including: *Un Amour maladroit* (Paris: Gallimard, 1961); *La Femme de Loth* (Paris: Laffont, 1970); *Sara Sage* (Montréal: Hurtubise HMH, 1986) and *Lamento* (Laval: Trois, 1997).

2. Régine Robin was born in France in 1939; she has lived in Québec for many years. She has published several books of critical reflection, two novels and a bio-fiction: *La Québécoite* (1983, republished, Montréal: XYZ, 1993); *L'Immense fatigue des pierres* (Montréal: XYZ, 1996); *Le Naufrage du siècle* followed by *Le Cheval blanc de Lénine ou l'Histoire autre* (Montréal: XYZ, 1995).

3. Nadine Ltaif was born in Cairo in 1961; she lives in Québec where she has published four volumes of poetry. The latest, *Le Livre des dunes* (Saint-Hippolyte, 1999), has just been published.

4. This is a reference to the idea of thought constructed as a system, and the notion of logocentric truth, such as that found in *La Condition postmoderne* by Lyotard. It is an idea that marks feminist writing of the decade 1975-1985. In the case of Québec, examples include Nicole Brossard and Louky Bersianik. In different variations, this questioning of entrenched thought marks the writing of François Charron, Édouard Glissant and the authors analyzed here.

5. Québec criticism is already inventing new categories; the need to classify and circumscribe is never far away. According to the latest issue of *Tangence*, the evolution of Ying Chen is typical in this respect: migrant literature, métis literature, the writing of identity (see the article by Christian Dubois and Christian Homel, as well as the article by Hans-Jürgen Greif). For some, it seems that migrant literature deals essentially with exile and the adaptation or lack of it to the destination country. For others, including L'Hérault, Lequin, Simon and Verthuy, it is more of an open concept that must be kept open.

WORKS CITED

Allard, Jacques. *Le Roman mauve*. Montréal: Québec-Amérique, 1997.

Bosco, Monique. *Babel-opéra*. Laval: Trois, 1989.

Chambers, Iain. "Signs of Silence, Lines of Listening." *The Post-Colonial Question. Common Skies/Divided Horizons*. Eds. Chambers and Lidia Curti. London/New York: Routledge, 1996. 47-62.

Charron, François. *La Passion d'autonomie* followed by *Une Décomposition tranquille*. Montréal: Les Herbes rouges, 1997.

Des Rosiers, Joël. *Théories Caraïbes*. Montréal: Triptyque, 1996.

Dubois, Christian, and Christian Hommel. "Vers une définition du texte migrant: l'exemple de Ying Chen." *Tangence*: "Écrivains d'ailleurs" 59 (hiver 1999): 38-49.

Ewald, François. "Le Renouveau de la philosophie morale." *Magazine littéraire* 361 (janvier 1998): 20.

Glissant, Édouard. *Introduction à une poétique du Divers*. Montréal: Presses de l'Université de Montréal, 1995.

Greif, Hans-Jürgen. "L'Identitaire allophone: les modèles allemand et québécois." *Tangence*: "Écrivains d'ailleurs" 59 (hiver 1999): 87-112.

Ltaif, Nadine. *Élégies du levant*. Saint-Hippolyte, 1995.

———. *Entre les fleuves*. Montréal: Guernica, 1991.

———. *Les Métamorphoses d'Ishtar*. Montréal: Guernica, 1987.

Médam, Alain. "Ethnicité et cité. Entre le "Co" et le "dis", le "Trans"?" *Métamorphoses d'une utopie*. Eds. Jean-Michel Lacroix and Fulvio Caccia. Paris/Montréal: Presses de la Sorbonne Nouvelle-Triptyque, 1992. 49-61.

Minh-ha, Trinh T., and Annamaria Morelli. "The Undone Interval." *The Post-Colonial Question. Common Skies/Divided Horizons*. Eds. Iain Chambers and Lidia Curti. London/New York: Routledge, 1996. 3-16.

Pelletier, Jacques. *Les Habits neufs de la droite culturelle*. Montréal: VLB éditeur, 1994.

Robin, Régine. "L'Écriture d'une allophone d'origine française." *Tangence*: "Écrivains d'ailleurs" 59 (hiver 1999): 26-38

———. *Le Roman mémoriel*. Montréal: Le préambule, 1989.

———. "Sortir de l'ethnicité." *Métamorphoses d'une utopie*. Eds. Jean-Michel Lacroix and Fulvio Caccia. Paris/Montréal: Presses de la Sorbonne Nouvelle-Triptyque, 1992. 25-42.

Simon, Sherry. *Le Trafic des langues. Traduction et culture dans la littérature québécoise*. Montréal: Boréal, 1994.

Cracking the Boundaries

Icelandic-Canadian Challenges to Canadian Literature

Daisy Neijmann

Icelandic-Canadian literature invites many of the questions which recently have come to be addressed by critics concerned with the development of a critical discourse on minority writing in Canada, the most urgent of which no doubt is: how do we conceptualize "Canadian minority writing"? As the comfortable notion of a homogeneous Canadian identity is no longer tenable, and even such binaries as "centre vs. periphery," "ethnic vs. mainstream" and "self vs. other" which have characterized more recent discussions of minority writing, seem too simple, too reductive, and too dependent on notions of cultural homogeneity and authenticity, the need to reexamine our approaches has become particularly acute. The breakdown of a homogeneous Canada, and its notions of cultural authenticity, forces us to redefine exactly what constitutes minority writing in Canada. The main concern of this essay will be this redefinition, viewed from the angle of Icelandic-Canadian literature.

On what basis do we define writers or texts as "minorities?" Do we do so on the basis of a perceived inscription in signature or text? What are the grounds for such perceptions? Is it solely a matter of origins, which, for many in Canada today, are becoming increasingly remote and increasingly diverse? During my explorations of Icelandic-Canadian literature, I have found that many Icelandic-Canadian texts have been begging these questions for years. In 1992 Kirsten Wolf, in a review of

Kristjana Gunnars's collection of new Icelandic-Canadian writing called *Unexpected Fictions*, raised questions about the implications involved in the use of "ethnic" or "Icelandic-Canadian" as literary banners, and their validity when the only basis for their use appears to be that of the author's ancestry rather than anything generated by the text itself. Wolf proceeded to ask the question whether ethnicity can form the basis for defining a literature ("Icelandic-Canadian Literature" 448). Francesco Loriggio has discussed the general complexities of these questions, suggesting that, decades after Barthes's claim that the author is dead, minority discourses have revived "the problematics of signature in a non-trivial manner" ("History" 592). Indeed, Loriggio argues that since ethnicity cannot reliably be defined by content, nor formally, our only clue is signature.

In this paper I would like to contribute to the larger discussion of Canadian minority writing by addressing some of these questions in relation to Icelandic-Canadian literature, a corpus which has a 125-year-old history and provides one frame of reference for generational continuity in minority literature.[1] After all, the history of Canadian multiculturalism is a narrative that has many beginnings, all of which contribute to a better understanding of its many and diverse patterns, as Smaro Kamboureli indicates in her introduction to *Making A Difference* (11). By using the broad term "Icelandic-Canadian literature," I realize, of course, that I am dangerously close to the generalizing approach that has plagued the study of Canadian literary diversity for so long, running the risk of effacing the differences that exist within the corpus. However, the onus of this paper is on discussing how writers of Icelandic descent have in various ways and over the course of time dealt with the question of their role and position in the larger field of Canadian literature and, in doing so, challenged generalizing and

confining classifications of themselves and their writings. In my discussion I will focus on the most promi-
nent writers who, taken together, span the history of
Icelandic-Canadian writing. Particular attention will be
given to Laura Goodman Salverson, whose work represents the transformation from Icelandic to anglophone
writing and evidences the complex dynamics underlying minority literature in Canada.

Enoch Padolsky is, even to date, one of few who has
made concerted attempts to create a critical framework
with which to approach minority writing, loosely defining "minority" on the basis of status in Canadian
society. His suggestions for a "pluralistic" approach are
illuminating when applied to Icelandic-Canadian literature, which has generally benefitted little by approaches
based solely on formal expressions of "otherness." The
fact that Icelandic-Canadian writing has, by now, a fairly
long history in Canada – nearly all Icelandic-Canadian
writers today are fourth-generation Canadians – un-
doubtedly plays a role here. What is striking, however,
about even some very early Icelandic-Canadian texts is
their stubborn resistance to being "othered" and, at the
same time, their strategies to proclaim their difference.
In fact, the majority of Icelandic people in Canada was
quick to infiltrate many levels of Canadian society, intermarriage became a common feature, and identities
were constructed to which Linda Hutcheon's description of "crypto-ethnicity"[2] corresponds, perhaps, the
closest. The slippery nature of many of these Icelandic-
Canadian texts in this respect could be held accountable
for the fact that many critics, both here in Canada as
well as in Iceland, have found it difficult to label them,
recognizing them as somehow "different" yet finding
that "difference" extremely hard to pin down. Trinh T.
Minh-ha has drawn attention to the blurring of divid-
ing lines generated by hyphenated identities and hybrid

realities; her description of the insider looking in from outside who is also looking out from inside seems particularly relevant to Icelandic-Canadian writers:

> Not quite the same, not quite the Other, she stands in that undetermined threshold place where she constantly drifts in and out. Undercutting the inside/outside opposition, her intervention is necessarily that of both a deceptive insider and a deceptive outsider. She is this Inappropriate Other/Same who moves about with always at least two/four gestures: that of affirming "I am like you" while persisting in her difference; and that of reminding "I am different" while unsettling every definition of otherness arrived at. (74)

Icelanders in Canada have tended to resist such simplified divisions from the beginning. Their settlement ideal, signified by their naming of "New Iceland" and "Gimli," was to contribute the best in their Icelandic heritage towards a new and better future in Canada.[3] Icelandic-Canadian literature became the main site for the negotiation and construction of an identity based on this ideal, an identity which embraced Canada while at the same time infusing it with an Icelandic legacy. While nostalgic writing tended to degenerate into the excesses of cultural pride and isolation, writers such as Jóhann Magnús Bjarnason, Stephan G. Stephansson, Guttormur Guttormsson and Gudrún H. Finnsdóttir engaged in literary explorations of the new geographical and social environment they inhabited. Still writing in their native Icelandic, they initiated the process of constructing a Canadian identity which allowed immigrants to both participate in and fully integrate into Canadian society while preserving what they considered valuable in their cultural heritage. The concept of Canadian identity these writers envisioned was one enriched by the heritages and differences of all that shared it.[4] It was largely based on the immigrant view of Canada as a land of possibilities and a new beginning, of freedom and equality, and, as a result, we find early expressions of profound concern over the prevailing attitudes of colonialism and imperialism which informed Anglo-Canadian culture.[5]

For the poets Stephansson and Guttormsson, the immigrant experience had significantly diminished their allegiance to any one country. They regarded themselves instead as citizens of the world, and their work tends to focus on such international issues as social justice, peace and the future of humanity, especially the disenfranchised, in an increasingly technological and materialistic society. Stephansson's ideological position led him into trouble during the First World War, which he regarded as a European imperialist game that used its own people as pawns. Stephansson's collection of anti-war poems, *Vígslóði* (*Battlefield*), was the most controversial contribution to what was probably the most painful clash in the Icelandic-Canadian community, which became hopelessly divided over the question of whether the War constituted a betrayal of Canada's ideals and a victory for Anglo-Canadian colonialism over the rights of those cultural groups with a history of pacifism; or whether it offered people in Canada a chance to prove their worth as Canadian citizens and to settle their sense of indebtedness to the country that offered them a new beginning. The First World War constituted the greatest challenge to the question of Icelandic identity in Canada, and it is therefore not surprising that it reverberates throughout the history of Icelandic-Canadian literature (see Gudsteins's "Stephan G. Stephansson's Legacy"). As David Arnason has pointed out, Stephansson's anti-war poetry constitutes also a significant challenge to the commonly held view that the modern sensibility from which it sprang did not find expression in Canada until much later ("Icelandic Canadian Literature" 61-2).

For immigrant short-story writer Gudrún H. Finnsdóttir, the most pressing concern was the deconstruction of de-

structive dichotomies contained in ethnic and gender boundaries through integration based on a healthy respect for self
and other, a concern she often and most powerfully depicted through the exploration of intermarriage. She
believed that segregation ultimately offered no solution,
but rather envisioned the continuation of the Icelandic
heritage through the constructive integration of future
generations in her emphasis on the importance of
matriarchal values and a nurturing vision for the
development of Canadian society.[6]

For most Icelanders, as apparently for Hutcheon
growing up in Toronto's Little Italy (see "Crypto-
ethnicity"), the "English" were just another cultural
group, and Icelandic immigrant literature became a site
to develop discursive strategies to counter majority assumptions and claims to Canadian culture. In Jóhann
Magnús Bjarnason's fiction, the "English" appear as
empty caricatures, characters who are culturally and
emotionally barren because they have consistently denied themselves the enrichment of cultural interaction
and the value of respect for self and others on which it is
based. Bjarnason, a school teacher, also used fairy-tales
and fables to adapt traditional Icelandic culture to its
new, Canadian social and physical environment.

These Icelandic-Canadian immigrant writers help
demonstrate that minority literatures written in nonofficial languages have engaged in explorations of Canadian society, culture and identity as much as
Anglo-Canadian writings have, and have indeed offered
challenges and alternative views to those advocated in
majority literature.[7] Noteworthy, too, is that the Iceland-
dic-Canadian critical examinations of Canada's social
make-up and the ideologies informing it find their basis
in a strong commitment to Canada and are conducted
from within that position, rather than stemming from
any fixed position outside of Canadian society as the

choice of language might suggest (see Neijmann's "In Search of the Canadian Icelander").

Laura Goodman Salverson, born in Canada to Icelandic immigrants, was the first to take this counter-discourse into the realm of English, thereby laying bare some of the complexities involved in minority writing in Canada. Writing in English about Icelanders suddenly acquired popularity with the larger Canadian audience, but also became an exposé of community secrets: an insider resorting to the outsider's explicative strategies. Salverson spoke the unspeakable, exposing the secrets only to be imparted to insiders to a readership of outsiders, in Minh-ha's words (74). As she broke the silence, Salverson felt maligned and rejected by members of the Icelandic community and stereotyped by her larger Canadian audience, yet always contributing herself to that rejection and stereotypification. Barbara Godard has pointed to the ideological as well as aesthetic implications involved in choice of language for minority writers. When Salverson chose to write in English, she also consciously opted for a different literary and cultural context, different aesthetic expectations, in order to disrupt them. At the same time, Salverson introduced the variable of gender, thus doubling her difference. As a writer, Salverson explicitly set herself up as an example for other aspiring minority writers, particularly women, to follow.[8]

As Gudrún Gudsteins has recently demonstrated, Salverson's first novel, *The Viking Heart* (1923), can fruitfully be read as "doubled" minority women's discourse trying to break the silence within the male realm of Canadian literature in English ("Laura Goodman Salverson's Vineland the Good"). Gudsteins uncovers an "exaggerated doublevoicedness" in what she regards as Salverson's most problematic and most interesting novel. The effects of Salverson's double muting, of not being "heard" by the dominant group as a member of a cultural minority and as a woman, are evidenced by a tendency towards overarticulation due to the effort involved in making muted concerns audible to the dominant majority on terms that it will accept.[9] Such overarticulation could account for the passages of cultural pompousness in *The Viking Heart* to which some critics have objected and which have led others, notably Eli Mandel in his otherwise groundbreaking article "Ethnic Voice in Canadian Writing," to dismiss Salverson's writing as ethnic since it is not concerned with problems of identity and self-definition but considers itself rather part of an authentic culture. As a text immersed in cultural as well as gender politics, however, the novel deals almost exclusively with issues of identity, the construction of a more comprehensive Canadian identity, in particular.

The Viking Heart in many ways continues the identity debate which had up to the novel's publication in 1923 been conducted within the linguistic security of Icelandic, as Salverson set out to establish a dialogue not only with a larger Canadian readership but also with her literary predecessors in the Icelandic-Canadian community. *The Viking Heart,* usually read as a romantic settlement saga, examines the painful process of becoming Canadian from various angles introduced earlier by writers like Stephansson and Finnsdóttir, which challenged majority views of Canadian identity based on an existing hierarchy of power and values. Gudsteins, for instance, has discussed Salverson's textual dialogue with Stephansson and other pacifists in *The Viking Heart*: the passage depicting Loki's slaughter of a calf echoes Stephansson's depiction in his anti-war poem *Vígslóði* of Britain's "reeking slaughter-pen" where blood-thirsty merchants "drink all the bloody profits off" ("Stephan G. Stephansson's Legacy"). Interestingly, the blood symbolism employed by Salverson in this passage is consid-

ered to be "ineffective" and "mechanical" by Alison
Hopwood in her introduction to the NCL edition of
the novel. Hopwood is obviously unaware of the literary dialogue embedded in the imagery. As critics, we need
to be sensitive to the fact that minority writing often
addresses two audiences and engages in cultural dialogues
on different levels.

Salverson also carries on Finnsdóttir's emphasis on
the importance of reuniting polarities through love and
nurturing, and her focus on the role of women in the
development of Canadian society. *The Viking Heart* re-
volves around the love and strength of several powerful
female characters who are the pillars of their community and strongly resist materialistic patriarchy as a betrayal of the promise held by Canada, emphasizing
instead the importance of social and cultural equality.
Like Finnsdóttir, Salverson also displays a resistance of
divisions, advocating the importance of what Gudsteins
has termed "the totality of self," a recognition of the
intrinsic value of self and other, based in a larger belief
in the constructive potential of impurity: good contained
within evil, past within present, destruction within construction, masculinity within femininity ("Wake-Pick
Weavers" 142). In *The Viking Heart*, as in Salverson's
later works, evil is redeemed by "the right effort."[10]

The fact that this has not always been clear to its
readers probably has much to do with the fact that
Salverson, in her attempt to make herself heard from
within, adopted a style and genre then considered appropriate for Canadian women writers by the Anglo-
male establishment (see Campbell; Gerson). She used the
popular form of the romance but infiltrated it with passages of social realism and cultural politics, disrupting
the narrative with Icelandic words indicative of the cultural alternatives suggested by the text. Through her
writing she also challenged majority representations of

Canada and of minority groups in Canadian culture and society. As she herself said:

> Fool or not I venture to believe that my own experience as an outsider member of a minority race has given me a more sympathetic insight into the touchy problem of racial adjustment than can be said of many writers who make use of a similar subject. Ralph Connor may have made a success with his Foreigner, but I should like to know where such a colony existed – and if the whole North End of Winnipeg did not rise up and mob him it only goes to prove that the people so misrepresented were his superiors in humor and forbearance . . .[11]

Her contribution has been important: at a time when ethnogenetic myth-making in Anglo-Canadian writing was reaching its zenith, Salverson challenged from within its own strictures and boundaries the very premise of those myths, helping to open up the field of Canadian literature in English for a larger, multicultural dialogue.

It is rather ironic, although telling, that Salverson has always been considered by non-Icelanders to be a reliable spokesperson, a true representative of her culture, evidencing the fallacy of a monolithic "I" representing an authentic culture (Minh-ha 76). As Salverson herself reveals in her autobiography, she was rejected by many from her community because of her "inaccurate" representation of Iceland in the introductory chapter of *The Viking Heart*.[12] Gender, of course, evidences one site of difference, and it probably exercised a significant influence on Salverson's reception within the Icelandic community (see Wolf's "Western Icelandic Women Writers"). Interestingly, however, Salverson seems to have partly constructed her own rejection by the Icelandic community, just as she condemned some of the same stereotypes of Icelanders she herself helped create or introduced into Canadian literature. This may well have been Salverson's own lived experience that, in Kamboureli's words, "cultural boundaries are porous, that cultural representation is contingent on the authors' singularity of imagination" (4), an imagination that, like identity, is in constant flux, and constantly being reinvented. Salverson continually courted and rejected the positions of insider and outsider, thus resisting being caught by either.

Salverson's writing in itself thus raises many issues important to a discussion of minority writing. While it has now come to be recognized that relations between writers and their cultural communities impinge on, indeed are inscribed in, their literature, critics have so far stayed away from the thorny issue of "popularity," a concern with community readership that translates itself into writing of a less experimental nature. The larger implications of the antagonistic relationship that has developed between academic and popular Canadian writing has fairly recently been discussed by Robert Lecker, and while the issue is, of course, much too large to discuss here in more detail, I believe it is of great pertinence to the field of Canadian minority writing. No one would, I think, deny the grass-roots of most minority cultures and, indeed, its occurrence in more experimental writing has been enthusiastically hailed by critics. However, writers who consciously choose more traditional forms of writing to address a community audience tend to be ignored by critics in the academy (see Padolsky's "Canadian Ethnic Minority Literature in English"). Since literature was a popular occupation among Icelandic immigrants (i.e., practised with enthusiasm by people from all social and occupational levels), a significant component of Icelandic-Canadian writing falls in the category of "popular writing."

Salverson is a good example of someone whose literary reputation has suffered among critics because of her popular appeal. More recently, W. D. Valgardson has experienced a similar lack of academic recognition for his writing, as he made a conscious choice not to alienate the audience which he felt had nourished his aspirations as a writer ("Personal Gods" 180). As Kristjana Gunnars points out in a discussion of the influence of critical reception, or lack thereof, on minority writers:

> The works of both Salverson and Valgardson have been popular as well as literary. But while the writings of both show considerable craftsmanship and artistry, there appears to be an invisible brick wall separating popular acceptance from academic intellectual consideration and absorption into the canon. It is easy to brush these matters off as a question of excellence. ("Ethnicity" 41)

Gunnars goes on to argue that the lack of dialogue with other cultures or with the literary establishment constitutes an "invisible assault" on the writer's self-confidence. Certainly this has been true for Salverson and Valgardson, who experienced their struggle for literary as well as cultural identity as painful.[13] During the current postcolonial climate, the politics informing notions of aesthetic excellence and artistic judgment have, of course, received closer attention. It is important for the development of a critical framework on minority writing that the hierarchies that have kept so many writers on the periphery are not copied but rather re-examined from a fresh perspective, so as not to limit or distort our understanding of minority writing.[14]

Contemporary works by W. D. Valgardson, Kristjana Gunnars and David Arnason bear testimony to the large diversity still existing among Canadian writers of Icelandic descent. Arnason is the only contemporary author of singly Icelandic origins. The issue of multiple origins and its influence on minority writing is one that has remained largely unexplored in Canada, at least among critics. This may be due to the fact that, as Trinh

Minh-ha points out, "Any mutation in identity, in essence, in regularity . . . poses a problem, if not a threat, in terms of classification and control" (73), and this may have been even more strongly the case in Canada where multiculturalism has tended to promote a view of Canada as a cultural mosaic made up of homogeneous ethnic communities. While Gunnars and Valgardson are both known as Icelandic-Canadian writers, Gunnars is in fact half Danish and Valgardson is half Anglo-Irish.

How is mixed heritage inscribed in literature? On the basis of a number of works written by Americans of multiple origins, Michael Fischer has formulated some observations of the writing of mixed heritage.[15] He suggests that "Openness to construction of new identities is promoted by the fact that almost all writers acknowledge a creative sense of being of mixed origins" (224-5):

> It is a matter of finding a voice or style that does not violate one's several components of identity. In part, such a process of assuming an ethnic identity is an insistence on a pluralist, multidimensional, or multi-faceted concept of self: one can be many different things, and this personal sense can be a crucible for a wider social ethos of pluralism. (196)

While it is likely that a plural heritage reinforces these aspects, the dual heritage implied in an Icelandic-Canadian identity, as I have argued, provided sufficient stimulus on its own for the creation of multifaceted concepts of self among Icelandic-Canadian writers. What is of particular interest here is that for a writer like Valgardson, the matter of "multiple origins" has been a traumatic, if ultimately constructive experience, something which he himself has attributed to "the Canadian experience," where segregation often triumphed over integration. Although Valgardson's first short-story collections and novel have almost exclusively been discussed in the light of his

Icelandic background, they deal in fact largely with the rural disenfranchised in an increasingly urban and materialistic society, harking back to the concerns that informed the work of writers like Stephansson and Guttormsson. The setting is decidedly multicultural and often not specifically Icelandic-Canadian. Indeed in many interviews Valgardson has tried to emphasize the fact that he was influenced by the various cultures that inhabit the Interlake area and their shared immigrant history in Canada. He has also claimed that, in spite of his perceived characteristic "saga style," he feels most influenced by Russian writing, conceivably in an attempt to escape the confining influence of the qualifier "Icelandic," like Salverson before him.[16]

In more recent works, Valgardson's concern with cultural dialogue and the construction of identities achieves more prominence, and here, the influence of mixed heritage appears as painful and the existing boundaries between cultural groups as exclusive and divisive. As he explains in an interview:

> Whenever you have a very strong ethnic community, if you are not 100 per cent genetically pure you are very aware: that is the Canadian experience. The whole thing about the integration into becoming Canadian, of course, is very difficult and is most difficult in those who are the first to cross the boundary . . . I have given up all the terrible despair that I felt over not being totally Icelandic and not being totally Irish. It would have been much easier if both parents had been Irish or both parents had been Icelandic. Belonging to two communities forces a kind of growth, and it forces a kind of struggle with something other people do not have to struggle with. That growth is painful, but that is part of the Canadian experience. (*Other Solitudes* 137-139)

The differences in emphasis and tone between his works and those of David Arnason are striking and can in part be explained, I believe, by the fact that Arnason, who also grew up in the Interlake area but in a fully Icelandic family, has been much more secure in his ancestral identity. Interestingly, although Arnason's work appears as multicultural as Valgardson's does, it is much less saliently "Icelandic" than Valgardson's has been perceived to be. Could it be that in Canada, at least for some writers, ethnicity becomes a bigger deal when multiple origins are involved?

Arnason has been quite emphatic about his desire to be regarded as a Canadian writer and, while he strongly identifies with his Icelandic background, he has been very careful to avoid classification solely as an Icelandic-Canadian author. When Arnason's work does deal explicitly with his Icelandic background, it is not in a traumatic but rather in an affectionately playful way, very much, in fact, in the way described by Fischer, where the construction of multiple selves is used to challenge dominant hegemonic ideologies, such as the prominence of Central Canada in representations of Canadian culture, the fallacy of a homogeneous Canadian identity, and inherited colonialisms which Arnason has termed "dreams of Empire" (*New Icelanders* 8). However, even his "non-Icelandic" works often have, on closer reading, a subtext which can be seen in the generational continuity of his Icelandic-Canadian literary heritage. Arnason's writings often revolve around the question of what it means to be Canadian in an increasingly urban, international and globalized culture, resisting the colonial heritage from the old world as well as the colonizing pull from the United States. Arnason's work thus continues to address many of the concerns that occupied his literary forbears. In *The Pagan Wall*, for instance, Arnason revisits the theme of the First World War, this time to examine what it has meant for Canada and its colonial heritage. Iceland makes a very brief appearance in the novel, although none of the main characters is

Icelandic. Gudsteins (see "'Kalda strídid'") has demonstrated how Arnason changes Iceland's geography to symbolize its legacy of encompassing contradictions, thus echoing Salverson's symbolic but inaccurate description of Iceland in *The Viking Heart*, and deconstructing the "sanctity," the cultural colonization imposed by the Icelandic mother country on the development of a separate Icelandic-Canadian culture.[17] Arnason has always made it very clear that, for him, his Icelandic heritage begins with the landing of the first immigrants in Canada in 1875. In this light, it is also interesting to note that Arnason, like his literary predecessor Bjarnason, has frequently created Canadianized versions of traditional fairy-tales and used the genre of the fable to parody mainstream Canadian politics.

Kristjana Gunnars's works, too, display a profound and continuous concern with the issues of identity and representation. She is the only contemporary Icelandic-Canadian writer who is herself an immigrant. When she came to Canada and began to write, she felt that she was automatically equated with the Icelandic community in Canada, although she did not share its history, was unfamiliar with the community, and had been partly moulded by an Iceland which was drastically different from the Iceland the original immigrants had left. These differences were generally ignored; instead, she felt pressured to make the community "her business," as she writes in "Words on Multilinguilism." Gunnars began researching Icelandic immigrant history in Canada, and created her own imaginative representations in *Settlement Poems 1/Settlement Poems 2* and *The Axe's Edge*. Interestingly, the reception of these works in the Icelandic community was one of bewilderment rather than recognition. Her "Icelandicness" was located not so much in an experience of cultural community but in individual displacement. This makes Gunnars's work significantly different from that of Valgardson and Arnason. With Icelandic as a native language Gunnars had direct access to Icelandic immigrant literature rather than receiving it filtered through community experience, and in her works she establishes a textual dialogue with her Icelandic immigrant forbears as part of a larger exploration of Canadian cultural history.

In *Wake-Pick Poems* and *The Prowler*, Gunnars deals with her mixed heritage which, as in Valgardson's works, appears as an outsider's experience. Unlike Valgardson, however, and more like her Icelandic immigrant "foremothers" Finnsdóttir and Salverson, Gunnars actively resists the insider/outsider dichotomy in her texts. In both works, the narrator continually reinvents herself and recreates her own past in order to avoid being trapped by borders, boundaries and stereotypes of all kinds, including generic ones, as she experiments with structure and form to find ways of writing difference, inscribing her multicultural and female identity into Canadian texts.[18]

Having Icelandic as a native language, Gunnars has also experimented with Canadian English, informing it with Icelandic words and Icelandic ways of speaking English. Fully aware of the immigrant past and present of Canada, she promotes the adoption of words and speech rhythms from the ancestral languages of Canada's many immigrants:

> What fascinated me when I began was the possibility of escaping the unilingual mode, expanding the language I wrote in by pushing out the boundaries. I made cracks on the surface of the English I wrote in by shifting into an Icelandic phrase or changing the structure of an English sentence in accordance with Icelandic sentence structure. This is possible in poetry and it is good to be able to let your language be informed by other modes of thought . . . In Canada it should happen with the native tongues and languages of the immi-

grants. Those rhythms should be allowed to enter, to alter the rhythms of English so we can start thinking in other ways. (Demchuk 32-34)

It would seem that in Icelandic-Canadian writing, as Michael Fischer has argued, "It is the inter-references, the interweaving of cultural threads from different arenas, that give ethnicity its phoenix-like capacities for re-invigoration and reinspiration" (230). In spite of many and various differences between individual writers of Icelandic descent, some clear patterns may be detected which appear to suggest a generational continuity in Icelandic-Canadian literature, even among fourth-generation Canadians. These patterns reveal an early and strong commitment to Canada, a profound concern with social and cultural equality, and an enduring resistance to totalizing, homogenizing and confining forces such as colonialism, imperialism and nationalism by continually devising strategies to challenge and escape simplified classifications and definitions. Can ethnicity form the basis for defining a literature? Icelandic-Canadian writers appear to suggest that such an approach by itself is too limiting, too "definitive," although it can contribute to a better understanding, a more diverse reading of a text. Perhaps the only definition that we can ultimately attach to minority literatures is that they are writings which force us back, in a variety of ways, to continually refocus, re-examine, redefine the adjective "Canadian" as a heterogeneous and transcultural concept which is in constant flux.

NOTES

1. See Padolsky's "Canadian Ethnic Minority Literature in English."
2. Hutcheon describes "crypto-ethnicity" as "the situation of immigrants whose family name was changed when they arrived in a new land or women like me who married at a time when social custom meant taking on a husband's surname and who suddenly found more than the nominal marker of their ethnicity altered" (32n). In spite of a vocal group of purists who advocated cultural isolation, a significant component of Icelandic immigrant literature almost immediately tried to accommodate these developments by constructing an Icelandic-Canadian identity which was based in cultural integration.
3. The naming of New Iceland, the original area of settlement along the west coast of Lake Winnipeg which existed as a republic with its own constitution during the first years of immigration, initially indicated the desire to found a new Iceland, but soon the majority of the immigrants changed their past-oriented attitude to a future-oriented one, and the adjective "new" became more important than the noun it qualified. It is the latter meaning that we find in, for instance, the title of David and Vincent Arnason's collection *The New Icelanders*. Gimli is part of a Norse post-apocalyptic myth, the name of the hall where only the best of gods and people will live after the old world has been destroyed, and they have been cleansed of its corruption.
4. For a more elaborate discussion of Icelandic-Canadian literary acculturation patterns see Neijmann's *The Icelandic Voice in Canadian Letters*; Delafenêtre and Neijmann.
5. This concern derived to a large extent from the fact that Iceland itself had been a colony for centuries and was, during the main wave of immigration to Canada, engaged in a nationalist struggle for independence from Denmark.
6. Palmer has discussed the role of matriarchal values in prairie immigrant fiction.
7. I agree with Padolsky's suggestion that minority writing in nonofficial languages can be fruitfully compared with contemporary Anglo-Canadian writing to explore the literary differences engendered by minority and majority positions in society ("Cultural Diversity" 115-16).
8. Indeed, this is the reason she gives for writing her autobiography (*Confessions* 414).
9. Gudsteins relies on Edward and Shirley Ardener's analysis of women as a muted group (see *Perceiving Women*), and on Helga Kress's application of this analysis to early Icelandic women's writing.
10. In *Confessions*, Salverson quotes her father's axiom: "That which people accomplished, whether good or evil, was the true substance of themselves, and could not perish" (214-15). For a more detailed discussion on this, see Gudsteins's "Wake-Pick Weavers."
11. Lorne Pierce Papers, Queen's University Archives, Kingston, box 16, folder 2, item 41, n.d.
12. Gudsteins has demonstrated how this kind of cultural colonialism has persisted in recent Icelandic translations of Icelandic-Canadian literature: in the translation of *Confessions of an Immigrant's Daughter*, for instance, perceived "inaccuracies" in Icelandic details were "corrected," to the detriment of the work's structural integrity (see "Kalda stríðid").
13. Salverson's correspondence with her editor, Lorne Pierce (Ryerson Press), collected in the Lorne Pierce Papers, bears testimony to this, as does her autobiography *Confessions*; Valgardson has fictionalized his painful struggle in *What Can't Be Changed Shouldn't Be Mourned* and *The Girl With The Botticelli Face*. Valgardson also shares with Salverson the difficult reception of his work in the Icelandic-Canadian community, at least, intially: Valgardson, although now well respected, was criticized for his unflattering depiction of the Interlake area and its inhabitants (see Brydon).
14. The role of community for many minority writers, whether in absent or present, negative or positive form, has often been noted, and relations with their cultural

communities and/or literary ancestors are often inscribed in their works. See also Padolsky's "Canadian Ethnic Minority Literature in English," and Kamboureli's introduction to *Making a Difference*.

15. It is telling in this respect that attention for the writing of diverse origins has come from American rather than Canadian critics, such as Sollors, Fischer and Minh-ha. Sollors uses mixed heritage as an argument against what he terms "pure pluralism."

16. Interview with Donna Danylchuk. Valgardson similarly claimed during a reading at "The Icelandic Connection" Conference held in Red Deer, 19-21 October 1995, that his story "The Man Who Always Ran Out of Toilet Paper," which has been perceived as reflecting the traditional Icelandic love and respect for reading and education, actually has a Ukrainian background, although the names of the characters were changed to Icelandic ones. For further comments on the influence of other cultural groups and the immigrant experience, see Valgardson ("An Immigrant Culture") and his interview with Judith Miller in *Other Solitudes* (133-40).

17. George Bisztray has drawn attention to the colonial influence often exercised by the mother countries of cultural minority groups: "Let us face one fact: what we call acculturation, mutual understanding, and good citizenship in this multicultural country, may appear to the cultural chauvinists overseas as bastardization of our ancestral tradition, language and heritage" (112).

18. The reinvention of her own past has significantly influenced the reception of Gunnars's work both in Iceland and in Canada. While the Icelandic-Canadian community does not appear to recognize its immigrant past in Gunnars's works, in Iceland there have been objections to Gunnars's "inaccurate" representations of Icelandic history; as a result, an Icelandic translation of *The Prowler* fell through (see Gudsteins's "Stephan G. Stephansson's Legacy"). For a more elaborate discussion of Gunnars's experiments in writing difference and how they carry on Salverson's earlier efforts in this direction, see Gudsteins's "Wake-Pick Weavers."

WORKS CITED

Arnason, David. *The Dragon and the Dry Goods Princess*. Winnipeg: Turnstone, 1994.

——. "Icelandic-Canadian Literature." *Identifications: Ethnicity and the Writer in Canada*. Ed. Jars Balan. Edmonton: Canadian Institute of Ukrainian Studies at the U of Alberta, 1982. 53-66.

——. *If Pigs Could Fly*. Winnipeg: Turnstone, 1995.

——. *The Pagan Wall*. Vancouver: Talonbooks, 1992.

Arnason, David, and Vincent Arnason, eds. *The New Icelanders: A North American Community*. Winnipeg: Turnstone, 1994.

Bisztray, George. "Comments." "A/PART: Papers from the 1984 Ottawa Conference on Language, Culture and Literary Identity in Canada." Ed. J. M. Bumsted. *Canadian Literature* Supplement 1 (May 1987): 111-13.

Bjarnason, Jóhann Magnús. *Karl litli: Saga frá Draumamörk/ AEvintyri* [*Little Karl: A Story from Dream Forest/Fairytales*]. 1935/1946. Rpt. as *Gimsteinaborgin* [*The City of Jewels*]. *Ritsafn* I. Akureyri: Bókaútgáfan Edda, 1977.

Brydon, Anne. "The Icelanders." *Encyclopaedia of Canada's Peoples*. Multicultural History Society of Ontario. Ed. Paul Robert Magocsi. Toronto: U of Toronto P, 1999. 685-700.

Campbell, Sandra. "Nationalism, Morality, and Gender: Lorne Pierce and the Canadian Literary Canon, 1920-1960." *Papers of the Bibliographical Society of Canada* 32.2 (1994): 135-60.

Danylchuk, Donna. "The Author and His Art." Interview with W. D. Valgardson. *The Icelandic Canadian* (Summer 1987): 32-34.

Delafenêtre, David G., and Daisy L. Neijmann. "The Netherlandic and Scandinavian Transition in Canada: A Sociological and Literary Perspective." *International Journal of Canadian Studies* 15 (1997): 209-30.

Demchuk, David. "Holding Two Ropes: Interview with Kristjana Gunnars." *Prairie Fire* 5.23 (1984): 32-37.

Finnsdóttir, Gudrún Helga. *Dagshríðar Spor [Tracks of Days Struggle]*. Akureyri: Árni Bjarnarson, 1946.

——. *Hillingalönd [Lands of Mirages]*. Reykjavík: Félagsprentsmidjan, 1938.

Fischer, Michael M. J. "Ethnicity and the Post-Modern Arts of Memory." *Writing Culture*. Ed. J. Clifford and G. E. Marcus. Berkeley: U of California P, 1986. 194-233.

Gerson, Carole. "The Canon Between the Wars: Fieldnotes of a Feminist Literary Archaeologist." *Canadian Canons: Essays in Literary Value*. Ed. Robert Lecker. Toronto: U of Toronto P, 1991. 46-56.

Godard, Barbara. "The Discourse of the Other: Canadian Literature and the Question of Ethnicity." *The Massachusetts Review* 31.12 (1990): 153-84.

Gudsteins, Gudrún Björk. "Kalda strídid' í pydingum á íslensk-kanadiskum bokmenntum 1923-1994." *Jón á Bœgisá* 3 (1997): 5-19.

——. "Laura Goodman Salverson's Vineland the Good." The Viking Connection Conference: Canada – Continentalist Perspectives. Ernst-Moritz-Arndt Universität, Greifswald. 3 May 1996.

——. "Stephan G. Stephansson's Legacy in Icelandic-Canadian Literature." The Icelandic Presence in Canada: A Story of Integration – Symposium organized by the U of Manitoba Icelandic Department. Gimli, MB. 24 May 1997.

——. "Wake-Pick Weavers: Laura G. Salverson and Kristjana Gunnars." *O Canada: Essays on Canadian Literature and Culture*. Ed. Jørn Carlsen. Dolphin 25. Aarhus, Denmark: Aarhus UP, 1995. 142-163.

Gunnars, Kristjana. *The Axe's Edge*. Victoria: Porcépic, 1983.

——. "Ethnicity and Canadian Women Writers." *Room of One's Own* 14.4 (1991): 40-50.

——. *The Prowler*. Red Deer: Red Deer College, 1989.

——. *Settlement Poems 1/Settlement Poems 2*. Winnipeg: Turnstone, 1980.

——. ed. *Unexpected Fictions: New Icelandic Canadian Writing*. Winnipeg: Turnstone, 1989.

——. *Wake-Pick Poems*. Toronto: Anansi, 1981.

——. "Words on Multilingualism." *Prairie Fire* 5.23 (1984): 78.

Hutcheon, Linda. "Crypto-ethnicity." *PMLA* 113.1 (1998): 28-33.

Kamboureli, Smaro. Introduction. *Making a Difference: Canadian Multicultural Literature*. Toronto: Oxford UP, 1996.

Kress, Helga. *Máttugar meyjar: íslensk fornbókmenntasaga [Mighty Maidens]*. Reykjavík: Háskólaútgáfan, Háskóla Íslands, 1993.

Lecker, Robert. *Making It Real: The Canonization of English-Canadian Literature*. Toronto: Anansi, 1995.

Loriggio, Francesco. "History, Literary History, and Ethnic Literature." *Canadian Review of Comparative Literature* 16.34 (1989): 575-99.

——. "The Question of the Corpus: Ethnicity and Canadian Literature." *Future Indicative: Literary Theory and Canadian Literature*. Ed. John Moss. Ottawa: U of Ottawa P, 1987. 5368.

Mandel, Eli. "Ethnic Voice in Canadian Writing." *Identities: The Impact of Ethnicity on Canadian Society*. Ed. Wsevolod Isajiw. Canadian Ethnic Studies Association 5. Toronto: Peter Martin, 1977. 57-68.

Neijmann, Daisy L. *The Icelandic Voice in Canadian Letters: The Contribution of Icelandic-Canadian Writers to Canadian Literature*. Ottawa: Carleton UP, 1997.

——. "In Search of the Canadian Icelander: Writing an Icelandic-Canadian Identity into Canadian Literature." *Canadian Ethnic Studies* 29.3 (1998): 64-74.

Minh-ha, Trinh T. "Outside In Inside Out." *When the Moon Waxes Red: Representation, Gender and Cultural Politics*. New York/London: Routledge, 1991. 65-78.

Other Solitudes: Canadian Multicultural Fictions. Ed. Linda Hutcheon and Marion Richmond. Toronto: Oxford UP, 1990.

Padolsky, Enoch. "Canadian Ethnic Minority Literature in English." *Ethnicity and*

Culture in Canada: The Research Landscape. Ed. J. W. Berry and J. A. Laponce. Toronto: U of Toronto P, 1994. 361-86.

——. "Canadian Minority Writing and Acculturation Options." *Literatures of Lesser Diffusion/Littératures de Moindre Diffusion*. Ed. Joseph Pivato. Edmonton: Research Institute for Comparative Literature at the U of Alberta, 1990. 46-64.

——. "Cultural Diversity and Canadian Literature: A Pluralistic Approach." *International Journal of Canadian Studies* 3 (Spring 1991): 111-28.

Palmer, Tamara. "Ethnic Response to the Canadian Prairies, 1900-1950: A Literary Perspective on Perceptions of the Physical and Social Environment." *Prairie Forum* 12.1 (1987): 49-73.

Perceiving Women. Ed. Shirley Ardener. New York: Halsted, 1975.

Salverson, Laura Goodman. *Confessions of an Immigrant's Daughter*. 1939. Social History of Canada 24. Toronto: U of Toronto P, 1981.

——. Correspondence with Lorne Pierce. Lorne Pierce Papers. Kingston: Queen's University Archives.

——. *The Viking Heart*. 1923. New Canadian Library 116. Toronto: McClelland, 1975.

Sollors, Werner. "A Critique of Pure Pluralism." *Reconstructing American Literary History*. Ed. Sacvan Bercovitch. *Harvard English Studies* 13. Cambridge: Harvard UP, 1986. 251-79.

Stephansson, Stephan G. *Selected Prose and Poetry*. Trans. and ed. Kristjana Gunnars. Writing West Series. Red Deer: Red Deer College, 1988.

——. *Vígslódi [Battlefield]*. Reykjavík: Bókaverzlun Ársaels Árnasonar, 1920.

Valgardson, W. D. "An Immigrant Culture: Reconciling Diverse Voices." St. John's College. Winnipeg, U of Manitoba. Nov. 1987.

——. "Personal Gods." *Essays on Canadian Writing* 16.2-3 (1979-80): 179-86.

——. *What Can't Be Changed Shouldn't Be Mourned*. Vancouver: Douglas, 1990.

Wolf, Kirsten. "Icelandic-Canadian Literature: Problems in Generic Classification." *Scandinavian Studies* 64.3 (1992): 439-53.

——. "Western Icelandic Women Writers: Their Contribution to the Literary Canon." *Scandinavian Studies* 66 (1994): 154-203.

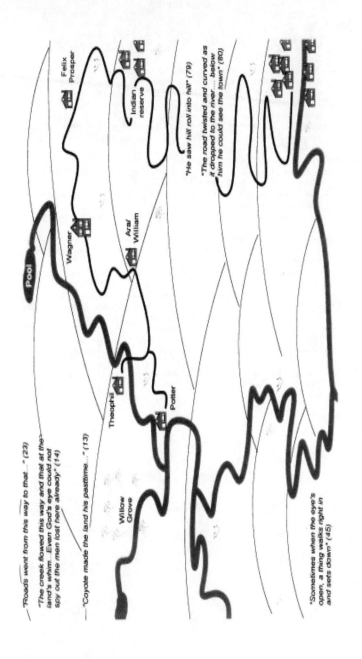

"Roads went from this way to that..." (23)

"The creek flowed this way and that at the land's whim... Even God's eye could not say out the men lost here already." (14)

"Coyote made the land his pastime..." (13)

Willow Grove

Theophil

Pool

Wagner

Ana' William

Potter

Felix Prosper

Indian reserve

"He saw hill roll into hill" (79)

"The road twisted and curved as it dropped to the river... below him he could see the town" (60)

"Sometimes when the eye's open, a thing walks right in and sets down" (45)

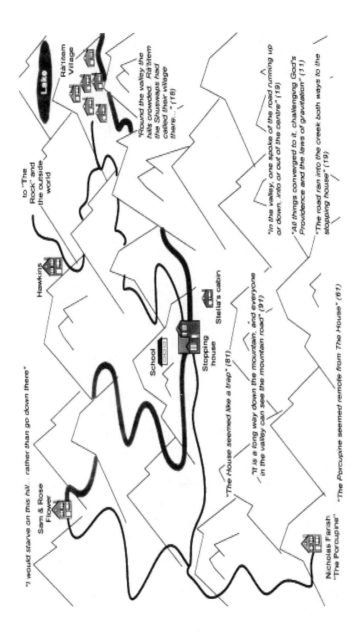

Lake

Ritíem Village

"Round the valley the hills crowded. Ritíem the Shuswaps had called their village there..." (18)

to "The Rock" and the outside world

"In the valley, one spoke of the road running up or down, into or out of the centre" (19)

"All things converged to it, challenging God's Providence and the laws of gravitation" (11)

"The road ran into the creek both ways to the stopping house" (19)

Hawkins

Stella's cabin

School

Stopping house

"I would starve on this hill... rather than go down there"

Sam & Rose Flower

"The House seemed like a trap" (81)

"It is a long way down the mountain, and everyone in the valley can see the mountain road" (91)

"The Porcupine seemed remote from The House" (61)

Nicholas Farish "The Porcupine"

Representations of the "Native Condition" in Watson's *The Double Hook* and *Deep Hollow Creek*

Samara Walbohm

Recently, Sheila Watson's novel *The Double Hook* has been read as a postcolonial text which enacts "the construction of a new world discourse . . . that allow[s] language to reclaim meaning and the new world to claim and sustain itself fully" (Turner 65). In her essay, "Between One Cliché and Another," Barbara Godard sees *The Double Hook* as "above all, a story of the coming of the Word, a dramatization of the beginnings of language and cultural order in a primitive people" (149). Like Turner, Godard situates *The Double Hook* within a discourse of postcolonial literary reaction to Empire. *The Double Hook* is based on "an interrogation of the origins of language" (153) which has set Watson "at odds with prevailing [European] modes of fiction as she attempts decreation" (149).[1] Such an interpretation sets *The Double Hook* against conventional (European/white) language and narrative modes, a critical move which empowers and revitalizes current readings (and rereadings) of Watson's 1959 novel.[2]

As a "postcolonial" novel, *The Double Hook* is firmly rooted within the Canadian literary mainstream. As its "mainstream" author, Sheila Watson writes from a Eurocentred English-Canadian literary tradition (Watson wrote her MA thesis on Addison and Steele). However, to read *The Double Hook* as a Canadian postcolonial text in this way erases Native voice, presence and power from Watson's postcolonial project. Although First Nations mythology is central to *The Double Hook*, the novel's postcolonial/Imperial tension is defined as a new world/white settler linguistic experimentalism which confronts and decreates an old world narrative. This linguistic rebellion excludes the First Nations experience narrative. As Linda Hutcheon suggests, "when Canadian Culture is called post-colonial today the reference is very rarely to the Native culture which might be the more historically accurate use of the term" (172). In effect, First Nations subjects in *The Double Hook* are "doubly colonized" (172). While *The Double Hook* enacts some type of new world experimentation against a narrative (European) norm, it is a reaction (albeit powerful) which appropriates Native myth to serve a white settler (critical) literary objective. The First Nations subject – as the voice and creator of this myth – is neither fully depicted nor recognized and celebrated.

However, a reading of *Deep Hollow Creek* – a novel written in the 1930s but published only in 1992 – problematizes the white settler postcolonial interpretation of *The Double Hook*. Watson's earlier novel reintroduces Native participation in the postcolonial agenda outlined in *The Double Hook*. *Deep Hollow Creek* foregrounds another type of postcolonial rebellion – that of First Nations peoples against the white settler community – and subsequently challenges recent postcolonial critiques of *The Double Hook* which only envision a type of white-on-white postcolonial tension. *Deep Hollow Creek* can be read as an alternative text to the potentially excluding metaphors of tradition suggested by *The Double Hook*. In *The Double Hook*'s metaphor of duality, a privileged, white Christian narrative overrules and ultimately disparages a First Nations, mythological, minority unwritten or unwriteable history. *The Double Hook*'s metaphorical duality exists smoothly with no obvious tension between the peripheral and the central narratives. There is an unproblematic appropriation of Native voice, character and history – the central white mythos dominates by the end of the story. In contrast, *Deep Hollow Creek* is situated in the interface between the peripheral and the central narratives. While *The Double Hook* seems to grant no distinction between the Native margin and the white mainstream (the centre has just subsumed the margin), *Deep Hollow Creek* attempts to include the unwritten, the peripheral. *Deep Hollow Creek* depends on the very contrast between the centre and the margin, between those who speak and those who are held voiceless, between those who write and those who are written about. Watson's emphasis on the silence and "unwriteability" of Native figures and history in *Deep Hollow Creek* suggests their importance to her story.

Read together, Sheila Watson's novels hold a unique place in the interstices between a mainstream and a peripheral Canadian literature. Moreover, because both *The Double Hook* and her recently published *Deep Hollow Creek* were actually written over fifty years ago, Watson's sensitivity to the problematics linked to representation of minority figures by a literary central text seems far ahead of its time and worthy of a retrospective glance. I do not dispute that either of the novels is a white person's story about First Nations people through and through – embedded with assumptions, duplicitous representations and fetishizations. However, a close comparison of Watson's novels suggests that her depictions of First Nations people and culture are not simply aesthetic instruments within mainstream texts. Specifically, Watson's representation of Native figures in *Deep Hollow Creek* grants First Nations people, their culture and their myths a narrative distinction and status not present in *The Double Hook*.[3]

Much Watson scholarship has praised the highly experimental aesthetic quality of *The Double Hook*.[4] It has been suggested that the unique linguistic strength of *The Double Hook* is gained precisely through the juxtaposition of Native myths and oral communicative modes with traditional European Judeo-Christian myths and modes of narration. I agree with these positions and see Native influence as both central and powerful to Watson's narrative process and to the text as a whole. However, it seems to me that the highly aestheticized narrative of *The Double Hook* actually diminishes Native presence and authority while reaffirming Imperial ideologies. Specifically, when read as a postcolonial novel, Watson's deployment of the Native myth of Coyote in *The Double Hook* becomes an act of narrative appropriation. However unintentional it may be, Watson's appropriation of Coyote supports the white settler postcolonial agenda and ultimately occludes a distinctively Native postcolonial experience. This reading situates Coyote in a highly ironized and contradictory role. Coyote symbolizes a condensed, reduced, less recognizable version of Native experience *and* represents the controlling narrative authority of a white text. When *The Double Hook* begins "In the folds of the hills under Coyote's eye lived . . ." (11), First Nations mythology becomes the cultural source from which the novel will grow. However, *The Double Hook* is not about First Nations people – at least, not obviously so. Native voice is represented most generally and metaphorically as the Coyote myth which ironically stifles any actual or individualized Native voice – all things Native are subsumed within this metaphor. The Coyote myth seems initially to centralize Native peoples, cultures and mythologies in the novel. However, the lack of clearly represented Native characters and the gradual disempowerment of the Coyote myth in the novel ultimately displaces Native presence to serve a settler postcolonial agenda. Native myth (and Native presence, more generally) is discarded once that agenda is fulfilled, ultimately erasing Native power both from the text and from any postcolonial readings of *The Double Hook* as a "new world" resistance to Empire.

The problematic displacement and disempowerment of Native people and mythologies in *The Double Hook* is made more explicit through a reading of Watson's *Deep Hollow Creek*. Like *The Double Hook*, *Deep Hollow Creek* explores the social, racial and linguistic problems of a small, isolated community somewhere in the British Columbian interior. But while *The Double Hook* reduces its landscape and characters to mythic abstraction and figurative symbols, *Deep Hollow Creek* depends on a spatial, cultural, historical and political specificity which offers its characters a distinct sense of power. As this paper will attempt to show, the characters, setting and Native relations of *Deep Hollow Creek* are highly realized while those of *The Double Hook* are highly abstracted. In a conscious shift towards a more crafted, aesthetic text, Watson creates characters in *The Double Hook* who are symbolic figures who move in what appears to be a generally depoliticized world. Not only do the unmarked Native figures seem to lack political agency but, by the end of the novel, they are either dead, blinded or smoothly absorbed into the cultural fabric of the white settler community.

While *The Double Hook* seems facilely to appropriate elements of First Nations history, culture and mythology, *Deep Hollow Creek* displays an awareness of how the Native voice/body is or is not representable in a white text. In *The Double Hook*, Native voice is represented metaphorically as the Coyote myth which precludes distinctive, realistically depicted Native characters. However, *Deep Hollow Creek* presents actual Native characters who engage in veritable confrontations – highlighted by Native silence and non-verbal dialogue (and possibly rebellion) – with settler characters. The issue of Native voice is made conspicuous by its very absence. This silenced Native voice is in stark contrast to the distinct narrative of its white mainstream protagonist – Stella, the writer (who can be interpreted, perhaps, as Watson herself). The Native characters of *Deep Hollow Creek* are silent and exist along the periphery of a central white settler community. Yet, this very marginalized silence suggests Watson's awareness of the problematics linked to depicting Native voice. *Deep Hollow Creek* reflects Watson's sensitivity towards Native/settler community relations, which is less apparent in her later novel. While *The Double Hook* seems to erase ethnic distinctions, Native relations are foregrounded in her earlier novel. Rereading *The Double Hook* alongside *Deep Hollow Creek* challenges the relation between a so-called literary periphery and centre. *Deep Hollow Creek* reflects the difficulties of Native representation and ultimately empowers a silent peripheral voice trapped in a white central text. Watson's earlier rendering of First Nations characters in *Deep Hollow Creek* reveals an awareness of the tensions between a literary mainstream and its marginalized fringe, which seems far ahead of both her most well-known work and the 1930s Canadian literary environment from which it emerged.

Watson's changing depiction of the periphery/centre metaphor from *Deep Hollow Creek* to *The Double Hook* parallels a shift in the representation of spatial landscape in the two novels. Both *The Double Hook* and *Deep Hollow Creek* are set in highly suggestive landscapes which can be visually translated into maps.[5] As Graham Huggan suggests, cartography demonstrates strategies for colonial policy implementation and can offer a paradigm for the critique of colonial discourse.

According to Huggan, "key rhetorical strategies imple-
mented in the production of the map such as
reinscription, enclosure and hierarchization of space . . .
provide an analogue for the acquisition, management
and reinforcement of colonial power" (115).[6] An analysis and comparison of the "maps" of *The Double Hook*
and *Deep Hollow Creek* reflects each novel's particular
use of central and marginal narratives and explores their
contrasting roles as postcolonial literary texts.

A visual translation of the geographical setting of
The Double Hook suggests a highly abstract quality – its
"spareness and immediacy" – which allows characters
to "simply be in their time and place" (Flahiff 123).
Despite its very porous and loose spatial configuration,
The Double Hook takes place in a closed community
system – there is no escape from this arid, desolate landscape. James comes close to leaving, but he returns. There
is no sense of anything beyond the surreal universe of
The Double Hook. But, within the community, there is
much interaction, so much that things become almost
claustrophobic. Although certain characters are less than
amicable (even murderous), everyone knows everyone
else; everyone sees everyone see everyone else's business.
The entire community, however remote, is connected by
winding roads and by William's postal delivery route:
"Roads went from this way to that" (23) . . . [and] "the
creek flowed this way and that at the land's whim" (14).
People move from one home to another not by open
invitation as much as through what seem to be perpetu-
ally open doors. There is an almost incestuous exchange
of bodies. The shifting, imminent presence of Old Mrs.
Potter is mistaken for a shadow; Angel moves from Felix
to Theophil and back to Felix; Lenchen sleeps with James
and names her baby after Felix with whom she has spent
the previous night. Ara, Angel and Lenchen shift alternatively in and out of Greta's house. In *The Double Hook*,

there is a lack of boundaries. Fences are continually breaking down and in need of repair. Heinrich's continual
fence-building seems to signify the futile erection of barriers and the need to create and maintain one's own
physical and spiritual space: "I'm going to put a fence
right across the creek, he said, so James Potter's mother
can't go up and down here anymore . . . The boy wrestled
with the roll of wire which curled in on itself seeking the
bend into which it had been twisted" (17,19). In *The
Double Hook* there are no geographical borders; there
seem to be no private spaces. Proximity is too close.

In *The Double Hook*'s abstracted setting – an arid,
spiritually desolate landscape shared by all the characters – there is no sense of historical or cultural specificity. Reflected in this floating, borderless landscape are
characters who, largely unidentifiable by race, history or
cultural markers – Widow Wagner being the exception –
appear as Watson herself has said, like "figures in a
ground." One may speculate that Kip is a Native "mes-
senger," or that the Potters are of Native descent, but the
only clear mention of a Native character in *The Double
Hook* is that of the "Indian reservation" on the way to
town with its "cabins huddled together" and its "bone-
thin dogs" (79). Although Native characters do not
physically participate in the text, Watson uses the Native myth of Coyote to create and symbolize an aesthetic and assumed "white" narrative landscape. This
abstract, boundless landscape frees the novel from any
distinct authorial voice and creates what Watson envisioned for *The Double Hook*: "a cry of voices – a *vox
clamatis* – voices crying out into the wilderness . . . voices
reaching beyond themselves" (Meyer and O'Riordan
158). *The Double Hook*'s surreal, almost transcendental
universe – both its landscape and its people – emerges
out of mythology itself, "In the folds of the hills / under
the eyes of Coyote" (11). It is the multiplicitous poetics

of Coyote's song which fuel the novel and control its
unpredictable, trickster-like rhythms – at least, initially.
But, although the Native myth of Coyote is so central
to *The Double Hook* (perhaps *because* it is), the novel
lacks any clearly marked or defined Native characters.
Something has happened to isolate Native characters in
their own landscape. Coyote not only emerges as the
central controlling narrative force, but also symbolizes a
condensed, all-inclusive version of Native voice, character, culture, history and mythology. Realistic, individual
depictions of Native character are concealed within myth.
It is a desire to articulate voices that are not one's own
that commits Watson (however powerful the result) to
an act of appropriation. Watson would later claim:

> I didn't want it to be an ethnic novel – not a novel about
> Indians or any other deprived group but rather about a
> group of people who had no ability to communicate because
> they had found little to replace the myths and rituals which
> might have bound them together. (Meyer and O'Riordan
> 159)

Although Watson's aim was not to write "an ethnic
novel," her use of the Coyote myth to represent "a group
of bodies that were virtually inarticulate" inevitably makes
The Double Hook an ethnic, political novel embedded
with cultural tensions.[7]

Critical emphasis on *The Double Hook* as a purely
abstract, mythological text seems to erase Native presence in the name of literary aesthetic experimentalism.
Glenn Deer suggests that "*The Double Hook* immerses
the reader in a world whose ontological status is myste-
rious and resistant to rational understanding . . . [where]
we might wonder 'Where are we?' 'What is the nature
of this world?'" ("Miracle" 29). In this abstract, prophetic world, "Watson's presentation creates a sense of
disconnection between cause and effect, agent and act,

act and consequence" (31). In an Afterword to the most recent edition of *The Double Hook* (1989), Fred Flahiff suggests that the high aesthetic level of Watson's novel erased the presence of (or need for) cultural and historical specificity:

> Gone now are the scraps of personal and family history and the details of national and racial origin by means of which the characters sought to locate and understand themselves and others . . . [Watson] moved against such guarantees as are provided by *possibility* and *causality* and *memory* in order to more fully realize that spareness and immediacy that come to characters when they have no alternative but to *be* in their time and place – when they are characters who have no history apart from the experience of their readers. (123, 125)[8]

It is precisely these interpretations of *The Double Hook* as aesthetic (and thus powerful) which enable Watson's appropriation of Native to remain unquestioned.[9] Flahiff's emphasis on the novel's abstract quality, its "spareness and immediacy" which allows characters to simply "*be* in their time and place," is linked to Barbara Godard's reading of *The Double Hook* as "decreation" or a "new way of seeing"(149). What Godard sees as Watson's "dramatization of the coming of the Word," or what Flahiff defines as a landscape without history, nation or race, is really an erasure of Native presence in the name of literary aestheticism. This attempt–whether on the part of critics or of Watson herself – to graft an aesthetic "newness" or an apolitical timelessness onto the literal and metaphorical landscape of *The Double Hook* instead points towards what came *before* the newness. They highlight the presence of a textual, cultural and ethnic history that pre-exists Watson's written account and actually sets up the central paradigm for the novel. The dramatic opening lines of the novel are written in the past tense: "In the folds of the hills / under

Coyote's eye liv*ed* . . ." Here, Watson's words suggest
that much has happened before the text even begins, that
much has happened before *The Double Hook*'s "dramatization of the beginnings of language and cultural order
in a primitive people" (Godard 149). This prior history
suggests a different kind of people than those Godard
refers to – the First Nations people. There is a sense of
history, identity, race and cultural order which pre-exists
that of the settler community depicted in *The Double
Hook*.

Reading *Deep Hollow Creek* as a type of blueprint
for the historical, narrative, spatial and political landscape of *The Double Hook* uncovers the ethnic tensions
beneath the latter's polished, seemingly unproblematic
aesthetic. Interestingly, *Deep Hollow Creek* was composed
before *The Double Hook*, yet, seems to offer a cultural
scenario that precedes it. *Deep Hollow Creek* depicts the
"past" which *The Double Hook* condenses, mythologizes,
appropriates and, indeed, colonizes. Watson's earlier
work presents a Native/settler community which is highly
stratified and distinctive. People are separated and identified by their geographical location, cultural history and/
or community status. Central to *Deep Hollow Creek* are
the cultural/racial tensions which threaten the cohesive-
ness of the community. However, this landscape, rich
with ethnic tension and cultural boundaries, has been
smoothed out by the opening lines of *The Double Hook*'s
abstract aesthetic. Watson's earlier novel reveals how *The
Double Hook*'s representation of Native peoples/myth
alongside a non-Native community or within a non-
Native text is inevitably grounded in some sort of political, historical and ethnic apparatus, although it seems
not to be – nor aims to be. Reading *Deep Hollow Creek*
as a pre-text to *The Double Hook* suggests that Watson's
later novel is grounded in events that occur before the
novel even begins – events which enable a non-Native

community (and a non-Native text) to emerge "In the folds of the hills" under the eye of a Native deity, events upon which *Deep Hollow Creek* are centred. As much as *The Double Hook* lacks specific historical, national or racial references, a reading of *Deep Hollow Creek* considers how Watson's later novel conceals political concerns beneath a narrative mask of aestheticism – a mask created through the appropriation of Native myths, oral narrative modes and symbolism.

The Double Hook's erasure of ethnic distinction and the condensation of Native representation within the Coyote myth removes the possibility for realized and individuated Native and/or white narrative space. The characters first appear as a collective, as an indexed dramatic personae, which suggests a type of colony-like existence. Presented as this genealogical list the characters do not initially possess any distinguishing features, which anticipates *The Double Hook*'s incestuous, borderless landscape. It is a narrative and physical landscape lacking both boundaries and the possibility for personal space. These "figures in a ground" all live together, unified within the symbolic, rejected city of Ninevah (24). Alternatively, *Deep Hollow Creek* foregrounds Native settler relations with detailed characters who live in a realistic and highly demarcated setting. The characters are introduced one by one, each inhabiting a different space within a variegated, hierarchical landscape. Each character has a detailed history and a distinct social past. Each character is politicized and participates in a social, economic and racial system. The contrasting depiction of character and community between *Deep Hollow Creek* and *The Double Hook* becomes more apparent at the end of the novels. While *The Double Hook* concludes with the same organic sense of cohesive community that opened the novel, the separate communities in *Deep Hollow Creek* remain as markedly distinctive at the end of the novel as at the beginning. Indeed, Stella, the one character who links the two geographic and narrative spaces in the novel, leaves the valley – and the text – altogether.

While *The Double Hook*'s nebulous community/narrative is reflected in a borderless, abstract landscape, the very distinctive cultural and narrative perimeters of *Deep Hollow Creek* are suggested in a highly demarcated spatial landscape. The narrative map of *Deep Hollow Creek* sets up a series of metaphors for peripheral and central spaces. Recently, W. H. New has suggested how "demarcations of lands cannot simply refer to physical phenomena, but necessarily include a historical and cultural relation" (8). Geographical boundaries create politically charged spaces that reflect ethnic tensions between a white settler Imperial centre and a First Nations cultural margin. New writes:

> Representations of "Canadian land" consequently illustrate many of the sociocultural and socioeconomic issues raised by post-colonial theory: the issues of colony and empire, wealth and power, centre and margin, the opportunity to speak and the likelihood of being heard. (11)

Land-based metaphors such as those which appear in Watson's fiction encode an assumed authority system based on ethnicity. In so-called mainstream texts, such metaphors assume a privileged perspective which might view the central position as natural or right.[10] While *Deep Hollow Creek* certainly depicts a society demarcated along stratified physical and ethnic boundaries, Watson also reveals how these boundaries hold the potential for confrontation. Watson's earlier novel suggests that the power relations signified by these boundaries may not be truly natural or right, nor are they necessarily fixed. Indeed, a questioning, transgression and breaking-down of these politically encoded narrative and physical spaces is apparent in the actions and writing of Stella – a clearly privileged subject.

The narrative map of *Deep Hollow Creek* is characterized by geographical, ethnic and social boundaries which clearly delineate a peripheral Other (mostly Native) from the white settler urban centre. This narrative, cultural, political and civilized centre lies in the heart of a deep valley surrounded by steep hills, which represent a fringe community of First Nations people and others looked down upon by the privileged centre. Here, Watson sets up a powerful visual paradigm for this periphery/centre metaphor. Stella, the main protagonist who comes "into the valley to find a life for herself" (7), initially lives with Sam and Rose Flower in the hills above the valley. She describes the journey into the hills – away from the centre:

> High up the road wound. Below on the left the river flowed between reddish banks . . . Up hill – the road crumbling away at the shoulder – they climbed, close into the bank . . . [and] all else tended to the river-like artery which twisted below as the land sloped off – fell off roughly – tumbled stones below. All things converged to it. Only the car climbed tenaciously up the slope, challenging God's providence and the laws of gravity. (11)

This realistically described landscape highlights a geographic separation that clearly distinguishes peripheral and central space. The force of the centre is so strong, in fact, that to move away from it (as a privileged subject) is akin to fighting upstream against some sort of natural "artery," to oppose one's religion and even to challenge laws of science.

The valley of Deep Hollow Creek is inhabited by a settler population, most of whom are first- or second-generation European immigrants. This community is often referred to as the centre of things: "In the valley, all things moved to a point . . . [O]ne spoke of the road running up or down, into or out of the centre" (19). Within the centre itself, "the road ran into the creek both ways to the stopping house" (19), a type of general store from which all action emerges. As Stella looks down to the village from her first house on the hill, she

> Could see the angled roof of the stopping house diagonally to the right against the down falling drop of the land which she thought seemed to contract and fall into the narrow valley from the flat outreaching land above. Only with difficulty, she thought, can I raise my eyes. They focus inevitably on the stopping house . . . (13)

The stopping house is run by the most cosmopolitan, European of characters, Mamie Flower, who is depicted as "arranging and rearranging the folds of black crepe to show a slim city-bred ankle," telling her story "with the abandoned fluency of the lady of quality in Smollet's – or was it Defoe's tale" (13). Mamie Flower is part of the privileged settler community which sees itself as the natural centre of civilization surrounded by a vast, uninhabited nothingness that displaces Native significance. However, beyond this naturally garrisoned centre, virtually defining the perimeters of Deep Hollow Creek, live the First Nations people: "Round the valley the hills crowded. Ra'tltem the Shuswaps had called their village there; they were the people of the deep hollow" (18). The distinct geographical boundaries in *Deep Hollow Creek* reflect a heightened tension between inhabitants of peripheral and central spaces. Rose Flower "would starve on this hill . . . rather than go down there" (19). Bill tells Stella, "Living up on the hill you're on their side" (54). From the centre, Mamie wonders, "What Sam wanted to do digging himself up into the hill I don't know . . . No one goes to see Rose . . . No one" (18). Of course, what Mamie means is that no one from the *centre* visits Rose.

The most powerful instances of inside/outside tension occur with the physical transgression of spatial borders – that is, during realistically depicted interactions between central and peripheral characters. Rather than symbolizing fixed, naturalized power relations, physical boundaries in *Deep Hollow Creek* become potential sites for confrontation. The interstices between the periphery and the centre – and the people who shift between these two spaces – appear to resist or to defy an encoded authority of privilege. The most telling challenges occur when Stella, the main protagonist who may or may not stand in for Watson herself, comes to experience a form of Native resistance against settler culture and authority.

As the novel begins, Stella is the outsider, a visiting school teacher brought in from the city. Stella's teacher status, her urban background and, perhaps most significantly, the depiction of her as a reader and a writer as well as the actual narrator of the novel, clearly portray her as a member of the privileged centre. However, Stella's journey of self shifts her away from this centre towards the novel's narrative fringe. Stella's outside position sets her apart from the community and allows her to enact the role of a detached observer. The portrayal of Native experience as different from and inaccessible to settler culture in *Deep Hollow Creek* is a direct result of this narrative perspective. Stella's roles as the external narrator, teacher, reader and writer inevitably address the problematics associated with representation of Native experience by a white writer in a white text.

While the (ostensibly) all-embracing narrative perspective of *The Double Hook* appears to erase ethnic tensions, Stella's dynamic position as both a fringe and a central character highlights these tensions and exposes the difficulties inherent in the attempt to portray an experience that is not one's own. In *The Double Hook*, Native representation is fully accessible to a white writer and a white text; indeed, Native characters, culture and history are appropriated by Watson's central narrative as the Coyote myth. The portrayal of Native experience is manipulable, obscure and held powerless as "Native" because it is grounded in myth – a myth viewed through a white narrative lens. There is no individualized, realistic Native voice. But, in *Deep Hollow Creek*, Native experience is depicted in highly realized interactions with settlers, particularly, with Stella. Stella's recorded, realistically presented interchanges with Native characters attest to the very unrepresentability of Native voice in a white narrative format and disallow a privileged narrative system to fully encode or appropriate First Nations voice.

Stella's relations with the Natives in *Deep Hollow Creek* highlight their narrative silence which contrasts with the gossipy, familiar dialogue of the settler community. For example, when Stella engages to buy a horse from Old Saul John, their interaction is marked by abrupt pauses, silences and voiceless gestures:

> Uncle Dick has sent an Indian . . . Old Saul John from Shallow Creek.
> Stella went out.
> The man said nothing.
> Well, she said.
> He jerked his head towards the horse.
> Gentle saddle horse, he said, resting his chin in the folds of cloth he wore knotted about this throat. Then he was silent again.
> Stella stepped up to the horse.
> I'd like to see him, Stella suggested.
> Look, he said, no touch. (56)

The awkward dynamics of this interaction signify both the problems associated with Native/settler relations in the novel and the difficulties of representing Native experience and culture in this sort of textual framework.

As in *The Double Hook*, Native voice is silent in *Deep Hollow Creek*. But Watson's earlier novel suggests that this silence is not a simple negation of Native voice by a white text. By choosing not to represent Native voice, Watson offers the possibility for a distinct Native experience – an Other cultural narrative from which the white narrative tradition is denied. The very inability to represent another's voice affords the Native an ironic (because it *is* silent) power that is beyond the restrictive authority of the white text. In this way, Stella (and/or Watson) seems sensitive to issues of appropriation – she does not attempt to speak in another's tongue. Old Saul John is silent in this interaction, not powerful in a traditional textual way. However, Watson offers him a type of personal narrative space – a void, perhaps – where his own narrative and experiences lie. Watson does not attempt to articulate the Native narrative for him; there is no translation for the white text. What remains so emphatically is silence. Although presented as fragmented and one-sided, Stella's interactions with Native characters resist the appropriation and encoding of the white experience narrative.

One night, after Stella had hired Elizabeth, a First Nations woman, to help around the house, she hears

> . . . a tap on the door – a tap between loud and soft, a tap between a demand and a request . . .
> He stood there holding his hat, his spurs dragging on the floor. She did not know him.
> There is a courage born of caste, of position, of prerogative. No one would dare to hurt me, she thought.
> Juno stood over the pups, rigid.
> Yes? She questioned.
> Leezbeeth, he said, I come to tell you Leezbeeth n-o come. I come to tell you I n-o let Leezbeeth come. I come to tell you Leezbeeth n-o work for other people. My woman n-o work for n-o-one. (136)

Here, Stella's sense of fear, alongside both her need for domestic labour and an articulation of racial and cultural superiority, reflects the contradictory representation of First Nations characters in *Deep Hollow Creek*. Stella identifies with a privilege "of caste, of position, of prerogative," yet Watson depicts a First Nations challenge to this assumed, encoded authority system. Within this inconsistent portrayal of Native and settler relations, Stella (Watson) imagines the potential for Native resistance and self-motivation in individual, highly realized scenes – a power which is decidedly lacking in *The Double Hook*.

As the novel progresses, Stella comes to situate herself further and further from the settler community centre. She leaves her boarding room at the Flowers' to live on her own, a move looked down upon by the privileged centre: "Women don't do it in this country . . . there's only one kind of woman lives alone and it's not for quiet's sake she does it" (72). Stella becomes more critical of the centre – she thinks that "Living in the valley is like living in a pit" (61), and that the "[boarding] House seemed like a trap" (81). At the end of the novel, Stella leaves the valley. She absently offers a cigarette to her dog remarking, "I don't know . . . I really don't know who is mad. It is time for us to get out of here" (141). Perhaps Stella is voicing a type of "madness" about the problematic community relations in Deep Hollow Creek. Perhaps she senses her inability to change these relations – her inability to fit within a physically outlined cultural landscape. Perhaps Stella (or Watson herself) expresses a sensitivity to the difficult relations between proximate marginal and central spaces. An inability to fully represent the peripheral experience in a white central narrative is reflected in the desire to get out – both of the valley and of the textual enterprise itself.[11]

It is Watson's awareness of ethnic tensions and the doubled portrayal of Natives in *Deep Hollow Creek* which necessarily inform one's reading of *The Double Hook*. However much *The Double Hook* seems to be an aestheticized, depoliticized text, *Deep Hollow Creek* reveals the ethnic tensions concealed beneath its polished, mythologized narrative mask. Watson's replacement of *Deep Hollow Creek*'s narrative perspective (Stella) with Coyote in *The Double Hook* ostensibly erases the distinction between peripheral Native and central settler cultures. It is Watson's vision of the *vox clamatis* in *The Double Hook* – a desire and self-professed ability to express voices which are not one's own – which commits her to an act of appropriation. This appropriation is clearly suggested when Watson, walking along Toronto's Bloor Street, fifteen years and four thousand kilometres away from these "voices," conceives *The Double Hook* and recalls, "I know what I am going to do – I can hear the voices" (Meyer and O'Riordan 159). While *The Double Hook* is a powerful watershed of Canadian literary experimentalism and has been read as a central (white) postcolonial text, it must also be considered in terms of its First Nations political, historical and cultural specificities.[12] What appears to be an unproblematic representation of First Nations myth and culture enables an unquestioned ideological triumph of the settler community and reaffirms Imperial authority. Indeed, while *The Double Hook* unfolds under the powerful eyes of a Native deity, this First Nations participation in the novel is gradually deflated. The once transcendent Coyote is demeaned from mythical status to a flesh and bone coyote. As Dawn Rae Downton has pointed out, Coyote loses "its mythical stature and its ability to intimidate and fragment in proportion to the demise of Kip [Coyote's 'servant']" (183).[13]

Despite what seems to be an apolitical, aestheticized

novel, the political nature of Sheila Watson's *The Double Hook* is made clear through a reading of her earlier novel, *Deep Hollow Creek*. Reading *Deep Hollow Creek* as a type of pretext problematizes *The Double Hook*'s appropriation of Native voice – an appropriation which necessarily submits representations of First Nations people, culture and myth to the power of a white central narrative and, ultimately, to its underlying moral order, values and cultural systems. Sheila Watson has spoken of *The Double Hook* as being concerned with "figures in a ground, from which they could not be separated" ("What I'm Going to Do" 15). *Deep Hollow Creek* asks what kind of figures and to what kind of ground she refers. *Deep Hollow Creek* reinterprets how landscape tropes encode political and ethnic power relations between a privileged, mainstream, white, narrative system and a marginal, First Nations unwritten culture and people. While *The Double Hook* seems to erase ethnic borders, appropriate the marginalized, and assume a natural historical, sociopolitical and cultural superiority, *Deep Hollow Creek* depicts boundaries as sites of confrontation, offering the peripheral experience an opportunity to resist an encoding authority narrative.

NOTES

1. See Grube; Kroetsch; Downton.
2. Although published in 1959, *The Double Hook* was written in the 1930s.
3. See Putzel for a detailed look at British Columbian Indian Coyote tales. Putzel's essay looks at "the new meaning these tales take on when filtered through the imaginations of the white settlers, and at the relationship between the Indian's trickster and the settlers' Judeo-Christian God" (8).
4. See Deer; Flahiff; Godard; Kreisel.
5. See maps by Samara Walbolm on pages 78-79. The first represents spatial references in *The Double Hook,* and the second, spatial references in *Deep Hollow Creek.*
6. See Huggan for a discussion of mimetic representation in cartography and colonialism and the "ironic and/or parodic treatment of maps as metaphors in postcolonial literary texts" (122).
7. George Bowering's suggestion that Watson's Coyote might be a "White Coast author's Coyote" (Putzel 7) reflects an awareness of these embedded cultural tensions.
8. See Godard; Kreisel.

9. I am not minimizing the power of this and other similar readings, but it seems to me that they ignore issues surrounding Native representation in the novel.
10. For a deeper analysis, see W. H. New (321).
11. It is of course interesting to contemplate Watson's decision not to publish *Deep Hollow Creek* earlier, especially after the success of *The Double Hook*.
12. See Putzel.
13. For a discussion of the rise of a new efficacy of language, see Downton; Godard.

WORKS CITED AND CONSULTED

Bowering, Angela. *Figures Cut in a Sacred Ground: Illuminati in* The Double Hook. Edmonton: NeWest, 1988.
Bowering, George. "Sheila Watson, Trickster." *The Mask in Place: Essays on Fiction in North America*. Winnipeg: Turnstone, 1982. 97-111.
Brydon, Diana. "The White Inuit Speaks: Contamination as Literary Strategy." *Past the Last Post: Theorizing Postcolonialism and Postmodernism*. Eds. I. Adam and H. Tiffin. New York/London: Harvester Wheatsheaf, 1991. 136-142.
Davidson, Arnold E. "*The Double Hook*'s Double Hooks." *Canadian Literature* 116 (1988): 29-41.
Deer, Glenn. "Miracle, Mystery and Authority: Rereading *The Double Hook*." *Open Letter* 6.8 (1987): 25-43.
——."Postmodern Canadian Fiction and the Rhetoric of Authority." *University of Toronto Quarterly* 65.1 (Winter 1995): 218-220.
Downton, Dawn Rae. "Message and Messengers in *The Double Hook*." *Sheila Watson and* The Double Hook. Ed. George Bowering. Ottawa: Golden Dog, 1985. 177-84.
During, Simon. "Postmodernism or postcolonialism?" *Landfall* 39.3 (September 1985): 366-80.
Flahiff, F. T. Afterword. *The Double Hook*. By Sheila Watson. 1959. Toronto: McClelland, 1989. 119-139.
Godard, Barbara. "Between One Cliché and Another: Language in *The Double Hook*." *Studies in Canadian Literature* 3.2 (1978): 149-65.
Grace, Sherrill E. *Regression and Apocalypse: Studies in North American Literary Expressionism*. Toronto/Buffalo/London: U of Toronto P, 1989.
Grube, John. Introduction. *The Double Hook*. By Sheila Watson. 1959. New Canadian Library. Toronto: McClelland, 1966. *Sheila Watson and* The Double Hook. Ed. George Bowering. Ottawa: Golden Dog, 1985. 73-82.
Huggan, Graham. "Decolonizing the Map: Post-Colonialism, Post-Structuralism and the Cartographic Connection." *Ariel* 20.4 (1989): 115-31.
Hutcheon, Linda. "Circling the Downspout of Empire: Postcolonialism and Postmodernism." *Ariel* 20.4 (1989): 149-75.
Kreisel, Henry. "Sheila Watson in Edmonton." *Figures in a Ground: Canadian Essays on Modern Literature Collected in Honour of Sheila Watson*. Eds. D. Bessai and D. Jackel. Saskatoon: Western Producer Prairie, 1978. 46.
Kroetsch, Robert. "Death is a Happy Ending: A Dialogue in 13 Parts." *Figures in a Ground: Canadian Essays on Modern Literature Collected in Honour of Sheila Watson*. Eds. D. Bessai and D. Jackel. Saskatoon: Western Producer Prairie, 1978. 207-215.
Meyer, Bruce, and Brian O'Riordan. "Sheila Watson: It's What You Say." *In Their Words: Interviews With Fourteen Canadian Writers*. Toronto: Anansi, 1984. 154-67.
Mitchell, Beverly. "Association and Allusion in *The Double Hook*." *Sheila Watson and* The Double Hook. Ed. George Bowering. Ottawa: Golden Dog, 1985. 99-114.
Monkman, Leslie. "Coyote as Trickster in *The Double Hook*." *Sheila Watson and* The Double Hook. Ed. George Bowering. Ottawa: Golden Dog, 1985. 63-72.
Neuman, Shirley. "Sheila Watson." *Profiles in Canadian Literature*. Vol. 4. Ed. Jeffrey M. Heath. Toronto/Charlottetown: Dundurn, 1982. 45-52.

New, W. H. *Land Sliding: Imagining Space, Presence and Power in Canadian Writing*. Toronto: U of Toronto P, 1997.

Ondaatje, Michael. Afterword. *Tay John*. By Howard OHagan. 1960. New Canadian Library. Toronto: McClelland, 1989. 265-72.

Putzel, Stephen. "Under Coyotes Eye: Indian Tales in Sheila Watsons *The Double Hook*." *Canadian Literature* 102 (1984): 716.

Rooke, Constance. "Women of *The Double Hook*." *Fear of the Open Heart: Essays on Contemporary Canadian Writing*. Toronto: Coach House, 1989. 82-92.

Scobie, Stephen. *Sheila Watson and Her Works*. Toronto: ECW, 1984.

Turner, Margaret E. *Imagining Culture: New World Narrative and the Writing of Canada*. Montreal/Kingston: McGill-Queens UP, 1995.

Watson, Sheila. *Deep Hollow Creek*. Toronto: McClelland, 1992.

——. *The Double Hook*. 1959. Toronto: McClelland, 1989.

——. "Close to the Truth." Interview with Pat Barclay. *Books in Canada* (Sept. 1992): 11-13.

——. "What Im Going to Do." *Sheila Watson and* The Double Hook. Ed. George Bowering. Ottawa: Golden Dog, 1985. 13-15

Wilmott, Glenn. "The Nature of Modernism in *Deep Hollow Creek*." *Canadian Literature* 146 (Autumn 1995): 30-48.

This Tormenting Time of Indecision

Performative Metaphors in Austin Clarke's The Origin of Waves

Heike Harting

> But as this withdrawal of the metaphoric leaves no place free for a discourse of the proper or the literal, it will have at the same time the sense of a re-fold . . . , of what retreats like a wave on the shoreline, and of a re-turn . . . , of the over-charging repetition of a supplementary trait, of yet another metaphor, a discourse whose rhetorical border is no longer determinable according to a simple and indivisible line, according to a linear and indecomposable trait.
>
> Jacques Derrida, "The Retrait of Metaphor."

The opening scene of Austin Clarke's latest novel *The Origin of Waves* (1997) takes the reader into a childhood memory of Tim, the novel's narrator. He remembers the time he spent with his friend John at a beach in their native Barbados, watching the waves advancing and receding. In their repetitive movement, the waves wash ashore a conch-shell, and an old, patched inner tube from a truck which becomes the boys' floating toy. At the beach the two friends contemplate their first and shared love, and their fears of drowning in the sea, as so many fishermen and relatives have done. As a medium of transportation, the sea also carries the boys' hopes to leave the island and its persisting shadow of colonialism for a more promising future in the US or in Canada. Though John and Tim do emigrate to these countries, respectively, their hopes for success and self-realization remain ambivalently

unfulfilled. During an unexpected meeting in Toronto
after forty-five years of lost contact, both men have to
face "the hurtful memory of those glorious, happy days"
(32).

The men retell the events of their past and become
the readers and the writers of their own life-stories. John
invents a tale of immigrant success and adventure. Having exploited the racist system of the southern US to his
advantage, he now pretends to be a successful psycho-
analyst and the proud father of a large number of children as a result of his various intercultural marriages.
Tim, in contrast, leads a life of self-reproach, isolation
and frustration caused by his failed relationship with a
Chinese woman, Lang, a law student whom he met
while he was a student at Trinity College. Although the
relationship between Tim and Lang must have ended
more than forty years prior to Tim's meeting with John,
Tim clings to the memory of his Trinity time and his
two- or three-month affair with Lang as the happiest
time he had in Canada. The various versions of his relationship with Lang that Tim conveys keep both John
and the reader unclear as to whether Lang actually died
or simply became lost as an object of Tim's love.[1] Each
account of Lang, however, is punctuated by metaphors
that originate in Tim's Caribbean past. Tim's narratives
of loss and memory suggest, as does the opening scene
of the novel, that the psychological configuration of
the novel's characters is marked by a nostalgia which
keeps them locked between the desire of return and an
aggressive need to foster old wounds.[2]

Both men's narratives, however, are frequently in-
terrupted by the recurrence of the conch-shell and inner
tube metaphors which, like the waves, recoil from and
re-enter Tim's and John's narratives. In Tim's memory
the conch-shell signals a loss of speech that is linked to
his fear of poverty and his apparently lost love, Lang. As

a marker of repression in Tim's psychic life the conch-shell determines the gaps and twists in Tim's narrative. The novel's rhetorical movements of withdrawal and doubling also figure in the structure of Tim's and John's dialogue because both characters advance life-stories based on fantasies of cultural authenticity and original-ity from which they eventually retreat through a repeated telling of their stories. Characterized by the motion of withdrawal and return, the symbolism of the conch-shell and the waves provides a theoretical intersection of psy-choanalysis, performativity and metaphor that shifts the novel's apparent focus of nostalgia to melancholia.

This shift combines discourses of the psychic and the social and enables a reading of how metaphor can intervene into rather than consolidate the binary struc-tures of processes of identity formation. If the conch-shell signifies speechlessness as the normative condition of Tim's life, then the constant return of this metaphor in Tim's memory also exposes practices of social and cultural containment that construct loss as untranslat-able. Instead of emphasizing metaphor's received divi-sion into tenor and vehicle and its self-identifying operations of substitution, the conch-shell and inner tube metaphors operate performatively. More precisely, they reiterate, disidentify and resignify the historically sedimented effects of their prior circulations in both Caribbean literature and hegemonic discourses of iden-tity production. A performative articulation of both of these metaphors facilitates a critical reading of how so-cial and psychic conformity to dominant notions of cultural authenticity governs the construction of ethnic subjectivities in Clarke's novel. At the same time, a performative reading of metaphor questions dominant theoretical conceptualizations of metaphor in the dis-course of ethnic Canadian writing by examining how one is interpellated as "ethnic."

As a trope of power, metaphor names, designates and produces memory to compel reductive and homogeneous identities. They construct, to use Judith Butler's phrase, "subjects in subjection" (*Excitable Speech* 34). More specifically, by hailing and classifying somebody as ethnic, metaphor serves to constitute and naturalize a cultural norm at whose margins the "ethnic" appears as the cultural Other. Yet, it is precisely from the social and political position assigned through an act of naming that it becomes possible to generate agency because "the reiterative operation" of interpellation, as Butler argues, "has the effect of sedimenting" the subject's social and cultural "'positionality' over time" (34). The conch-shell metaphor, for example, not only indicates how Tim's identity is produced historically through exile and migration, but also marks his liminal and defying social position within Canada's multicultural mosaic. Performative metaphors, I suggest, negotiate how agency can emerge from within the constraints of power, not by merging into or mimicking the structures of power but by reiterating and disidentifying their operative modes and effects. While the conch-shell signifies a normative configuration of cultural Otherness in Tim's psychic life, its constant reiteration in Clarke's novel undermines the binary concepts that govern the production of cultural Otherness.

The novel introduces the conch-shell as a silent participant in the boys' beach conversations. Subsequently triggering both the narrative and the memories of the narrator, the conch-shell functions as the novel's metaphorical marker and carrier of Caribbean history, which, as Edward Kamau Brathwaite argues, is "submarine" (1). In the discourse of Caribbean history and literature the sea signifies the absence of an empirical archive of historical data and designates both a history of loss and relation inaugurated by the middle passage and the slave trade. It points toward the construction of a Caribbean national identity based on cultural and racial hybridity.[3] In Tim's memory, as well as in a wider discourse of Caribbean history, the conch-shell already carries the normative traits of an imagined cultural belonging and originality. In the Caribbean setting of Tim's childhood, however, the conch-shell cannot be linked to one singular cultural origin. The exoticizing and authenticizing connotations and effects of the conch-shell, that retrospectively turn Tim's childhood and cultural origins into an idealized past, only emerge once Tim migrates to Canada.

Symbolically speaking, the process of migration is, of course, also a metaphorical movement of displacement and idealization.[4] From the beginning of Clarke's novel, then, the conch-shell does not fully comply to an essentialist notion of cultural belonging. On the contrary, being itself displaced on the beach, the conch assumes a liminal position, emphasizing borders and spaces of inbetweenness, prior movements and sounds purporting to echo the sea while, in fact, reflecting the listener's own inner blood stream. It bears the traces of other histories and memories such as the death of Tim's uncle, the fear of drowning, the hope for a safe return from the sea, the colonial "Combermere School for Boys" (*Origin* 11), the dream of Chermadene (38), and Tim and John's childhood love. The conch-shell, then, dramatizes and maintains the conflict between Tim's desire for an identity of unequivocal cultural origins and identity formation processes that can neither generate nor emerge from subjective autonomy.

Both metaphors, the conch-shell and the inner tube, explore the multiply split postcolonial and ethnic subject-positions while altering metaphor's conventional definition[5] as a binary trope of substitution and resemblance into performative operations. The practice of performative reiteration and citation of the conch-shell's various signifying traces places the normalizing effects of the conch-shell metaphor in culturally and histori- cally specific discourses and simultaneously opens it to- ward a discursive process of resignification. The conch and the inner tube negotiate the cultural and psycho- logical losses and gains of those "tormenting time[s] of indecision" (22) which mark the historical and contem- porary experience of Caribbean exile and emigration. At the same time, a performative reading of these meta- phors contests the privileged use of tropes such as irony, mimicry, satire and allegory in theoretical conceptu- alizations of ethnic Canadian texts to examine some exclusionary practices of cultural representation.

If it is true that one cannot write outside of meta- phor, it seems necessary to probe why a theoretical evalu- ation of metaphor is so frequently absent from the discourses of ethnic Canadian literary criticism. For a tentative answer I would like to turn to Gilles Deleuze and Félix Guattari's ground-breaking and widely used concept of a "minor literature" because, since its publi- cation in 1986, it has significantly shaped the works of various ethnic Canadian literary critics.[6] The revolution- izing and deterritorializing practices Deleuze and Guattari assign to ethnic writing often determine to what degree metaphor, as well as other forms of symbolism, are marginalized in ethnic literary discourses. The authors' exclusion of metaphor from what they define as an "in- tensive utilization of language" (22) participates in what Smaro Kamboureli refers to as the "technology of ethnicity" (202), that is, the dominant practices of con- structing ethnicity.

Departing from Kafka's rejection of metaphor as a trope of power and containment, Deleuze and Guattari equally classify metaphor as a nominal trope of substi- tution and binary representation. With their view of the writing practices of minor literatures as machine-like or rhizomatic they, by and large, oppose metaphor to the polysemous uses of metamorphosis. Rather than refer- ring to a proper and figurative referentiality, metamorphosis denotes "a distribution of states" (22), or an "*intensive utilization* of language." Intensive writing, Deleuze and Guattari propose, depends on "*a collective assemblage of enunciation*" which eliminates the writing subject and establishes the "revolutionary conditions" (18) of ethnic literature. Underscoring the intrinsic tensions of language, intensive forms of writing disjoin the nodal points at which the reference between the vehicle and tenor of a metaphor appears as a proper and natural relation. The deterritorializing effects of intensive writing result from privileging the signifier because an intensive use of language "directly links the word to the image" (23) and denaturalizes the relation between signifier and signified. Although the notion of an ethnic "intensive" writing rightly calls into question the authority of the proper name and referentiality, it can only do so by excluding the "intensive" uses of metaphor on grounds of an exclusively binary and non-discursive definition of metaphor. What this approach overlooks are the disruptive effects of metaphorical punning that, for instance, characterize John's language. The one thing, John explains to Tim, the "Eye-talians can't face" is that "*Hannibal cross the fucking Alps*" (97). Interestingly, further on in the novel, John tries to break through his previous ethnocentric and universalizing comment on the "Eye-talians" by musing on the particularities of language: "[T]*ransgresserat*," as he remembers from reciting "Virgil *Aeneid* and Livy XXI and Caesar *Gallic War*" (97), "ha[s] a connection to *transgression,* in a figurative sense, although the strict sense is *crossing*? I suppose a crossing-over is a crossing-over, even if one is crossing the Alps, or crossing-over a man's woman!" (149). The passage clarifies that metaphor, which etymologically designates a crossing-over, participates in "intensive" forms of writing. The several semantic and catachrestical connotations and repetitions of "crossing-over" in John's sentence, for example, destabilize the previous reference of *transgresserat* to national conquest.

To exclude metaphor from intensive writing practices also corresponds to the obliteration of the subject and, thus, leads to a dehistoricized practice of ethnic writing in which identities are articulated outside the constraints of power. By overlooking the rhetorical particularities of ethnic texts, especially within their dominant modes of realist writing, Deleuze and Guattari's exclusionary notion of ethnic "intensive" writing participates in hegemonic constructions of ethnicity. In other words, a concept of writing that sidesteps the symbolic and metaphorical power of language erases the traces of those conflictual and divided discourses that make ethnicity, in Kamboureli's words, a productive discourse "where contestation occurs and where alternate lines of action ought to be sought" (203). The perpetual reoccurrence of the conch-shell metaphor in Tim's narrative and memory suggests that the traces of the various intersecting and contesting discourses inscribed in the conch-shell – namely, Tim's diasporic life and history, his withdrawal into silence and his desire for cultural authenticity – function as identity-effects and defy obliteration.

By relinquishing metaphor Deleuze and Guattari also abandon an empowering tool of writing and overlook how metaphor operates through various turns and detours that open it toward catachresis. Metaphor literally operates as what Tim's mother calls a "'friction' of . . . imagination" (*Origin* 87), a tension or impediment within language that breaks with conventional referentiality and enables the circulations of previously hidden meanings within metaphor. The pun Tim cites illustrates that to disrupt "proper" referentiality does not necessarily emphasize the signifier or vehicle of a metaphor. Instead, the mis-citation of an idiomatic expression, such as the turn from "a figment of one's imagination" to a "friction of imagination," opens metaphor towards its multiple circulations in different literary and philosophical discourses. "Friction" underscores the contestation and provisionality of meanings that emerge from the unstable relation between vehicle and tenor rather than just foregrounding the vehicle. Metaphor precisely enables "intensive" forms of writing because it participates in the discursive production of power and, thereby, in the formation of ethnic subjectivities.

If metaphor functions as a crucial agent in the production of power, it also guarantees that the power it produces can never attain an absolute status. Metaphors, such as the conch-shell and the inner tube, stress the formation of an ethnic subjectivity that, as Kamboureli contends, "is never utterly free and of itself" (204) but part of the power structures by which it is produced. For example, if in Tim's unconscious the conch-shell figures as an internalized pressure to conform to a politics of multiculturalism organized around distinct cultural origins, it also enables Tim to recognize that this demand is what constructs him as ethnic. The conch-shell, therefore, signifies an ethnic subject that "when it speaks of and through itself it also speaks back to what defines, and thus delimits, it as ethnic" (Kamboureli 204).

How, then, can one conceptualize metaphor within the context of ethnic writing other than in homogenizing terms? Sylvia Söderlind's acute study *Margin/Alias* examines "linguistic effects of alterity" (8) in a number of Canadian literary texts. Söderlind outlines a rhetoric of ethnicity that measures how marginality or territoriality, namely cultural homogeneity, produces or is produced by the texts under consideration. Looking at the extent to which certain tropes can effect territoriality more or less, Söderlind attributes a low coefficient of homogeneity to metaphor because its tension between "similarity and dissimilarity" always generates ambiguity and engages in "a kind of translation" (25). She further argues that metaphor operates similarly to the Freudian "uncanny" by "simultaneously indicat[ing] identity and difference . . . [the] strange and familiar." Söderlind, however, locates the symbolic value of metaphor's simultaneous operations in a prelinguistic stage of consciousness, "where distinctions between proper and improper are not yet operative because property and identity do not exist" (24). Her view presupposes that metaphorical signification can be divided into proper and improper, literal and figurative meaning. This division also leads her to exclude catachresis from metaphorical operations.

Söderlind perhaps underestimates the interventive potential of catachresis within both ethnic and postcolonial texts when she dismisses the trope as being merely a "[tenorless] vehicle" (25). In contrast to Söderlind, Gayatri Spivak convincingly argues that catachreses rework metaphorical excess, namely that which is absent in metaphor or remains as a trace or *différance* within metaphor and makes its prior discursive circulations accessible.[7] On the one hand, then, Söderlind's study usefully underscores the differentiating properties of metaphor and, in contrast to Deleuze and Guattari, resituates metaphor in a psychoanalytical discourse of alterity and ethnicity. For a reading of metaphor in Clarke's novel this shift is crucial because it accommodates the dialogical structure of the novel in which John becomes Tim's "therapist" (181). On the other, *The Origin of Waves* contains a number of examples that articulate metaphor through catachresis and suggest that metaphor helps construct an unconscious of past experiences in retrospect.

While John's analytical capacities are part of his charade and frequently lead to a reductive reading of Tim's dreams and loss of Lang, his unwitting misnaming connects Tim's psychic life to his social position. John compares Tim's obsession with killing black ants to the introverted sinologist Peter Kien, the protagonist of Elias Canetti's novel *Auto Da Fé*, who becomes the victim of both a psychoanalytical misdiagnosis and his dissociation from and disdain for his social environment. Mistakenly referring to Kien as "Klein" (96), John states that Tim, as well as Klein, suffers from "love gone so far that it turn-into hate and hatred" (97). John's catachrestic approach towards naming contains several implications that help us to read metaphor in performative terms. First, John subverts his own narrative because the allusion to Kien's misdiagnosis also introduces the likely failure of John's analytical insights. Second, the act of misnaming produces agency because it employs the instability of identities in order to read and reread them catachrestically as texts. Further, a catachrestic reciting of names intervenes into the formerly established and normalizing referentiality of language and designates a core element of what Judith Butler theorizes as the performative production of power and agency in and through language.

The production of power, Butler argues, is always discursive because the normative and regulatory effects of power not only control but also produce the subjects they seek to contain. She emphasizes that power "works through the foreclosure of effects, the production of an 'outside' . . . that bounds the domain of intelligible effects" (*Bodies That Matter* 22). In other words, power effects blind spots or silences that seem to be untranslatable and regulate what can and cannot be articulated. Being products of power, these loci of unspeakability safeguard the normative operations of power and simultaneously foreground the inherent instability of power. What is foreclosed or appears to be untranslatable in the operations of power is precisely the process through which power legitimates itself. A constitutive "outside" is never neutral or ahistorical but discursively produced which, in Butler's words, configures "the constituting effect of regulatory power as reiterated and reiterable" (22). By repeating and reiterating those "constitutive instabilities," or the excess of meaning, within regulatory power structures, the stabilizing effects of power shift their own norms "into a potentially productive crisis" (10).

A performative understanding of metaphor, then, does not deny metaphor's regulatory and derivative properties. Instead, it interrupts metaphor's circulation in hegemonic power discourses by reiterating its excess of meaning. Concurrently, metaphors that mark sites of untranslatability indicate how a subject is produced in subjection. In Tim's psychology the conch-shell signals the disavowal of what Tim perceives as a lost ideal and original cultural belonging, while the reiteration of the metaphor emphasizes the impossibility of cultural authenticity. Similarly, Tim's misquotation of "common sense" as "comma-sense" (20) recodes normative effects of power as forged within language.[8] Tim's catachresis engages the restrictive effects associated with "common sense" in a discursive production of power because it commits "a disloyalty against identity – a catachresis – in order to secure . . . the iterable or temporal conditions" (Butler, *Bodies That Matter* 220) of identity formation processes.

Experimenting with the various effects of a prescriptive and internalized notion of ethnic "purity," Clarke's novel investigates what Winfried Siemerling calls the "symbolic boundaries" (15) necessary for the perpetuation of cultural homogeneity within a pluralist constitution of multiculturalism. The constitution and utilization of these boundaries in a normative discourse of multiculturalism, however, also depend on how subject-positions are psychologically constituted prior to the

experience of emigration. As Janice Kulyk Keefer suggests, it is the notion of a trauma or lost ideal that is
reworked in the process of both immigration and the
discovery of ethnicity, which significantly influences the
fashioning of ethnic "multiple selves" (86). In Tim's case,
however, the disavowed loss of cultural belonging does
not lead to but rather inhibits heterogeneous identity
formation processes. The inner tube and, more explicitly, the conch-shell metaphors mediate between the need
for multiaccentuated and provisional identity formations and the desire for an unequivocal origin which,
through the melancholic lens of distance and time is
projected into either the memory of the Caribbean or
the figure of Lang, Tim's lost love. In fact, Tim's psychic
life is regulated by a series of losses that substitute for
each other and are symbolized in the conch-shell metaphor which at once cancels and preserves the memory of
loss. What Tim fails to acknowledge is that the loss of
his Barbados childhood and his lost love, which substitutes for Tim's originary loss of belonging, constitute
him as a subject. This failure of self-recognition also prohibits him from generating an identity based on cultural
heterogeneity. At the same time, a recognition of loss
does not and cannot eradicate the experience of loss.
For that reason the conch-shell metaphor does not un-
dergo a final process of sublation. Instead, Tim severs
his libidinal attachments from it and transfers them to a
related but less regulatory object – the inner tube. At the
end of the novel Tim observes an inner tube, similar to
the one Tim tried to save from the sea in Barbados, floating on Lake Ontario. The sight of the inner tube prevents him from committing suicide and opens the
possibility of scripting an identity of "multiple selves."
The various narrative repetitions and effects of the conch-
shell and the inner tube suggest that metaphor itself denotes a case of "tormenting indecision" (22).

The reader first encounters the conch-shell in the
novel's prologue which retrospectively recounts the last
afternoon Tim and John spend together at the Barbadian beach. The prologue signals both a narrative of

memory and, in Tim's unconscious, the cathectic configurations of the conch-shell and the inner tube as "the
flotsam and the jetsam of the sea" (1). Washed ashore,
the empty conch-shell does not move with the rhythm
of the waves but is twice hidden from the boys' sight:
"Once, when the wave brought the sand in its thrust, . .
. and once again, the second dying time, when the wave
went back out to sea, . . . the conch-shell was hardly
moved from its stubborn and insistent posture of voicelessness" (1-2). The catachrestic void of the conch-shell,
however, seems ambivalent. On the one hand, as a silent
witness of Caribbean history, the conch-shell indicates
the dispossession of language experienced through the
middle passage, colonialism and immigration. The
"voicelessness" of the conch-shell also conveys an image
of death through Tim's predominant association with it
as the harbinger of the death of his uncle, who drowned
at sea. On the other hand, the movement of a "second
dying time" engages with metaphor in a self-reflexive
way, proposing narrative operations of repetition and
negation without change. The notion of a "second dying time" also stands as a reminder of metaphor's differential movement in the form of a detour tending
towards self-destruction. The ambivalence of the conch-
shell, then, resides in those differential value inscriptions
which generate, according to Butler, an abject yet func-
tional outside. In Tim's early memory the conch-shell is
cathected with a fear of death and the belief in possess-
ing a natural, unwavering and, thus, non-discursive identity. Yet, from the beginning, the doubled movement of
the metaphor undermines the normalizing effects of the
conch-shell.

Clarke's novel recites the differential value inscriptions of the conch-shell through its intertextual echoes.
In Derek Walcott's epic poem *Omeros*, for instance, the
conch-shell not only links former colonial desires to the
contemporary exotic market value of the Caribbean as
tourist paradise, but the "conch's moan" (12) also envi-
sions the desire to reinvent language. In the Greek name

for Homer, Omeros, "O was the conch-shell's invocation" (14), a sigh that projects an imaginary space without claims to originality but appeals to an inevitable cultural hybridity. The conch-shell's invocation, however, is also troublesome. It reverberates with the wordlessness and silence of the sea that the four Barbadian boys in George Lamming's novel *In the Castle of My Skin* encounter, and which they try to read through their own history and expectations. Eventually, however, the sea does not yield more than the fear "*of being part of what you could not become*" (308). The invocation of the conch-shell, then, is an uncertain one, also cross-cut by a third reference that highlights the metaphor's "constitutive instability." In Michelle Cliff's novel *Abeng,* the conch allegorizes a Jamaican girl's struggle to come to terms with her racially and culturally mixed heritage. Here, the conch invokes both the instrument that ordered the slaves to the canefields and a vital means of liberation and communication used within Maroon communities. With respect to Clarke's novel, then, the conch-shell functions as a continuous catachrestic void in the libidinal organization of Tim's unconscious. More precisely, it generates an excess of culturally heterogeneous meanings which Tim's unconscious censors and curtails in order to preserve the normative inscriptions of cultural authenticity initially attached to the conch-shell. Simultaneously, the conch-shell's connotations of resistance, uncertainty and invocation mediate the notion of identity as an open field of contesting subject-positions, a field that, in the Caribbean context, is always already hybrid. While a performative reiteration of those values and positions entails the possibility of agency, that possibility remains partially frustrated by Tim's incapacity to envision non-essentialist identities outside the normative system of multiculturalism and his own perpetual disavowal of loss.

His eventual agency does not derive from the performative potential of the conch-shell but from the regulatory modes of the inner tube metaphor which designate the inscription and recognition of an originary loss. A floating toy made of an old truck tire, the inner tube interrupts the exotic imagination of a pastoral Caribbean landscape. "[P]atched in many different colours of rubber, black, brown, and red" (5), the inner tube simultaneously marks Barbadian economic deprivation, and cultural and racial heterogeneity. Furthermore, the flexible and floating properties of the tube link the metaphor to John, whom Tim perceives as a "double-jointed" (5) "soldier-crab" (4). Thus, the inner tube not only points at John's multiple migrations but relates him to the equally double-jointed Lang. The image further recalls Lamming's character, Boy Blue, and his fascination with crabs. With their "transparent" (*Castle* 128) eye colour and transportable crustacean home (146), they suggest the conditions and necessities of migration. Yet, the image turns on itself because it also implies the loneliness and compartmentalization of exclusive forms of multiculturalism that cherish the exoticism of Otherness but keep the demands and effects of cultural difference at bay. Those regulatory properties of the inner tube metaphor are further enhanced when Tim, who is unable to swim, cannot save the tube from floating out into the sea. The resulting feeling of impotence and fear interwoven with the presumption that he does not belong to the "'flotsam of [his Barbadian] society'" (20) estranges him from his own culturally mixed background. It also invests the conch and the inner tube with a traumatic desire for cultural and physical "purity" which, in turn, foregrounds material values and a Naipaulesque distance toward other Caribbean Canadians.

Once Tim has migrated to Canada, this traumatic investment of the conch-shell is psychically reconfigured as a melancholic[9] state which both compels Tim's cultural assimilation and prohibits cross-cultural identification processes. In his essay "Mourning and Melancholia," Freud suggests that the driving forces of melancholia are "fears . . . of becoming poor" (248) and the refusal to give up one's love, memory and expectations attached to a lost object. Melancholy thus organizes psychic life through pressures of social adaptation. In Tim's psyche both domains, the psychic and the social, are connected through the conch-shell. Contemplating the value of money and love as a measurement of social prosperity and successful integration, Tim links these values to his Caribbean past and to his presumed failure: "Money and love flow past us, like the waves on that beach with that inner tube that drowned at sea; or was lost. And no man came to put the voiceless conch-shell to his lips" (24). Not only is Tim's diction of lamentation and self-debasement common in melancholic persons, but it also, as John aptly observes, "g[ives]-[him]-way" (127). John's remark is ambiguous because it suggests that language hides something that should not be given away, and yet language gives way to or enables speech. Judith Butler considers this double function of language characteristic of melancholia when she argues that "melancholia is the effect of an unavowable loss" which, in turn, generates "a withdrawal . . . from speech that makes speech possible" (*The Psychic Life of Power* 170). The conch-shell, then, signifies a loss that cannot be articulated but whose untranslatability indicates how Tim's psychic life is governed through dominant social norms.

The recitation of the conch-shell primarily appears in the specific context of Tim and Lang's story and effects a further catachresis in which both Lang and the conch-shell emerge as culturally untranslatable and, finally, vanish from the narrative. Initially, the reader en-

counters Lang in Tim's almost pathetic memory for she
becomes "the sail that gives [him] movement" (14). Not
only is Lang immediately absorbed into Tim's idealizing
memory of an imaginary Caribbean, but an equally
essentialized idea of Lang as the rather undefined "Chinese woman" (100) of his dream becomes Tim's cause
for life, for an "injury" that "never heals" (204), and
for living in the "psychotic silence" (167) and isolation
of a racist and hostile society. He has "[n]o *consolation*"
(180), is "a *lost* cause" (185) and finally amounts to
"nothing" (213). Lang gradually takes the place of Tim's
ego and, framed in melancholic lamentations, she only
figures as a photo, a representation, with a "crease" that
looks like "a wound that will not heal" (59). If Lang
represents the substitution of a prior loss, namely the
loss of an ideal cultural belonging, then her representation as a photo signals that the objects of losses cannot
be traced to an origin but are derivates. What melancholia and loss produce is a profound ambivalence, a
"tormenting time of indecision" (22), which constitutes
Tim as a subject at the expense of Lang.

The lost object the melancholic substitutes for his or
her ego, as Freud reminds us, is "of a more ideal kind"
and "has not perhaps actually died" but has been lost as
an object of love. Indeed, Tim admits that Lang is actually "not dead" (199) so that Tim, as a melancholic, in
Freud's words, "knows *whom* he has lost but not *what*
he has lost in him" (245). In fact, Tim's melancholia
determines how he can represent Lang, namely, only as
a "face recorded in the faces of all the Chinese women
[he] pass[es]" (206). This descriptive generalization is
significant for two reasons: first, it reduces Lang to a
homogeneous and racialized category that defines the
loss of Tim's social world; second, it designates the post-
poned sublation of loss characteristic of melancholia so
that, to paraphrase Butler, the refusal to acknowledge

loss emerges as the preservation of the "lost object as psychic effects" (*Psychic Life* 182). While Tim's confession that he "live[s] the past as if it is the present" (81) partly acknowledges his melancholic state, he cannot see how it regulates the construction of his social life and, in particular, of Lang. He remembers that during a failed attempt at sexual intercourse with Lang he smelled "*incense from Beijing, China*" and heard his name "called out in chilling, plaintive, forcing screams of someone drowning, like how [his] uncle was drowning, of someone going-down, down, down" (86). The plaintive lamentation is, of course, the voice of Tim's melancholia. In this particular encounter, Tim's melancholia effects a speechlessness or untranslatability of a loss that is linked to Tim's Caribbean past and, simultaneously, "preclude[s] the loss of the addressee" (Butler, *Psychic Life* 182), that is, Lang, the new and foreclosed object of love. Through the process of melancholic substitution which takes Lang for Tim's ego, Tim not only objectifies Lang but also constructs her and his own identity in essentialist terms of cultural belonging. This process ensures that the authority of a normative and liberal multiculturalism[10] can be naturalized in Tim's psychic life and thus prevents him from articulating alternative notions of cultural identification.

Tim's vision of the dead Lang perpetuates his acts of narcissistic self-consolidation and turns Lang into the concept-metaphor of "ethnic woman."[11] The repetition of Lang in the syntax of melancholia re-enacts what Elisabeth Bronfen sees as a "*lost object*" which does not necessarily refer to a "presence" but to an "absence" (105). A "*dead woman*," Bronfen argues, "is denied her own body and is thus only a figure for a meaning other than herself . . . a living cipher for her lover's desired lost object" (108). In contrast to Bronfen's argument, however, Clarke's text suggests that a lost object cannot be recovered through repetition. When Lang dies the first thing Tim remembers "was the old conch-shell lying on the beach. I wonder who blows it, now? Lang has the same colour almost – had – and it is strange that I would compare the colour of a conch-shell . . . to the complexion of Lang. I think about that, all the time . . ." (226). Lang and the conch-shell act as mutual proxies for Tim's failure to come to terms with the multiplicity of cultural meanings and relations inscribed in the conch-shell, that is, with the inescapability of cultural difference, hybridity and the acceptance that waves have no other origins but the wind. Although Tim finally articulates the connections between his melancholic mourning for Lang and his Caribbean childhood, he cannot disentangle them because he still does not know *what* he has lost in Lang.

Instead, the end of the novel suggests a further substitution of metaphors which leads Tim to give up his melancholic attachment to his prior losses. Contemplating drowning himself in Lake Ontario, Tim recognizes an "old, black, patched inner tube" (245) floating on the lake and, for the first time, is able to respond to John in a compassionate way. The displacement and reiteration of the inner tube metaphor signals a provisional agency because it avows but does not eradicate the experience of loss. The constitutive ambivalence generated through loss equally remains because, to a certain extent, Tim's process of self-recognition requires that he abandon his distorted memories of both Lang and the conch-shell. What Tim gains is the capacity to make choices of cultural identification and to re-evaluate the pain of indecision as a productive contestation of culturally heterogeneous borders.

Tim, then, produces Lang and the conch-shell as a constitutive outside which safeguards the reproduction of his essentialist conceptions of ethnicity. Within his narrative the untranslatability of Lang and the conch-shell does not directly derive from an unspeakable and catachrestic trauma, but from Tim's melancholic insistence on traditions and origins that never existed in the first place. A successful intercultural translation however presupposes, as Rey Chow reminds us, the transmissibility of texts through the word as arcade,[12] that is, through a transparent palimpsest of cultural inscriptions which always already participate in modes of ethnic commodification. "Arcade," in Benjamin's sense, designates a passageway through which the production of meaning through translation always remains somehow provisional. As I noted at the outset of this essay, a performative conceptualization of metaphor employs and reiterates those culturally and historically sedimented effects of metaphorical meaning that extend and foreground the transparency and translatability of words. Rey Chow emphasizes that the transmissibility of cultural texts "is what *intensifies* in direct proportion to the sickness, the weakening of tradition" (199). This decay of traditions, then, largely depends on an increased transparency of metaphors on the one-word level in order to destabilize given binary modes of referentiality.

In Clarke's novel the reiteration and differential value inscriptions of the conch-shell and the figure of Lang, and their subsequent exclusion from the text, dissolve the binary cultural identifications Tim seeks to assign to them. While Tim participates in the multicultural commodification of ethnicity by authorizing imagined origins and traditions, the performative operative modes of Lang and the conch-shell metaphor dramatize the weakening of culturally essentialist traditions. They constantly intervene in Tim's homogenizing discourse and expose how Tim's psychic life is regulated through social norms. The performative effect of both the conch-shell and the inner tube depends on their inclusion within discursive power formations. This position enables re-

peated citations and disidentifications of these metaphors which both intervene in the received binary reference modus of tenor and vehicle, and help us to reread
the normative effects of power in a productive way. A
performative understanding of metaphor in the context
of ethnic writing perhaps emphasizes a catachrestic notion of identity based on cultural difference and allows
for a conceptualization of metaphor in less homogenizing forms. Metaphor's "tormenting times of indecision,"
then, can certainly not be resolved but may be performed
beyond the conventional binary coding in ways that suggest a different kind of intensive writing.

NOTES

1. In Tim's guilty imagination the turning point in his relationship with Lang
   occurs when he does not answer a telephone call while isolating himself in his
   garden to kill black ants with a spray can of Black Flag. He assumes that the
   caller is Lang and later interprets his failure to answer the call as a failure to
   save Lang's life. The guilt Tim generates correlates with a similar feeling of
   failure he experienced when he was a boy and unable to swim into the sea to
   rescue the inner tube. A detailed discussion of the metaphorical significance of
   black ants in relation to Tim's denial and simultaneous construction of cultural
   difference would require a separate essay. The present paper, therefore, excludes an analysis of Tim's obsessive character in favour of a clearer focus on the
   conch-shell and inner tube metaphors.
2. For the significance of nostalgia in multicultural writing see Daphne Marlatt,
   "Entering In: The Immigrant Imagination," *Readings From the Labyrinth*
   (Edmonton: NeWest, 1998) 17-35.
3. In the context of Caribbean writing and historiography, the metaphor of the sea
   harbours a complex net of contesting and contested ideas and discourses. In
   Brathwaite's usage, for example, it connotes a pan-Africanist Caribbean identity
   which seeks to unify cultural differences through shared historical roots. In
   Derek Walcott's famous poem "The Sea is History," the sea suggests a new
   beginning beyond the lamentations of historical loss, shame and guilt. In more
   recent uses of the metaphor, as for instance in David Dabydeen's long poem
   Turner, the sea signifies the frustrated hope of an absolute cultural and historical
   originality. The metaphor's connotation of Caribbean cultural hybridity, however, should be read with caution because it frequently relates to the construction of a cohesive national consciousness organized around a pluralist notion of
   difference in unity. For a discussion of Caribbean national hybridity see Édouard
   Glissant, *Poetics of Relation*, trans. Betsy Wing (Ann Arbor: U of Michigan P,
   1997). For a detailed discussion of cultural hybridity see Homi Bhabha, *The
   Location of Culture* (London: Routledge, 1994), esp. ch. 6; Robert J. C. Young,
   Colonial Desire: Hybridity in Theory, Culture and Race (London/New York:
   Routledge, 1995); and the special issue on hybridity of *Third Text* 32 (1995).
4. Derrida argues that the power of metaphor resides in its dialectical function of

sublation and idealization. In the process the exterior or physical origins of a metaphor are erased and transposed into a spiritual and interiorized "proper" ("White Mythology" 25) and, thus, true meaning.

5. I primarily refer to the Aristotelian notion of metaphor as well as to the structuralist and hermeneutic theories of metaphor, particularly those proposed by Roman Jakobson and Paul Ricoeur. For a communicative approach to metaphor see George Lakoff and Mark Johnson, *Metaphors We Live By* (London/ Chicago: Chicago UP, 1980). For a structuralist discussion of metaphor that emphasizes the trope's faculties of difference and resemblance, see Gérard Genette, *Figures of Literary Discourse*, trans. Alan Sheridan (New York: Columbia UP, 1982), esp. ch. 10. See also Tzvetan Todorov, *Theories of the Symbol*, trans. Catherine Porter (New York: Cornell UP, 1982).

6. For example, see Fulvio Caccia, "The Italian Writer and Language," *Contrasts: Comparative Essays on Italian-Canadian Writing*, ed. Joseph Pivato (Montreal: Guernica, 1995) 153-167; E. D. Blodgett, "Ethnic Writing in Canadian Literature as Paratext," *Signature* 3 (Summer 1990): 13-27; Allison Conway, "Ethnic Writing and Canadian Criticism," *Open Letter* 5 (1989): 52-66; and Sylvia Söderlind.

7. In the conclusion of her study Söderlind moves away from her categorical exclusion of catachresis from the operations of metaphor. Metaphor, she says, entails "a simultaneous naming and gesture towards unnaming, a kind of maiming" that cannot occur "outside the centre" (232). In other words, the catachrestic power of unnaming can only proceed from within the paradigms of power, namely, from within metaphor. Here, Söderlind comes close to Gayatri Spivak's argument that, in a postcolonial context, catachreses are those metaphors for which "no historically adequate referent may be advanced from postcolonial space" (60). Catachresis, Spivak emphasizes, "enables the recoding of value as the differential possibility of exchange and the channeling of surplus," that is, the excess of meaning produced through *différance* (65).

8. The play between "common sense" and "commasense" also refers to a syntax of separations, conjunctions, and permutations which symbolically defines ethnic subjectivities and which Austin Clarke cites in his essay as the necessity to live in the "semicolon of the North" (255).

9. My reading of how the conch-shell configures Tim's melancholia as a regulatory force of identity formation processes employs Judith Butler's rereading of Freud's analysis of melancholia. For reasons of clarity I briefly summarize here Freud's reading of melancholia. In contrast to mourning, melancholia designates the inability to detach libidinal energies from a lost object, person, ideal or country. The melancholic person refuses to break the attachment to what is lost and withdraws his or her attachment to the lost object "into the ego" and, according to Freud, "establishes an *identification* of the ego with the abandoned object" (249). The ego, in other words, substitutes for the lost object. In the process of substitution the ego splits off a critical agency (the super-ego) that regulates, structures and judges the ego. The melancholic who identifies with the lost object punishes him – or herself for the loss of the object so that the object-loss becomes an ego-loss and the ego emerges as being ambivalently and inextricably divided between "the critical activity of the ego," that is, the self-berating revocation and conservation of what is lost, and "the ego as altered by identification" (249) with the lost object. My discussion departs from Butler's suggestion that the substitutional operations and the profoundly "metaphorical language" (*Psychic Life* 178) of melancholia constitute the ego as a "history of loss, the sedimentation of relations of substitutions over time" (169). For a reading of melancholia in the context of ethnic Canadian criticism, see Smaro Kamboureli, "Of Black Angels and Melancholy Lovers: Ethnicity and Writing in Canada," *Feminism and the Politics of Difference*, ed. Sneja Gunew and Anna Yeatman (St. Leonards, Austral.: Allen, 1993) 143-56.

10. Following Homi Bhabha I distinguish between a conceptualization of multiculturalism based on liberal and pluralistic values of cultural diversity

that locates difference only within sameness, and a definition of multiculturalism based on cultural difference with its emphasis on cultural translation and split enunciative processes that question the legitimacy of received power structures. For a detailed discussion see Bhabha, "The Commitment to Theory," *The Location of Culture* (London: Routledge, 1994) 19-39; Anthony K. Appiah, "Identity, Authenticity, Survival: Multicultural Societies and Social Reproduction," *Multiculturalism: Examining the Politics of Recognition*, ed. Charles Taylor and Amy Gutmann (New Jersey: Princeton UP, 1994) 149-63; and David Bennett, ed., *Multicultural States: Rethinking Difference and Identity* (London/New York: Routledge, 1998).

11. I use the term "ethnic woman" in analogy to Chandra Talpade Mohanty's definition of the "'third-world woman'." She argues that dominant Western feminist discourses "colonize the material and historical heterogeneities of the lives of women in the third world . . . producing/representing a composite, singular . . . image which appears arbitrarily constructed but nevertheless carries with it the authorizing signature of western humanist discourse" (197). The effects of Tim's melancholia, read as an effect of normative power constellations, generates an equally singular image of Chinese women in Canada.

12. Chow's argument of cultural transmissibility is principally based on the following section of Walter Benjamin's essay "The Task of the Translator": A real translation is transparent; it does not cover the original, does not block its light, but allows the pure language, as though reinforced by its own medium, to shine upon the original all the more fully. This may be achieved, above all, by a literal rendering of the syntax which proves words rather than sentences to be the primary element of the translator. For if the sentence is the wall before the language of the original, literalness is the arcade (79).

WORKS CITED

Benjamin, Walter. "The Task of the Translator." *Illuminations*. Trans. Harry Zohn. Ed. and intro. Hannah Arendt. New York: Harcourt, 1968. 69-82.

Brathwaite, Edward Kamau. "Caribbean Man In Space And Time." *Savacou* 11-12 (1975): 1-11, 106-8.

Bronfen, Elisabeth. "Risky Resemblances: On Repetition, Mourning, and Representation." *Death and Representation*. Eds. Sarah Webster Goodwin and Bronfen. Baltimore: Johns Hopkins UP, 1993. 103-129.

Butler, Judith. *Bodies That Matter: On the Discursive Limits of "Sex."* London/New York: Routledge, 1993.

——. *Excitable Speech: Politics of the Performative*. New York/London: Routledge, 1997.

——. *The Psychic Life of Power: Theories in Subjection*. Stanford, CA: Stanford UP, 1997.

Chow, Rey. *Primitive Passions: Visuality, Sexuality, Ethnography, and Contemporary Chinese Cinema*. New York: Columbia UP, 1995.

Clarke, Austin. "In the Semicolon of the North." *The Austin Clarke Reader*. Ed. Barry Callaghan. Toronto: Exile, 1996. 255-63.

——. *The Origin of Waves*. Toronto: McClelland, 1997.

Cliff, Michelle. *Abeng*. New York: Crossing, 1984.

Deleuze, Gilles, and Félix Guattari. *Kafka: Toward a Minor Literature*. Trans. Dana Polan. Minneapolis: U of Minnesota P, 1986.

Derrida, Jacques. "The Retrait of Metaphor." *Enclitic* (1978): 5-33.

——."White Mythology: Metaphor in the Text of Philosophy." *New Literary History* 6 (1974-75): 5-73.

Freud, Sigmund. "Mourning and Melancholia." *The Standard Edition of the Complete Psychological Works of Sigmund Freud*. Ed. and trans. James Strachey. Vol. 14. London: Hogarth, 1957. 237-58.

Kamboureli, Smaro. "The Technology of Ethnicity: Law and Discourse." *Open Letter* 8.5-6 (1993): 202-17.

Keefer, Janice Kulyk. "'Coming Across Bones': Historiographic Ethnofiction." *Writing Ethnicity: Cross-Cultural Consciousness in Canadian and Québécois Literature*. Ed. Winfried Siemerling. Toronto: ECW, 1996. 84-104.

Lamming, George. *In The Castle of My Skin*. London/New York: McGraw-Hill, 1954.

Mohanty, Chandra Talpade. "Under Western Eyes: Feminist Scholarship and Colonial Discourses." *Colonial Discourse and Postcolonial Theory: A Reader*. Ed. Patrick Williams and Laura Chrisman. New York: Columbia UP, 1994. 196-220.

Siemerling, Winfried. Introduction. *Writing Ethnicity: Cross-Cultural Consciousness in Canadian and Québécois Literature*. Ed. Siemerling. Toronto: ECW, 1996. 1-32.

Söderlind, Sylvia. *Margin/Alias: Language and Colonization in Canadian and Québécois Fiction*. Toronto: U of Toronto P, 1991.

Spivak, Gayatri Chakravorty. *Outside In The Teaching Machine*. London/New York: Routledge, 1993.

Walcott, Derek. *Omeros*. London/Boston: Faber, 1990.

Ondaatje Goes to Hollywood

The Costs of Mainstream Arrival for the Representation of Cultural Difference

Don Randall

My most noteworthy memory of the 1996 Academy Awards broadcast is that awkward prelude to the acceptance of "Best Picture" by *The English Patient* producer Saul Zaentz. Director Anthony Minghella hovers anxiously a few feet from the main microphone and, in a low but audible voice, reminds Zaentz to thank "Michael." This moment both signals and confirms Michael Ondaatje's effective absence from the culminating scene of his "arrival" in the cultural field of major-market cinema. Acknowledging "Michael," thanking "Michael" – these, evidently, are gestures of "good form" that might be forgotten. "Michael" is not present, on stage, as, say, the indispensable collaborator that both Minghella and Zaentz evoke in other contexts, notably in their prefatory writings for Minghella's published screenplay (Foreword xi, xii; Preface xiii-xiv). At the Awards, "Michael" needs to be restored, if only briefly, to the cinematic consecration of *The English Patient*, a title that once belonged to him. In recollecting this little Awards moment, my primary concern is not then with "Michael" as a sign of the minority writer, but rather with "Michael" as a sign that attaches, metonymically, to the literary text of *The English Patient*, a work which has, evidently, no necessary place in the crowning moment of the film version's success story. The moment stages (quite literally) the potentially problematic relationship between the literary work and its high-profile filmic reproduction, raising questions about the shared title: after 1996, what meanings, what contents, does *The English Patient* assemble? what has been altered, what added, what lost?

In this essay, I consider how the major-market cinematic reproduction of *The English Patient* transforms, elides and partially effaces important aspects of the cultural impact and agency of Ondaatje's literary text. Notwithstanding his professed commitment to the underdog, particularly the cultural "mongrel" (Bush 244), and the "international bastards – born in one place and choosing to live elsewhere" (*The English Patient* 176), Ondaatje and his writing have recently "arrived" in relation to the cultural mainstream both in Canada and internationally. However, this arrival has been mediated, crucially, by the cultural apparatus of major-market film production. What then, I ask, are the cultural effects of this mediation? If the translation from Booker Prize novel to Oscar-winning hit movie transforms the meanings and values that attach to the title "The English Patient," what cultural work is being performed at present under the aegis of that title? After 1996, what changes mark the place and purpose of Ondaatje's novel in what Pierre Bourdieu has called "the field of cultural production"? This field is a dynamic network of situations and contexts in which the meanings of cultural works are multiply mediated. Bourdieu's insistence on mediation points not only to objective historical and institutional conditions of production but also to conditions of reception. Moreover, Bourdieu articulates "culture," particularly in *The Field of Cultural Production*, as a field of competitions among differently positioned social actors, as a field of competitions that restage more broadly structured social relations of power. In the light of Bourdieu's contribution, then, one would consider the film of *The*

English Patient not as an instance of docile derivation but, rather, as a potent remediation of the literary predecessor, a remediation which plays for – competes for – decently high sociocultural stakes, and one which may play *against* its predecessor. Similarly, one would expect the film to restructure, significantly, the literary document's overall participation in the cultural field.

At issue, in the first instance, are the cultural effects arising from the novel's visualization, which transports that "vision" we typically ascribe to authors and literary works from the realm of metaphor to that of concrete materiality. In the most baldly simple sense, as spectator-participants in contemporary cultural processes, we first *see* a narrative bearing the title "The English Patient" when the Miramax film comes out. But there *is* another distinct, visual and imagistic presentation of the text that is more intimately, more inescapably linked to its status as contemporary literature – the book cover or, rather, in the present case, the covers. The most recent of these manifests, unmistakably, the defining impact of *The English Patient*'s translation across the fields of its production, effectively staging a transformation of the conditions of reading and interpretation by high-profile film reproduction.

The initial Vintage paperback cover shows a non-European man – his garb suggests he is Indian or perhaps North African – climbing a difficult escarpment, as Kip does in one of the novel's passages (70). Another cover, which circulates after the Booker Prize announcement, evokes the desert-wanderer caught up in a sandstorm that obscures our view of him. This cover seems to me to point to Almásy's status as a troubled, latter-day version of the European imperial adventurer, as an imperial figure caught up in crisis and faced with the threat of dissolution.[1] The more recent, and now the most broadly circulated, Vintage cover features a photographic reproduction that is duly copyrighted by Miramax films. Here, the film's two European principals, Ralph Fiennes and Kristin Scott Thomas, engage in the glowing close-up kiss of classic Hollywood romance. It is crucial to note, however, that an image answering closely to this cover shot never appears in the film. That is, the image is not an appetizing *synecdoche*, a tasty part for the whole, but something more like a luminescent metaphorical condensation of the overall narrative design. This visual metaphor proposes itself as a stand-in for the literary narrative as much as for the filmic one.

The alluring graininess in the presentation of the flesh, in the faces and in Scott Thomas's luminescent shoulder, recapitulates the imagery of the film's opening sequences – the desert landscape as an expanse of grainy, golden, flesh-evoking contours, as an obviously eroticized place of contemporary neocolonial, touristic, fantasy-inspiring romance. As Minghella's screenplay specifies, "The late sun turns the sand every color from crimson to black and makes the dunes look like bodies pressed against each other" (1). The cover image's setting sun, which is literally contingent upon the brows of the kissing faces, seems thus to invite our indulgence in a delicious, nostalgic yearning for forms of erotic experience that seem almost constitutively incompatible with our late-twentieth-century urban lives in urban spaces.[2] The book now extends to its readers a splendid promise of pleasure framed in terms that are notably distinct from those put forward by the earlier austere, sparely detailed covers, both of which withhold almost as much visual information as they offer.

I would also draw attention, however, to less alluring, but nonetheless noteworthy, aspects of the most recent cover. There is the sticker, appended to copies distributed after the 1996 Academy Awards: "#1 Bestseller; Academy Award Winner." The sticker's unabashed elision of difference between the book and the film is important: one single thing called *The English Patient* is a bestseller and an award-winning movie. The promotional slogan at the bottom of the front cover reiterates this message – "The Bestselling Novel Now A Major Motion Picture" – as does the back cover layout, which presents glowing excerpts from book reviews paired with film credits as they would appear on a promotional poster – "Miramax Films presents a Saul Zaentz production . . ." All these elements of presentation are, of course, starkly promotional: the film is being used to sell the book and, thus, consumers are tacitly invited to read the book in relation to the film. The novel is now offered as an object reconstituted by desires, pleasures and also lines of interpretation for which the film is the primary referent. Moreover, references to instances of literary consecration – the Governor General's Award, the Booker Prize – which figured quite prominently on earlier covers are now entirely absent. Market achievement, the bottom line for the major motion picture, reframes the novel's presentation – it is now a "#1 Bestseller."

Particularly because this primary cultural reproduction tends to insist on the sameness of novel and film – or at least on their fundamental, prevailing similarity – it is worthwhile to note some of the key differences that distinguish the book from the film. As I briefly noted earlier, one of the pre-1996 covers suggests that the narrative is crucially about the text's non-white, non-European character – Kip, the Sikh sapper. Arguably, this cover does not mislead, does not belie the contents it heralds, notwithstanding a title foregrounding another character, the so-called "English patient," Almásy.[3] Kip, in the novel, is certainly a fulcrum upon which the narrative shifts and then redistributes its emphases. One reads about a fifth of the book before he appears but, thereafter, he figures prominently in or, indeed, dominates four of the book's remaining eight chapters. Most notably, in "August," the final chapter, the young Sikh spurs and definitively shapes the narrative's resolution. Indeed, I would assert that Kip's crucial importance founds the study of Ondaatje's text as postcolonial literature. Kip also is a figure who signals the pertinence of postcoloniality within considerations of minority experience. In so saying, I am suggesting that the examination of minority literature and culture can be supplemented, in certain instances, with the vocabulary and conceptual formations characterizing contemporary postcolonial criticism and theory. Considerations of cultural migrancy or diaspora, hybridity and on-going hybridization mark contemporary postcolonial debate, as does an insistently international frame of reference (which situates Canada amongst other nations of a decolonizing world). In the absence of a self-consciously postcolonial perspective, it would be difficult to situate a text like *The English Patient* in relation to contemporary developments of Canadian culture and to determine the implications, for national and international cultural processes, of the recent film adaptation. Certainly, the ascription of minority or postcolonial status should not depend, in a quite questionable, essentialist way, upon the author's Sri-Lankan roots; it should not lean – all too trustingly – upon that deliberate, if ironical spectacularization of "exotic" heritage, Ondaatje's canny 1982 autobiography, *Running in the Family*. The text of *The English Patient* makes, however, its own case, which even a cursory reading would reveal. When, for example, Kip is nicknamed "Kip" because Kirpal, his birth name, is rather too taxing for English tongues, one detects a move into the realm of minority experience. Similarly, Kip's discovery of minority status is evident in his recognition that his visible difference renders him culturally invisible in England, an "anonymous member of another race, a part of the invisible world" (Ondaatje 196). Later in the novel when Kip, in his rage, unequivocally equates "Englishness" with racist, imperial violence, one must take note of the distinctly postcolonial perspective. Incontestably, Kip plays the part of the postcolonial migrant: he is the outsider, the newcomer, the initiate, who pieces his way through the maze of modern English culture and then through the more historically resonant cultural maze which is war-ravaged Italy.

The novel's Kip demands to be considered in relation to questions of migrancy and the impact of migrancy upon technologically advanced, postindustrial and postimperial societies. Stating the more general case, of which Ondaatje's Kip is a representative, Iain Chambers writes:

> When the "Third World" is no longer maintained at a distance "out there" but begins to appear "in here", when the encounter between diverse cultures, histories, religions and languages no longer occurs along the peripheries, . . . but emerges at the centre of our daily lives, in the cities and cultures of the so-called "advanced", or "First", world, then we can perhaps begin to talk of a significant interruption in the preceding sense of our own lives, cultures, languages and futures. (2)

This late-twentieth-century cultural process Chambers suggests, which moves through "interruption" to the possibility of cultural revaluation, can contribute significantly to the interpretation of Kip's narrative role. It elucidates the purpose of Kip's extensive training in England and accounts for the allegorical import of his work: he is a sapper, a bomb defuser, trained to engage with and disarm modern Europe's complex technologies of violence. Once in Italy, and still pursuing his work, Kip situates himself at the centre of a multifaceted engagement with questions of colonial and postcolonial cultures and identities – the questions that emerge within the ruins of San Girolamo from the interactions of characters with diverse national, ethnic and class backgrounds. The narrative resolution turns, moreover, upon Kip's recognition of the impossibility of his relation with "Europe" – with European cultural codes and meanings – and his decisive withdrawal from participation in the project of salvaging and remaking the Western world.

But if I propose that Ondaatje's Kip figures forth the cultural agency of the contemporary postcolonial migrant – the migrant, moreover, who ultimately says "no" to "Europe" – I must also note that, in the film, he is little more than a "sexy Sikh" or, to use Pandit and McGuire's terminology, an example of "the commodification of alterities" (7). The cinematic Kip represents the cultural other as fantasy object to be consumed and enjoyed. Mingella's film presents an imaginary postcolonial environment in which cultural differences have no apparent disruptive or transformative potential, an environment where recognition across difference is immediate and unequivocal, unproblematic and fairly much unproblematized. Consider, for example, Hana and Kip's cross-cultural romance. In its inaugural moment Hana follows a luminous path of "shell lamps" (filled with oil) to the place of the first tryst. Kip, like the yearned-for Biblical bridegroom, says, "Hana," as he "steps out of the darkness" into light; Hana blissfully responds, "Kip" (Minghella, *English* 123). A love affair develops straightforwardly. Kip suffers a crisis, not due to the news of the A-bombings in Japan, but because of the sudden death of his English sapper cohort. He eventually departs from Villa San Girolamo, not in a furore of anti-European protest, but simply because he has been transferred – to Florence. And, of course, the film's resolution promises reunion: Hana, after the death of her patient, takes to the road, headed for Florence.[4]

If one allows, however, that Minghella's film participates in contemporary cultural processes in ways that differ significantly from those that are evident in the novel, one needs then to consider questions of legibility: how, and to what degree, do differences register; how do actual readers and viewers apprehend and evaluate the relationship between the two versions of *The English Patient*? While teaching Ondaatje's novel at Queen's University in 1998, I dedicated a portion of discussion time to examining the relationship between the literary text and the film. Many students chose to continue with this examination in their journal writing, which they produced at a rate of one page per week. This writing sheds light, I find, on the problem of reading Ondaatje's *The English Patient* in 1998 – that is, in the wake of the progress of the immensely successful film. (I cite the students by name, to make clear that I am putting forward a reasonably diversified assembly of critical responses rather than producing some generic version of "the student view.") Edwina O'Shea notes "the over-emphasis of the Katharine/Almásy love affair" in a film that "meets all of Hollywood's requirements for a larger than life romance." A sense that the film conforms to norms of Hollywood narrative is also present in the writing of several others. Elizabeth Frogley admits that she first decided to read the book "because [she] liked the movie so much." Yet she goes on to note that the Katharine/Almásy affair "dominates the movie," reflecting, "Maybe this is because the Kip-Hana relationship . . . is less acceptable" to audiences. "Or maybe," she then suggests, "the people who made the movie just assumed it would be less acceptable or less interesting to movie viewers, which is a major problem in itself." Niana McNalley, Sonya Melim and Ian Busch object in various ways to the film's depleted presentation of Kip, Hana and Caravaggio. Busch's treatment makes an issue of the pursuit of "big bucks" and, indeed, other writers touch on the question of commercial viability, albeit, in passing. I will conclude this selection of students' contributions by quoting Nikki Shaver at some length because she concentrates on the novel/film comparison with a noteworthy intensity:

> While Ondaatje's novel undoubtedly explores love under the unusual circumstances of war and exile, *The English Patient* is a work primarily concerned with issues of nationhood and identity. This becomes clear through many conversations in the book, such as Kip's speech about England near the end: "You and then the Americans converted us. With your missionary rules. And Indian soldiers wasted their lives as heroes so they could be *pukkah*. You had wars like cricket.". . . Ondaatje focuses much of the novel on telling the histories of Kip . . . in England, and of Hana and Caravaggio . . . However, in the film these histories are neglected. Movie-Kip seems to have no qualms about working for the English, and his . . . notable statement about nationality is: "Hardy and the patient, they represent all that is good about England." Similarly, Caravaggio's history with Hana's father is completely left out of the film, and Hana's Canadian nationality is downplayed enormously. Instead, the film magnifies the romance of Katharine and the patient, focusing on the Hollywood tropes which reside amidst the complexities of the novel.

To begin a processing of my students' writings, I note first that these reader/viewers have some sense of the issues Pierre Bourdieu confronts in relation to "the field of cultural production." They seem, clearly, to understand that a work of serious literature and a major-market movie do not take place culturally in quite the same way. In Bourdieu's terms, the two inhabit distinct subfields of cultural production: the ambitious novel plays for stakes that are not exclusively but predominantly symbolic – cultural prestige, critical consecration and the like; the film, whose production costs exceed thirty million dollars, must form a tighter bond with broad-based marketing potential and measure much of its success in dollar revenues. Moreover, as Frogley suggests, the film-maker works with distinct expectations as to his audience's sensibilities, tastes and levels of cultural competence. Also apparent in the students' contributions is an awareness that the shift from novel to film entails, to use a musical figure, a shift from minor to major: the soaring romance between the European principals comes to the fore, and the characters, situations and scenes that treat minority experience recede or disappear. Similarly, as Shaver's commentary makes particularly clear, the film version has no use for the novel's distinctly postcolonial perspectives on nation and nationality, cultural identity and history.[5] Shaver also recognizes that the depleted representation of non-European elements in the film coincides with the reduced presence of the "minor" nation, Canada, within the narrative's imagined world. To extend from this enabling observation, one may observe that the filmic Hana, now a francophone from Montreal, is not re-envisioned with the commitment to culturally specific characterization that marks Ondaatje's Anglo-Canadian original – as is evidenced in a primary way by the casting of a well-known *French* actress in the role. Hana's intensely fraught relationship with the English cultural archive and her consequently ambivalent relationship with her "English patient" are lost elements in the film version. Also lost – given that the filmic Hana is neither Anglo-Canadian nor convincingly *montréalaise* – is the interpretive path that would treat the Hana/Kip relationship as an allegorical rendering of possibilities for cross-cultural encounter and exchange in contemporary Canada.

But to deal directly again with my students' writings – what should one make of them overall? My original design had been to use them as an initial approach to a conclusion that would delineate major-market cultural production as a subfield that is still closed to complex, nuanced treatments of minority and postcolonial topics. I intended to emphasize that the productive address of such topics still tends to be restricted to enclaves of literary culture, to works of relatively limited cultural dissemination – a point that emerges from the general thrust of the students' commentary. I knew that I would not be offering anything particularly surprising, but I thought that the film version of *The English Patient*, with its tremendous popular success and its profit margin of more than a hundred million and counting, would provide a single instance compelling enough to make the argument worthwhile. But, in any case, that conclusion, as it happens, has become the road not travelled. As I worked through the student material, editing, assembling and rearranging, it occurred to me that often if not invariably the journal writings demonstrate that the film, by its redistribution of emphases, by its elisions and omissions, brings certain aspects of the novel into sharper focus. In the realm of literary experience, this novel's concerns with cross-cultural encounter and the forging of postcolonial consciousness become more thoroughly evident, more *legible*, because the film version puts these aspects aside or treats them inadequately. The film's advent within the field of cultural production thus spurs the reading of Ondaatje's novel as a work that is crucially concerned with postcolonial experience and, notably, with the negotiation of cultural differences. And, I should add, it makes clearer the cultural and political stakes of such a reading.

In closing, however, I must place limits upon my new optimism. As I noted earlier, since its release in 1996 the film is being used to promote the book – and very successfully.[6] What will readers discover, then, who come to the novel from the film? I would now conclude that the cultural effects of that promotional initiative are, to some degree, encouragingly unpredictable. But it still troubles me to think that for many consumers of cultural products *The English Patient* is and will remain exclusively a film experience. Returning one more time to Bourdieu, I recall his arguing that patterns of production and consumption emerge not independently, but contingently, interdependently. The production of cultural goods is directly, ineluctably, linked to the production of taste. Moreover, "the appropriation of cultural products presupposes dispositions and competences which are not distributed universally" (*Distinction* 228). Appropriations are marked by inclusions and exclusions. If one allows that the film of *The English Patient* has forged a place for itself within "the legitimate culture" of class-divided North American society, one must also remember that this legitimate culture is itself "a product of domination predisposed to express or legitimate domination" (228). Consumer participation in stagings of legitimate culture will yield for some, and not for others, what Bourdieu calls "a profit in legitimacy," which is "the fact of feeling justified in being (what one is), being what it is right to be" (231). Viewed in the light of this commentary, Minghella's film must appear as a victory of the cultural mainstream over initiatives of minority and postcolonial representation.[7] The filmic Kip does not challenge or "interrupt" (to use Chambers's figure) the experience of selfhood and culture that the European principals represent. Indeed, in being presented as a spectacle, "a sexy Sikh," he effectively recedes into cultural invisibility, the very invisibility the novel presents as a problem, a matter for encounter, negotiation across difference, learning. Yet this mainstream victory I speak of can and should be considered a limited victory, limited because it provokes countering effects in the cultural field. The film produces and, presumably, will continue to produce new or renewed readings of the literary text, by readers newly and, perhaps, differently disposed to the reading. It may be that, at least for some readers, Ondaatje's novel manifests concerns with minority and postcolonial experience more clearly after 1996, precisely because of the film's selective reworking of its contents.

NOTES

1. Wachtel, in her 1994 interview, alludes to the novel's use of "a peculiarly British mythology—the exoticism of Lawrence of Arabia." Ondaatje responds by affirming that this "English take on the desert" is indeed "very central" to his development of the narrative (255).

2. The *Seinfeld* treatment of "The English Patient" phenomenon, particularly the intense antipathy Elaine feels for the suddenly unavoidable must-see film, presents the other side of the nostalgia coin. Elaine's squirming response to the film's portrayals of eroticism and romance counters the curious, emotionally expansive "wetness" of this desert film—a "wetness" entirely incompatible with the unrelenting urban, edgy and ironical "dryness" of the *Seinfeld* scene. It is worth noting, however, that Elaine's evidently unswerving commitment to the prevailing norms of *Seinfeld* sensibility makes her unpopular, first with the boyfriend who dumps her (as a result of her anti-*English Patient* position), and subsequently with virtually every other character, major and minor. In a fateful turn of events, Elaine's boss, Peterman, takes up the project of her sentimental education, obliging her to go to the Tunisian desert to live, for an unspecified time, in a cave.

3. I feel a need to pose here a qualifying question: is not "English Patientness," in different ways, a condition that one can ascribe to other major characters? Hana and Kip, I would affirm, are also obliged to discover and work through their relation with the English cultural legacy, obliged to be, in a sense, "patients" of the cultural conditions of Englishness.

4. At this point, I have clearly opted in favour of the novel over the film with respect to the representation of minority and postcolonial concerns. However, I should emphasize that my thinking *is* comparative and does not entail a thorough approbation of Ondaatje's treatment of those concerns. Ondaatje's presentation of his young Sikh, as one who has an instinctive affinity with machines, certainly bears traces of exoticism. The relation between Caravaggio's particular talents and his ethnicity needs to be pondered. Certainly, the notion that continents touch when Hana and Kip caress seems to me a too easy, too romantic portrayal of the negotiation of cultural differences. I hold, however, to my overall sense that Ondaatje's novel, unlike Minghella's film, is quite complex in its envisioning of cultural identity and cross-cultural exchange.

5. I have had to make selective use of my students' input, leaving out or rendering rather too briefly a good deal of what my journal reading had brought to my attention. I would like to take this opportunity to acknowledge and thank, as a group, the participants in my 1997-98 English 282 course at Queen's University.

6. In a March 1997 *Globe and Mail* article, Elizabeth Renzetti puts forward the following input obtained from publishers. Since its appearance in 1992, Ondaatje's novel has sold 300,000 copies in Canada, "half of those since the film was released." Vintage sold 200,000 in the United States before the film release and, in response to market demand, "has shipped a million copies since." Interestingly, bookstore owners also informed Renzetti of an astonishingly intense demand, backed by substantial money offers, for their film-derived window display materials.

7. Particularly disheartening, with respect to this mainstream "victory" and its
    public mediation, is the chorus of enraptured reviews that have greeted the film
    (see Corliss; Howe; Schulgasser). Many of these give attention to the film's
    status as an adaptation and generally speak in its favour in this respect. In
    Canada, the noteworthy "lone voice" of dissent is Thomas Hurka, who created
    a small flurry of *Globe and Mail* debate, by publishing in that paper in early
    1997 a short condemnation of the film's ethics and politics. However, even
    Hurka's more ample reflection on the same topic in the *Queen's Quarterly* ends,
    in my view, just where it should begin. Having detailed the film's choosing of
    the personal over the political, Hurka closes his writing by too briefly observ-
    ing that *The English Patient* film is "a product of its time, one in which people
    have abandoned concern for those in other countries or even for less fortunate
    members of their own society" (55).

WORKS CITED

Bourdieu, Pierre. *Distinction: A Social Critique of the Judgement of Taste*. Trans.
    Richard Nice. Cambridge: Harvard UP, 1984.
——. *The Field of Cultural Production: Essays on Art and Literature*. Ed. Randal
    Johnson. Cambridge: Polity, 1993.
Chambers, Iain. *Migrancy, Culture, Identity*. London/New York: Routledge, 1994.
Corliss, Richard. "Rapture in the Dunes." *Time* 11 Nov. 1996: 82.
The English Patient. Dir. Anthony Minghella. Perf. Ralph Fiennes, Juliette Binoche,
    Willem Dafoe and Kristin Scott Thomas. Miramax, 1996.
"The English Patient." *Seinfeld*. Writ. Steve Koren. Dir. Andy Ackerman. NBC. 13
    Mar. 1997.
Howe, Desson. "'English Patient': Love is the Drug." *Washington Post* 22 Nov. 1996:
    N42.
Hurka, Thomas. "The Moral Superiority of Casablanca over *The English Patient*."
    Globe and Mail 25 Jan. 1997: D5.
——. "Philosophy, Morality, and The English Patient." *Queen's Quarterly* 104.1
    (Spring 1997): 44-55.
Minghella, Anthony. The English Patient: *A Screenplay*. New York: Hyperion-Miramax,
    1996.
Ondaatje, Michael. *The English Patient*. New York/Toronto: Vintage, 1993.
——. "An Interview with Michael Ondaatje." By Eleanor Wachtel. *Essays on Cana-
    dian Writing* 52 (Summer 1994): 250-61.
——. "Michael Ondaatje: An Interview." By Catherine Bush. *Essays on Canadian
    Writing* 53 (Summer 1994): 238-49.
——. *Running in the Family*. Toronto: McClelland, 1982.
Pandit, Lalita, and Jerry McGuire. Introduction. *Order and Partialities: Theory,
    Pedagogy, and the "Postcolonial."* Ed. Kostas Myrsiades and Jerry McGuire.
    Albany: State U of New York P, 1995. 1-12.
Renzetti, Elizabeth. "Oscars Revive English Patient." *Globe and Mail* 26 Mar. 1997:
    C1.
Schulgasser, Barbara. "Masterful 'English Patient'." *San Francisco Examiner* 22 Nov.
    1996: C1.

The Clash of Languages in the Italian-Canadian Novel

Licia Canton

In recent years, ethnic minority writing has played a major role in shedding light on the complexity of the Canadian identity. Italian-Canadians figure among the numerous communities active on the Canadian literary scene. In the last decade in particular the Italian-Canadian literary corpus, which traces its development alongside the growing Italian-Canadian community, has seen numerous publications, especially novels.

This paper discusses language, specifically the tension arising from the Italian word invading the Canadian text, as a representation of hyphenated identity in the following Italian-Canadian novels: Frank Paci's *The Italians* (1978), *Black Madonna* (1982) and *The Father* (1984), Caterina Edwards' *The Lion's Mouth* (1982), Mary Melfi's *Infertility Rites* (1991), Nino Ricci's *In a Glass House* (1993) and Antonio D'Alfonso's *Fabrizio's Passion* (1995). The novels trace the process towards defining an identity which is torn between two conflicting cultures, the Italian and the Canadian. The analysis of these narratives shows that the tension and the negotiation between the Italian and the Canadian components of the bicultural identity represented at the level of the events narrated are also at work in the texture of the writing. Language causes friction between the two cultures presented in the narratives: the question of identity is played out in the weaving of the words.

In the Italian-Canadian novel, Italian elements are an impediment in the quest towards Canadianness. Although the new generation embraces Canadianness through education, friends and lifestyle, the presence of the old country remains through the influence of parents, customs and language. Otherness as represented by the old country can never be completely erased even in the second generation. The Italian component, therefore, is something of a weed which keeps resurfacing. The same occurs at the level of the writing. The novels discussed are written in English – Canadian English as opposed to American, British or Australian English – in a Canadian context and for a Canadian audience. The Italian word surfaces now and then thereby breaking the flow of the English-Canadian text. The presence of the heritage language in the English text is what Francesco Loriggio calls "the device of the stone" (39) or, to use Enoch Padolsky's words, the "linguistic stone" (56). The Italian word within the English text is like a stone or a stumbling block. The presence of the "heritage" language within the "ethnic text" is a device used by the writer to illustrate the tension and negotiation at work in a bicultural identity.

Italian may take up as little space as a word or as much as a sentence, but in each case there is a noticeable effect on the narrative. Italian surfaces in different forms to break the flow of the English text: as a translated or untranslated word; as a literal translation of a phrase or sentence given in English; and as an English sentence having a latinate structure. There are two major reasons for the Italian word "contaminating" the English text: the first is purely to give the text an Italian flavour – to mark *l'italianità* of the writing; the second, which I focus on in this paper, serves a specific function in illustrating the duality inherent in the Italian-Canadian identity. The Italian word is present when there is no appropriate English equivalent: this points to the difference and, in extreme cases, to the incompatibility between the two cultures expressed within Italian-Canadian reality. And, the Italian presence, either as a word on the page or in the nuances of the sentence structure, points to the fact that within an Italian-Canadian reality there exists a constant process of translation.

The tension existing between elements of the Italian culture and the Canadian society in which the characters must constantly negotiate a space for their identity is especially evident in what I call "the irreplaceable Italian word." In such instances the English translation would not do justice to the Italian original. Examples include the following discussion of *polpi* in Frank Paci's *The Father*, *polenta* in Paci's *The Italians*, *calle* and *vaporetto* in Caterina Edwards' *The Lion's Mouth*, and *la busta* in Antonio D'Alfonso's *Fabrizio's Passion*.

In Paci's *The Father*, Oreste Mancuso who represents Italy, wants to instill a strong sense of the Italian heritage in his sons, whereas his wife Maddalena upholds Canadianness or the Canadian way. The tension between these two characters, and therefore between the two cultures, is illustrated in the following passage:

> He [Oreste] brought up a bowl of dark grapes and set them on the table beside the *polpi*, a dish of fish stewed in large quantities of oil and red peppers . . . The dish was so strong that no-one else in the family could eat it. A fresh loaf from the bakery rested beside his favourite dish. (63-64)

In this passage, the word *polpi* breaks both the English language and the Canadian culture by highlighting the Italian one. The word *polpi* refers to Oreste's favourite dish, something from the old country that he will not give up, like making his own bread and wine. In this scene the bread was made by Oreste in his bakery, and he has just finished making wine. The word *polpi* also emphasizes the tension between the members of the family: Oreste who represents the ways of the old country, and

Maddalena and Stefano who want to become Canadianized. It is significant, then, that no one besides Oreste can eat the *polpi* because they are too strong, signifying "too old country." The rejection of the *polpi* by the rest of the family is symbolically a rejection of Oreste and of the old country.

In *The Italians*, the narrator (speaking from Alberto's perspective) comments on Giulia's tendency to prepare too much food: "To judge from the meal's size, she still hadn't got over the years in the old country when they had been forced to eat *polenta* almost every day. They had scarcely seen meat then . . ." (74). The word *polenta* disrupts the English passage in two ways. First, the mere presence of the Italian word causes tension within the first sentence. Second, the word *polenta* causes a shift in setting, from the overabundant Christmas meal that Giulia has prepared in the present to the poverty experienced in the Italy of the past. The presence of the Italian word results in the juxtaposition of the Italian setting and the Canadian one, thereby pointing to the fact that the Italian past (the poverty which caused a diet of cornmeal and bread) is an undeniable component of Italian-Canadian identity. In other words, the Italian past is responsible for the behaviour of the present, in this case Giulia's fear of regression.

The inclusion of specific Italian words in Caterina Edwards' *The Lion's Mouth* also takes the reader back to the Italian setting. In the subordinate narrative (Marco's story), the author uses nouns such as *vaporetto* and *calle* that are specific to the Venetian setting:

> Seeing the floating station for the *vaporetto* before him, Marco realized he had been going in the wrong direction . . . (21) Stopping at the top of a bridge and gazing down at the twisting *calle*, he saw the last of the evening crowd . . . He began running, pushing his way down the calle, then turning off down a narrow, empty *fondamento* (30). He broke into a

slight run. *Calle*. Bridge. One more – the last narrow street was blocked off. (37)

In this passage the Italian words which describe Marco's Venice cause the reader to experience the Italian component of the novel. The *vaporetto* is a common means of transportation in the water city. An English equivalent such as "boat" or "little steamer" could have been included, but no English word could do justice to the image created by the word *vaporetto*. Similarly, the word *calle* could be replaced by "narrow street," as in the last sentence quoted above. The *calle*, however, is one of Venice's specific attributes. In fact, *The Collins Concise Italian-English Dictionary* gives the meaning for *calle* as "narrow street (in Venice)." The *fondamento* refers to the platform or quay at the edge of the water – where manmade construction meets one of the natural elements, water. The *fondamento* represents stability, a product of man's rationality, whereas water represents nature's uncontrollability and unpredictability – as in the recurring Venetian floods, one of which is described in Edwards' novel.

The presence of Italian words in the above passage, as in the novel itself, which are very specific to the city of Venice, creates an image of the setting inhabited by Marco, a setting which is at the root of Bianca's (the Italian-Canadian protagonist) quest for identity. Venice – the *calle*, the *vaporetto*, the water – is an ineffaceable component of Bianca's identity as well as Marco's. The passage quoted above reflects Marco's unstable and precarious situation: his lack of direction, psychological and physical (given that "he had been going in the wrong direction"), and his sense of panic are indications of his impending nervous breakdown. The words italicized in the above passage are simultaneously associated with motion – the constant motion, therefore instability –

and the maze which qualifies Marco's psychological state. The author has chosen these specific Italian words to create a detailed image of the Italian water city and to illustrate the vulnerability of an individual's identity.

In the last chapter of *Fabrizio's Passion*, the narrator takes the time to explain the connotations of the *busta* (the envelope) which is an integral part of Lucia Notte's wedding as of many Italian-Canadian weddings:

> Peter is tripping over Lucia, their hands encumbered by white envelopes handed to them by the guests after the handshakes. Those famous Italian envelopes. . . *La busta*. How to describe this seemingly simple object intrinsically linked to Italian-American weddings? This tiny white envelope seals what consideration or dislike one family holds for another . . . Each envelope is a potential time bomb. It can celebrate a friendship or insinuate a subtle disenchantment. All confessed, yet nothing ever openly spelled out – one family's unbreakable loyalty to you as well as another's hypocrisy. (226-7)

The *busta* holds nuances and connotations that the "envelope" does not. What the narrator does not spell out is that the *busta* is the carrier of a monetary amount given to the newlyweds as a gift. It is the specific amount of money contained in the envelope which "can celebrate a friendship or insinuate a subtle disenchantment." The word *busta* in the above passage is more than a simple envelope; it is a symbol of the traditional Italian wedding in Canada. It brings together the friends and relatives from the old country in the setting of the new country.

The word *paesano*, or *paesani* in the plural, which appears in several instances in the novels has several connotations. In Italian a *paesano* is a person who is from the same town, or nearby town, in Italy. For instance, in commenting on his first weeks in Mersea the narrator of *In a Glass House* points to "the strange half-familiar faces of the *paesani* who came to visit" (3). Here, the word *paesani* refers to people originally from Valle del

Sole, Vittorio's hometown, or from neighbouring towns. For the Italian living abroad, such as the Italian-Canadian, the word *paesano* has taken on a broader meaning to refer to Italians of the same region. And, in regions outside of Italy inhabited by few Italians, *paesano* refers to Italians in general. This meaning of *paesano* has also been adopted by non-Italians to show kinship or goodwill, be it sincere or not. It is sometimes used to make fun of the Italian as well. Mario Innocente (*In a Glass House*) comments on the non-Italian's use of the word *paesano* in the passage below:

> "Mario," he [the German] said. "Mario, Mario, *como stai, paesano?*" . . .
> "That was the guy I bought the farm from," he [Mario] said. "Those Germans – *paesano* this, *paesano* that, everyone's a *paesano*. But the old bastard just wanted to make sure I don't forget to pay him." (31)

The passage shows the Italian's mistrust of non-Italians who try to ingratiate themselves by relying on the inherent friendship implied in the word *paesano*. Although Mario Innocente is not fooled by this, his young son Vittorio is lured into a false sense of friendship by the bullies on the school bus:

> "*Italiano*," I [Vittorio] said, clutching at the familiar word.
> "Ah, Italiano!" He thumped a hand on his chest. "*Me speak Italiano mucho mucho. Me paesano.*"
> When the other boys got on the bus and came to the back, the black-haired boy said they were *paesani* as well, and each in turn smiled broadly at me and shook my hand. (49)

Vittorio soon discovers that the pretense of friendship is simply a way of making fun of him.

The word *paesano*, then, brings together the Italian and the non-Italian, be it positive or negative, sincere or not. For the Italian-Canadian, the word creates a link between the new country and Italy by defining and uniting those of the same origin; at the same time the word allows the non-Italian, or the Canadian, to enter into the Italian culture albeit under false pretense. The word *paesano* brings together the two components of Italian-Canadian identity in uniting the true sense of the word with the meaning adopted by non-Italians. In each of the examples quoted above, the presence of the Italian word highlights something specifically Italian within Italian-Canadian reality and emphasizes the fact that this component cannot be erased or replaced within a Canadian context.

The author's choice to include the translation of an Italian word or sentence renders the text accessible to the reader who does not read Italian. It therefore establishes a certain openness – the will to reach beyond a minority audience. On the other hand, the absence of the translation renders inaccessible certain sections of the novel to readers who do not read Italian. In this case, it can be argued that the author risks alienating the non-Italian speaking reader, thereby establishing a certain degree of elitism for the novel. Arun Mukherjee distinguishes between the two by labelling the reader a "cultural insider" or a "cultural outsider" (44). Of course, in certain instances in which the Italian word appears without the translation the meaning is not lost for the reader. In other cases, the translation is necessary to understand the allusion made and the nuances of the action. In *The Italians*, for instance, it is necessary for the reader to know the meaning of the words "*ero ubriaco*" (20; "I was drunk") in order to understand the reason Lorenzo gives for raping his wife. Another such instance occurs in *The Lion's Mouth: Stasera mi butto* is the title of "the silly pop song" Marco and his bride-to-be had danced to the summer before their wedding (30). The reference to the pop song has a number of implications that the reader who does not read Italian will miss. The English equivalent of *Stasera mi butto* is "Tonight I throw myself" or "I abandon myself tonight." The meaning is very important because it refers to Marco's status in his marriage: by marrying Paola – a wealthy but overly demanding and domineering wife, whom he does not love – Marco abandons "his" self, losing his own identity in order to improve his social status. At the same time, the reference to the song foreshadows Marco's one night stand with Elena, the woman he has loved since childhood: Marco abandons himself to Elena that same night (*stasera*), thereby unknowingly entangling himself in a terrorist plot and jeopardizing his marriage and his reputation.

The process of translating is an undeniable step in writing for the Italian-Canadian author. Joseph Pivato makes this point in *Echo: Essays on Other Literatures:* "Independently of the language or languages the Italian writer uses, he or she is always translating. It often seems that the translating process becomes more important than the distant Italian reality that it may be evoking" (125). Translation is a way of bringing together the two worlds which make up the Italian-Canadian reality. Bianca, the narrator in *The Lion's Mouth,* is very conscious of the activity of translating inherent in the process of narration and in her Italian-Canadian reality. Edwards' novel highlights the complexity of the presence of Italian words, and their English equivalents: Bianca simultaneously reads her aunt's letter written in Italian and translates it into English for herself:

> "Bianca, *se sapessi, se sapessi,*" if you knew, if you knew, "*Que* [sic, *Che*] *disgrazia di Dio.*" God's disgrace? I must be translating incorrectly, a disgrace from God. "Barbara *scossa.*" Barbara has been shocked? hit? shaken? . . . "Worse, Marco (you, you) suffered a nervous breakdown." *Esaurimento nervoso,* the words translated literally as an exhaustion of the nerves. (9-10)

This passage illustrates the interplay between levels of the text and the complications resulting from the presence of Italian as well as the negotiation involved between "the Italian" and "the Canadian" components of the narrator's Italian-Canadian reality. The narrator translates for her own benefit: to ascertain that she understands the written Italian word, she feels compelled to find the English equivalent. This illustrates the constant need to bring together the two components of her reality in an attempt to better understand herself. The narrator points to the importance of the translation process necessary when the Italian word, in this case her aunt's letter, enters her own Canadian context. The narrator takes her role as translator very seriously in finding the appropriate word, which testifies to the notion that the Italian-Canadian lives in a state of constant translation.

Fabrizio, the narrator in *Fabrizio's Passion,* shares the same attention to detail in the act of translating: "When I finish the pasta, *faccio la scarpetta*. (Literally, this translates as 'to wet one's shoe,' that is, to soak a piece of bread in the tomato sauce, and wipe clean one's plate!)" (65). In the two examples mentioned, the act of translating is an attempt to unite the two worlds which comprise the narrator's reality, that of the Italian-Canadian. This is done in two simultaneous ways: first, by stating in Italian that which has its origin in the Italian world (the aunt's letter; the way one cleans the plate with bread); and second, by giving the English equivalent so that the non-Italian reader, rather than feel alienated, feels connected to that Italian world being described.

The tension existing between the Italian and the Canadian is rooted as deeply as the structure of the sentence, virtually beneath the texture of the writing. The stilted sentence is an English sentence which sounds Italian – a sentence which has a latinate structure as opposed to an anglosaxon or germanic structure. It is important to stress that the stilted sentence is different from the literal translation. In *Infertility Rites*, for instance, Nina is asked "When are you going to buy your baby?" (11) which is a direct translation from the Italian idiom meaning "when will you have a baby." This is a literal translation purposely used to maintain the Italian flavour and to indicate that the words were spoken in Italian. The same is true of the following: "I pour myself another cup of American coffee – what mother calls 'coloured water'"(137). The expression "coloured water" is a direct translation for the Italian cliché on American coffee. In *The Lion's Mouth*, Bianca reads in her aunt's letter that her cousin Marco has had "an exhaustion of the nerves" – the literal translation of *esaurimento nervoso* meaning a nervous breakdown (10). In these examples, the objective is not to sound English but to transmit the Italian idiom into English words without remaining faithful to the nuances of each language. This is usually done to indicate that the words are originally spoken in Italian.

In the stilted sentence, on the other hand, Italian is not present as words but at the level of the sentence structure, a characteristic which has been criticized as badly written English, or simply bad writing. I would suggest, instead, that the presence of latinate structures within the Italian-Canadian novel represents, to use Pasquale Verdicchio's words, "the utterances of immigrant culture" (214) and mirrors the reality of the Italian-Canadian experience.

The following passage from *Black Madonna* illustrates the latinate structure present in a conversation between Assunta and Marie, who represent polar opposites of the Italian-Canadian duality:

> "Ma, I'm going to Toronto," Marie said abruptly. "They . . ." She couldn't find the Italian word for "accepted." [sic] "They took me . . ."

> "Ma, I have to go. More times I go to school, better job."
> "You tell to your father . . . These things, I don't under-
> stand . . . You go to school – good. You smart – good. But you
> crazy. Your head in the clouds. The older you get, the crazier
> you get. I don't understand you. To *Toronto* you want to
> go?" (70-1)

In order to communicate with her mother, Marie is forced
to speak like her. Although Marie's "More times I go to
school, better job" is not correct English, the structure is
correct in Italian. Likewise, Assunta's "These things, I
don't understand." and "To *Toronto* you want to go?"
(where the (in)direct object precedes the verb) have an
Italian structure. The sentence "You tell to your father,"
on the other hand, is a direct translation of the Italian.
Moreover, the subject of their conversation consists of
the "push and pull" characteristic of the old way versus
the new way: the traditional Italian mother does not
want her daughter to leave home, whereas Marie wants
to experience the freedom of Canadian society.

In *Fabrizio's Passion*, Fabrizio uses an Italian sentence structure when he says "I am fourteen years old
but am thirty in my head" (72). This does not work
grammatically in English but is often used in Italian.
Likewise, in *The Lion's Mouth*: "But where have you
been? . . . We waited an hour, but since you didn't have
the courtesy to even phone . . ." (37-38) and "So loud
you have to have that record?" (42) have an Italian sentence structure. Such a structure is appropriate here given
that the sentences are spoken by an Italian, Marco's
mother. Bianca, too, is guilty of using the latinate sentence structure: "Her bedroom, that evening I visited,
was sparse, cell-like" (116). The following passage appears at the end of *The Lion's Mouth*, in the Epilogue:

> This week, Barbara arrived and I must play the wise aunt
> with a trunkful of distractions. Poor child – as I write she is
> standing in the living room, staring out the window at the

still leafless trees and mud-filled garden, *wondering what place is this . . . So I begin again my life in this city, this land.* (my italics, 178)

Even though narrating her tale has given Bianca a clear focus on both components of her cultural makeup, the stiltedness of the italicized words emphasize the influence of Bianca's Italian heritage. It is also significant that the first phrase, "wondering what place is this," refers to Barbara, the Italian girl visiting from Venice, taking in the novelty and difference of western Canada.

The presence of the heritage language within the "ethnic text" has led to accusations of bad writing, and the use of the stilted sentence may be perceived as the writer's inability to master the English language. On the contrary, these "ethnic markers" or "linguistic stones" are devices purposely used by the writer to illustrate the tension and negotiation at work in a bicultural identity. As Pasquale Verdicchio argues:

> By stressing latinate vocabulary, by the insertion of Italian syntactical forms, and by the inclusion of linguistic elements that represent the utterances of immigrant culture, these [Italian-Canadian] writers have altered the semantic field of English, thereby denying expected meaning. (214)

The fact that the Italian word interrupts the flow of the English text is a way of illustrating the symptoms of otherness which are an undeniable characteristic of Italian-Canadian reality. The presence of the Italian word within the English text should not be interpreted as a barrier between the two (Italian and Canadian) cultures. Rather, the meshing of Italian words with English words should be seen as the negotiation necessary in order to bring the two cultures together. Arun Mukherjee writes that "Ethnic minority texts inform their readers, through the presence of other languages . . . about the multicultural and multilingual nature of Canadian society" (46). Through their fiction Italian-Canadian writers suggest that in order to come to terms with the element of "schizophrenia" inherent in a bicultural identity, the individual must undertake the process of reevaluating the heritage culture. By using the "device of the stone," the Italian-Canadian writer attempts to illustrate the continuous transfer from one culture/language to the other experienced by bicultural individuals.

WORKS CITED

D'Alfonso, Antonio. *Fabrizio's Passion*. Toronto: Guernica, 1995.

Edwards, Caterina. *The Lion's Mouth*. Edmonton: NeWest, 1982.

Loriggio, Francesco. "History, Literary History, and Ethnic Literature." *Literatures of Lesser Diffusion*. Eds. Joseph Pivato et al. Edmonton: University of Alberta Press, 1990.

Melfi, Mary. *Infertility Rites*. Montreal: Guernica, 1991.

Mukherjee, Arun. "Teaching Ethnic Minority Writing: A Report from the Classroom." *Journal of Canadian Studies* 31.3 (1996): 38-47.

Paci, Frank. *Black Madonna*. Ottawa: Oberon, 1982.

——. *The Father*. Ottawa: Oberon, 1984.

——. *The Italians*. Ottawa: Oberon, 1978.

Padolsky, Enoch. "Canadian Minority Writing and Acculturation Options." *Literatures of Lesser Diffusion*. Eds. Joseph Pivato et al. Edmonton: University of Alberta Press, 1990.

Pivato, Joseph. *Echo: Essays on Other Literatures*. Toronto: Guernica, 1994.

Ricci, Nino. *In a Glass House*. Toronto: McClelland and Stewart, 1993.

Verdicchio, Pasquale. "Subalterns Abroad: Writing Between Nations and Cultures." *Social Pluralism and Literary History*. Ed. Francesco Loriggio. Toronto: Guernica, 1996. 206-226.

Tongue in Cheek

Dutch in Aritha van Herk's Writing

Christl Verduyn

Aritha van Herk is well known as a feisty feminist writer concerned with gender, a postmodern writer of wicked word-play prowess, and a prairie writer whose work reconfigures the Canadian West. She is not widely known as a writer whose development is closely linked to "an obscure language practised by barely eighteen million people"[1] in a country on the other side of the ocean, the Netherlands, where Dutch is the official language. On the one hand, this is an understandable reflection of contemporary critical contexts and current debates about multiculturalism, with the recent interrogation of ethnicity and discursive shifts to vocabularies of race. On the other hand, there has been the author's own resistance to being "pigeonholed" by her Dutch background, a resistance shared by many other Canadian and Quebec authors who are not of British or French background.[2] In this essay I consider "Dutch" – the use, place and importance of the Dutch language – in Aritha van Herk's writing, in particular, her essays. Author of five novels, including the award-winning *Judith*[3] and the recent *Restlessness*, van Herk is also an intelligent and refreshingly irreverent essayist. Her 1991 collection *In Visible Ink: Crypto-frictions* was followed a year later by a second book of essays entitled *A Frozen Tongue*.[4] With respect to the Dutch language, several essays are of particular interest. "Writing the Immigrant Self: Disguise and Damnation" (in *In Visible Ink*) features a long passage written in

Dutch, my response to which was in large part the starting point of my explorations. "A Frozen Tongue" is the lead essay in the eponymous collection, and the origin of my title here. Its unforgettable anecdote of the girl who boldly touches her tongue to a metal fence in sub-zero Canadian winter weather – a forbidden act of exploration that is simultaneously an exploration of the forbidden – captures an element of the relationship to the Dutch language expressed by van Herk as a writer, and experienced by myself as her reader. The essays "Edging Off the Cliff," "The Ethnic Gasp/The Disenchanted Eye Unstoried," and "Of Dykes and Boers and Drowning" further contribute to an examination of the author's writing and the Dutch language.

Language in the broadest sense is unquestionably central to Aritha van Herk's work. As for many of her contemporaries, for van Herk language precedes reality, brings the world into existence – by naming. "Language is the ultimate arbiter," the author states; "language, by naming a place, gives it life, existence" (*Frozen* 25). In this respect, language is comparable to mapping – a well-studied feature of van Herk's work[5] Language and mapping alike bring into relief and give contour to the indefinite. "Mapping, like language, is creation more than representation," van Herk asserts (58).

That the world which language creates seems to favour men more than women, and that the vehicle of delivery – language itself – reflects that favour, are observations van Herk shares with numerous feminist writers and critics. In this sense, van Herk's frozen tongue is, as she writes, "tied to the mast of gender . . . the world male-worded, and all tonguing confined to the masculine eye of history, biology, philosophy, a maelstrom" (21). It is this analysis of language that contributes to the prevailing, and not inaccurate, view of van Herk as a feminist writer.

In addition to being a key ingredient in feminist and postmodern analysis, language has been a major focus of postcolonial critique. Among its many accomplishments, postcolonial theory has been instrumental in establishing the importance and vitality of non-standard English and French in writing in Canada and Quebec. Recent years have brought deserved attention to native and nation languages alike.[6] One of the most significant and welcome developments in Canadian and Quebec literatures has been the publication of more work by Native writers and, also, more work written in national languages. When whole novels in the latter, such as Dionne Brand's 1996 *In Another Place, Not Here*, are taken up by major publishing houses, it is possible to say that new avenues have opened in Canadian/Quebec literatures.

In all this, Dutch has hardly been a critical concern, neither in debates about language and minority writing in general, nor in regard to van Herk's writing in particular. This is not surprising. As van Herk has observed, Dutch is an obscure language spoken by fewer than 50 million people in the world (*In Visible* 182). Canadians who still speak it are an invisible minority, widely considered to constitute the most assimilable of immigrants.[7] Who in Canada is interested in Dutch – that indignant-sounding language van Herk describes as "gutteral" and "spit-phlegm-sorted" ("Of Dykes" 422)? The language issues that bedevil Canadians revolve around the "official languages," French and English, while current critical discourse has turned its attention to native and nation languages.

As a participant in and contributor to the discussion, I am aware of this linguistic landscape. For van Herk, it has long been familiar terrain. Awareness and familiarity, however, do not fully account for the recurring reflection on the Dutch language in van Herk's writing, nor for the intensity of my response to her use of Dutch in writing. In both cases, the use of this language goes beyond a consciousness and concern for gender and critical acumen, to a realm where words like "emotion" and "ethnic sensibility" do not seem inappropriate. Closer reading reveals that Dutch is startlingly central to van Herk's overall literary trajectory.

In "A Frozen Tongue" van Herk recalls how she was born and learned to walk and talk in Dutch. As a child, she loved the Dutch books her parents had brought with them from Holland and is heartbroken when English replacements are provided so that van Herk and her siblings might learn English. "We live here now, in Canada," is the parental declaration, "these kids better learn English, Dutch will only confuse them" (19). In contrast to this familiar immigrant logic, van Herk's vocabulary for the required linguistic reorientation is strikingly emotional. She uses words like "need," "neglected," "abandoned," "forsaken," and "illegitimate" (19), and refers to the experience as "an excisement, speak English, however malformed and accented . . . the original language of blood and bone relegated to silence, forgettingness, obscurity" (19). A painful process of erosion begins: "English, the English of the prairies, was all around me, and it took over, lay on my tongue like a stone that needed to be spit out" (47); "Dutch buried itself in the pre-natal sack and blurred sound and I lost my tongue" (19).

The loss of the Dutch language is linked to one of the most important and definitive developments in the author's life, namely, writing: "Language was the key to the world . . . [but] no one used *my* language . . . So, I began to write myself, using the only language I knew – emotion" (34). Thus, at the heart of the writing life that was to become van Herk's is not, as might be expected, the discovery and mastery of the English language. Rather, the author's essays indicate that it is the loss and, as the following anecdote suggests, the subsequent (partial) recovery of the Dutch language:

> When I was twelve, some relatives came to spend the summer with us. They spoke only Dutch, nothing but Dutch, not a word of English at all. It was a curious summer. I was at first tongue-tied, unable to communicate, but then I discovered that the words formed themselves on my tongue, the language was there. I *knew* the language, it had rested in my head somewhere like a still pod, waiting to blossom, waiting for the opportunity. I had never learned it, but it was there. It was a gift; it was also a curse. The displacement I thought I had circumvented was there in me all along in the language I carried around, the words I knew, but did not know I knew. That epiphany, that realization, consolidated my pact with fabulation, with fiction. (47)

The pact with fiction is a deal with Dutch, that "evil/beguiling genie that still ambushes [van Herk] with its idiosyncratic voice and cultural nuance" (*In Visible* 129).

The link between Dutch and writing is presented from a playful but no less portentous perspective in "Edging off the Cliff." In this essay about the challenges to women who dare to declare themselves publicly as artists, van Herk explores the desire that fired her writing. Two items are of note: a gold fountain pen brought by her father from Holland, and the family bible, written in Dutch. Remembering clearly her father reading from the bible, "his voice weaving the heavy aspirations of Dutch, the language he was daily having to replace with a brash Canadian English that spoke in mouth much more than tongue" ("Edging" 214), van Herk also recalls the terrible temptation of the Dutch fountain pen, eventually and inevitably stolen and broken. Writing, van Herk explains, has been for her an act "larger than faith and more defiant than edging off a precipice" (211).

If becoming a Canadian writer entailed breaking old

European fountain pens (220), remembering the act has since generated a large body of writing. This may be said not only of van Herk but of other writers of "acculturated third and fourth generations"[8] as well. But as second- or third-generation writers, can their work appropriately be described, as sometimes it is, as 'ethnic writing'? And does this writing attest to second or third solitudes?

After a decade of working and teaching courses on Canadian and Quebec "ethnic" writers, I would like to move beyond the vocabulary of solitudes, the two of Hugh MacLennan's 1945 novel, and the "other solitudes" of Linda Hutcheon and Marion Richmond's 1990 anthology. Ten years ago I did not think this way. In the late 1980s and early 1990s, it seemed necessary or, at least, useful to delineate within the body of Canadian and Quebec literature a corpus that ended up being called "minority writing."[9] But with Governor General's and Gillers going to writers like Dionne Brand and Rohinton Mistry, I too wish to declare the terminology of minority, ethnicity and solitude obsolete. But I am cautioned in my desire to toll the knell of a third order of solitude in our literatures because, wish and want to the contrary, it is still there – where it might least be expected. Aritha van Herk's writing is a case in point. Her Dutch "ethnic background" is held to be among the most assimilable. But "the effects of displacement only begin to appear in the children or the grandchildren," van Herk counters. "Some people would say it is only a matter of adapting to a new environment, or adjusting to custom, of learning a language. I maintain that it is much more profound, a displacement so far-reaching that it only vanishes after several generations" (*Frozen* 46).

"Holland's insistence in my life was a slow revelation to me," van Herk states in *A Frozen Tongue* (45). There is in this no tongue-in-cheek – little of the levity implied by that puzzling English expression. Rather, there is a profound sense of loss and displacement:

> I have tried to unearth my lost Dutch, and to some extent I have, re-membered, re-learned, re-named the object of the world in my not-quite-forgotten language . . . the one I knew when I was born, before the excrescences of the verbal world. I try perpetually to re-capture that language, to give it tongue. It is both irrevocably lost and eternally present. (20)

A gift and a curse, irrevocably lost and eternally present, Dutch is clearly a problematic by which van Herk feels "bound" (*In Visible* 129). Her "first (and other) language (Dutch)" (129) remains a longing (*Frozen* 22) and a "perfect muteness, a pre-immortal memory that by its silence promise[s] another articulation, one that will perhaps teach [her] tongue its own treachery" (19-20).

In "The Ethnic Gasp/The Disenchanted Eye Unstoried" van Herk takes another tack on the problematic "gift" of Dutch, and the associated issue of ethnicity. The essay explores the author's thoughts and feelings at a funeral for Bezal Jesudason. Born in Calcutta, educated in Germany, Jesudason immigrated to Canada, settling in Resolute Bay where he became fluent in Inuktituk as well as German, Tamil, English and Japanese. In Jesudason's life – and in his death – van Herk confronts "wildly contradictory evidence" of ethnicity that can be both embraced and ignored ("Ethnic Gasp" 99). Ethnicity is perceived in terms of "the fluency of the look, the gasp of the eye before the tongue finds its root" (100). The funeral ceremony provides an "epiphanic seeing of Bezal as ethnic subject both central and other" (98), and prompts van Herk to consider her "own problematized and imprisoned ethnic, reconstructing her lost and imprisoned narrative." "This ethnic gasp of pain, I am repeatedly told," van Herk writes, "is nothing much, meaningless, without substance. But that era-

sure I repudiate, refusing to succumb to the powerless-
ness of invalidating my own invalidation" (101).

This refusal is pursued in "Of Dykes and Boers and
Drowning," where van Herk begins the articulation of a
final crucial significance that the Dutch language holds
for her.[10] This is its association with class, in particular,
working class. Much more than gender, in my view, class
is extremely difficult to render in literature, where language, as van Herk notes, "is a high-strung, well-bred
instrument" ("Of Dykes" 424). The author herself must
use that instrument to express the class connotations
Dutch represents for her, and she does it with trademark
fustian flare:

> And oh, the mouth so full of words that never say them-
> selves, bundled up in a backwash of that other language,
> forbidden, choking, the one that everyone laughs at: Dutch,
> Dutch, Dutch, as ugly as its sound and the throaty gutterals
> of its pronunciation. Full of connotations of lowness, levelity;
> Netherlandish the bottom . . . the duplicities of Dutch con-
> certs and Dutch courage, Dutch treats and Dutch cousins,
> Dutch collars and Dutch flight . . . Ah, to be a Dutchman; I'm
> a Dutchman if I do. Synonymous with all despicabilities . . .
> not to mention meanness, going Dutch going Dutch going
> Dutch going going gone . . . damned to this Dutchness, this
> thick-tongued accusation of the floundering sea against dykes
> and dykes and dykes . . . Tied to this tongue is a cartage of
> humiliation . . . oh the sheer thickheaded, cleanser-coated
> blue serge milkcowedness of it, so boorish, it is better to be
> not. (424)

The idea of "boorishness" develops from the Dutch for
farmer – boer – a family background van Herk has shared
with many immigrants, for whom it has often meant
economic hardship, and just as often been perceived as
cultural clumsiness, lack of class. The lowly farmer, the
"declassée" farmer's daughter, Dutch-speaking to boot.
The Dutch language has "another accent, classness" (422)
and, for van Herk, the class in question is decidedly "dirt-

on-the-hands-working-class" ("Ethnic Gasp" 101) with all its attendant connotations of uncultured, uncouth, coarse and common. "Examining these connotative figurations now," van Herk writes, "under the glass of *Inglish*, I begin to see and to understand that, in the powerfully Anglo world that my parents (Dutch *boers*) chose to emigrate to, displacing themselves from the comfort and safety of their known context, Dutch as place and language, I have tried and remarkably succeeded in effacing as much as possible of both my Dutch and my *boer*" ("Of Dykes" 425).

As the essays explored here indicate, however, at another, deeper level Dutch has been and remains central to van Herk's experience and creative expression. The author's most recent novel, *Restlessness*, suggests that in future this influence may figure more prominently in her fiction. To date, it has appeared mainly in her essays. In a memorable scene near the beginning of *Restlessness*, the narrator, who is staying at a hotel in Amsterdam, finds she needs a safety pin. She composes a grammatically perfect question in what she declares "one of the most difficult languages on earth" (*Restlessness* 21). The Dutch word for safety pin is the impossibly long *veiligheidspelden*. "Reduced to a question mark," the narrator reports, the sonorous construction flakes away until finally the mouth holds "only the stone of a noun" (22).

The foreign word as a stone in the mouth is an image that recurs with striking frequency in writing by Canadians of immigrant or "ethnic minority" background – so much so that in Italian-Canadian criticism, Francesco Loriggio has suggested that it has become known as the device of the stone. This is "after a phrase by Mary di Michele who, during a reading, explained that the Italian words in her poems were like little stones she had dropped in the flow of the English" (Loriggio, "History" 39). For Loriggio, the device or use of foreign language gives substance to potentialities of "ethnic literature" that would still seem to hold. The textual gap created by the

foreign tongue confronts the readers with the reality and
the history which are the author's and the characters',
Loriggio explains, and which preside over their enunciation, their linguistic, expressive options (40). Stretched as
far as it will go, the foreign tongue "will come to rest
finally on ground that is blatantly epistemological" (40).
Or, van Herk suggests, on frozen metal from which, when
torn away it will leave a strip of burning skin and gain
"the knowledge of a frozen tongue" (*Frozen* 12).

These observations have returned me to my sense of
earlier years that while we need not, perhaps, use terms
such as "ethnic literature" or "third solitudes," we do need
to read our writers' work very carefully, and to listen closely
when frozen tongues unthaw. For they still have a powerful capacity to speak and articulate the pain of lost language – however obscure it might be!

NOTES

1. This is van Herk's own description (*Frozen* 19). Smaro Kamboureli puts the
   question of ethnicity on the table in her brief introduction to van Herk, but
   within the context of the anthology the topic cannot be explored in depth. Van
   Herk's text "Of Dykes and Boers and Drowning" contributes to the argument I
   make in this paper that Dutch is central to the author's life and work.
2. When asked in an interview with Janice Williamson whether she would call
   herself an ethnic writer, Kristjana Gunnars, for instance, exclaimed, "Never!"
   She went on to explain, "It's the visitor impulse. I don't want to be a visitor!"
   (102-103).
3. This 1978 novel won the Seal Book First Novel Award and propelled van Herk
   to international fame. She went on to publish *The Tent Peg* (1981), *No Fixed
   Address: An Amorous Journey* (1986) and *Places Far from Ellesmere* (1990).
4. I looked at these two works in a paper presented at the ACSUS conference in
   Minneapolis, 21 November 1997, as part of a larger project examining the
   significance of essay collections by contemporary Canadian women writers. The
   overall thesis of the project is that the authors' essay collections are integral to
   their challenge to both literary and social traditions. As much as the writers'
   works of fiction – and because they work in tandem with them – Canadian
   women's essay collections deserve readers' and critics' attentions.
5. See Goldman (133-168).
6. Nation language denotes what others may refer to as Caribbean dialect or
   vernacular or the demotic. For more on nation language, see Brathwaite.
7. But wrongly. See Schryer for an indepth study of how Canadians of Dutch
   descent, despite appearances to the contrary, maintain an identifiable ethnicity.
8. This was the phrasing in the call for papers for the Third Solitudes conference,
   held at the U of Montreal, March 1998.
9. Or in Quebec "écriture migrante." The question of terminology has been an
   issue all along and it is not my purpose to enter the debate here. For a useful
   discussion, see Jonassaint.
10. But not for me. The sense of Dutch signifying boorishness or backwardness is
    not one that applies across the ("acculturated immigrant") board.

WORKS CITED

Brand, Dionne. *In Another Place, Not Here*. Toronto: Knopf, 1996.

Brathwaite, Edward Kamau. *History of the Voice: The Development of Nation Language in Anglophone Caribbean Poetry*. London: New Beacon, 1984.

Goldman, Marlene. "Abandoning the Map: From Cartography to Nomadology-the Fictions of Aritha van Herk." *Paths of Desire: Images of Exploration and Mapping in Canadian Women's Writing*. Toronto: U of Toronto P, 1997. 133-168.

Gunnars, Kristjana. "In That Gap Where One Searches, the Muse Hangs Around..." *Sounding Differences: Conversations with Seventeen Canadian Women Writers*. Toronto: U of Toronto P, 1993. 99-109.

Hutcheon, Linda, and Marion Richmond, eds. *Other Solitudes: Canadian Multicultural Fictions*. Don Mills, ON: Oxford UP, 1990.

Jonassaint, Jean. "Migration et études littéraires: Essai de théorisation d'un problème ancien aux contours nouveaux." *Journal of Canadian Studies* 31.3 (Fall 1996): 9-21. Rpt. in *Literary Pluralities*. Ed. C. Verduyn. Peterborough, ON: Journal of Canadian Studies-Broadview, 1998.

Kamboureli, Smaro, ed. *Making a Difference: Canadian Multicultural Literature*. Don Mills, ON: Oxford UP, 1996.

Loriggio, Francesco. "History, Literary History, and Ethnic Literature." *Literatures of Lesser Diffusion/Littératures de Moindre Diffusion*. Ed. Joseph Pivato. Edmonton: Research Institute for Comparative Literature at the U of Alberta, 1990: 21-45.

MacLennan, Hugh. *Two Solitudes*. 1945. Toronto: Macmillan, 1986.

Schryer, Frans J. *The Netherlandic Presence in Ontario: Pillars, Class and Dutch Ethnicity*. Waterloo, ON: Wilfrid Laurier UP, 1998.

Van Herk, Aritha. "Edging Off the Cliff." *Woman as Artist: Papers in Honour of Marsha Hanen*. Ed. Christine M. Sutherland and Beverly J. Rasporich. Calgary: U of Calgary P, 1993. 211–222.

——. "The Ethnic Gasp/The Disenchanted Eye Unstoried." *Journal of Canadian Studies* 31.3 (Fall 1996): 97-102. Rpt. in *Literary Pluralities*. Ed. C. Verduyn. Peterborough, ON: Journal of Canadian Studies-Broadview, 1998.

——. *A Frozen Tongue*. Sydney, Austral.: Dangaroo, 1992.

——. *In Visible Ink: Crypto-frictions*. Edmonton: NeWest, 1991.

——. "Of Dykes and Boers and Drowning." Kamboureli 421-426.

——. *Restlessness*. Red Deer, AB: Red Deer College, 1998.

Williamson, Janice. *Sounding Differences: Conversations with Seventeen Canadian Women Writers*. Toronto: U of Toronto P, 1993.

Unexpected Adjacencies

Robert Majzels's City of Forgetting

Lianne Moyes

"Barbarophones," writes Robert Majzels in the Montreal literary magazine *Matrix*, is Homer's word for "those folks from Asia Minor whose speech, to Greek ears, was an incomprehensible *bara bara*." He asks that "in this place of 'anglophones' and 'francophones'," he might be allowed to be a barbarophone ("Anglophones, Francophones, Barbarophones" 59). From this position of cultural difference and accented speech, Majzels locates himself between the famous solitudes. But, importantly, he does not make an argument for what Michael Greenstein has called the "third solitudes." To make such an argument would be to affirm the internal coherence and symmetry of the first two. For Majzels, the interferences, translations and self-divisions which constitute any language or culture[1] do not admit of coherence and symmetry. Majzels writes in an English which has French in its ears, an English which insists upon its "deterritorialization," its dislocation from major sites of English-language culture (Deleuze and Guattari 16).[2] Yet he does not identify as a minority writer. Rather, following Deleuze and Guattari's work on Franz Kafka, he understands his writing as a minor or marked practice of English, a major language of culture (18). Both Majzels's introduction to the 1994 *Moosehead Anthology* and his 1998 article "Anglophones, Francophones, Barbarophones" emphasize the *possibilities* for an innovative practice of English opened by living and writing amidst a

French-speaking majority, itself a minority within North America. The essays do not dwell upon the difficulties of working in the language of a linguistic minority. If there is a note of anxiety, it lies rather in Majzels's need to decentre his own linguistic and cultural identity, indeed, to destabilize any aspect of his identity that participates in dominant relations.

Like his critical essays, Majzels's novels *Hellman's Scrapbook* (1992) and *City of Forgetting* (1997) resist grand narratives and totalizing critiques, even those grand narratives and totalizing critiques which are themselves elaborated in resistance to prevailing discourses and practices. *Hellman's Scrapbook* stages what Sherry Simon calls the "traffic" between languages and cultures in Montreal (*Le Trafic des langues*), and *City of Forgetting*, the focus of this discussion, presents an international cast of characters who are homeless in Montreal and who dramatize the contradictions inherent in narratives of colonization, marxism, modernism, immigration, feminism, sexuality and gender. Although the novels are written in the spirit of modernity's critique of categories of identity and discourses of cultural belonging, neither is content simply to deconstruct identity. Both explore a fluid tactics of identity, a notion drawn from feminist thought: "You have to identify yourself," Majzels explains. "So you construct on the barricades a shifting position and you build it long enough to speak, then you dismantle it quickly and move on and rebuild it" ("This Could Be What a Conversation Is" 24). *City of Forgetting*, in particular, reminds us that the problematic of identity involves more than questions of language and cultural inheritance. Social and political projects, religious investments, sexual desires, sartorial habits, employment and literacy, to name only a few, intersect and overlap with language and culture in ways that shape subjects' access to positions in discourse and modes of identification. Also relevant to a discussion of minority writing is *City of Forgetting*'s in-

quiry into the material effects of figures of marginality
privileged by writings on/of modernity. In Majzels's
novel, homelessness and otherness – cultural, gender and
sexual otherness – are not only metaphors; as I will demonstrate in the section which follows, they are also part
of the lived experience of various characters.

Homeless: rethinking modernity

Clytæmnestra, Lady Macbeth, Suzy Creamcheez,
Rudolph Valentino, Ernesto Guevara, Le Corbusier, Governor de Maisonneuve: homeless in contemporary
Montreal, each of these figures has a dream or a radical
scheme and each struggles with the relative bankruptcy
of his or her own emancipatory narrative. Clytæmnestra,
an aging pickpocket, dreams of killing her husband the
King and reigning over her own kingdom until she is
killed by the riot police at Valentino's funeral cum gay
pride parade. Lady Macbeth, who would be Queen in
spite of her husband's cowardice, ultimately stabs herself
on the roof of a women's shelter rather than give in to
the men in the street below. Suzy Creamcheez, a character from Frank Zappa's songs, is Clytæmnestra's devoted
apprentice and sometime lover; the only character alive
at the end of the novel (aside from Pilote, de
Maisonneuve's dog), she has a tendency to forget who
she is and endlessly to reconstruct herself, sometimes as a
boy, sometimes as a girl. The gender identity of her friend
Rudy (Valentino) is equally ambivalent. Known as
Hollywood's King of Romance, Rudy tries repeatedly
and in vain to defend his manhood, dies young, and
comes "to symbolize the failure of the American dream"
(Hansen 26n3). Guevara, an uncompromising revolutionary who fights imperialism wherever it is (*City of
Forgetting* 93), takes a job in an insurance company as an

agent who investigates disability cases and eventually dies in a sea of discarded books. Le Corbusier dreams of a universal measurement and of cities built in straight lines to avoid what he calls "chaos, anarchy, [and] the overthrow of ruling classes" (98); an architect without a return address, Le Corbusier cannot get an audience with those who finance urban planning and development. De Maisonneuve's mission is to convert the Iroquois in the vicinity of his settlement on the island of what is now Montreal. As he carries a cross through the streets of downtown Montreal toward the summit of Mount Royal bent on claiming the settlement for France and for his God, he is unable to get the Mohawk language of prayer, a different belief system, out of his head.

Insofar as these characters are homeless, the novel suggests that there is no space within the contemporary context for their projects, for their revolutions. As I suggested earlier, homelessness is not just a metaphor, not just a way of figuring the exhaustion of the characters' emancipatory narratives.[3] The novel reincarnates its characters as homeless people whom many Montrealers will recognize, for example, the woman who plays the harmonica on rue Prince Arthur or the man who travels on a tricycle with a dog, a cat and a rack of prints and paintings.

Homelessness is, of course, also a metaphor. More specifically, it is a figure of exile, a figure crucial to the writing of modernity. As Sherry Simon observes in a discussion key to my thinking in this section:

> Telle que décrite . . . par tout un ensemble de critiques à partir des années 60, l'écriture de la modernité est celle qui se maintient dans un espace entre identités, dans un espace *hors*-identitaire. Ce ne sont pas les régimes d'appartenance, mais les espaces de l'exil, réel ou imaginé, qu'expriment les grandes oeuvres de la modernité. ("Espaces incertains de la culture" 41)

In drawing together characters from different cultural traditions and different epochs within the time and space of contemporary Montreal, *City of Forgetting* imagines Montreal as an inter-national city, a cosmopolitan space which fosters relationships between and beyond cultural communities. If one tries to read the characters as oblique references to the Greek, French, Latin American, Italian and Scottish communities in Montreal, one finds that the characters cannot be made to "represent" or "belong to" those communities. Majzels's novel is allegorical, but allegorical in the sense of generating movement between historical moments, between the mythic and the historical, more than in the sense of symbolically representing Montreal's contemporary cultural/language politics. In fact, a preoccupation with the latter politics is notably absent from the pages of *City of Forgetting*; the characters' principal struggles and identifications lie elsewhere. Not only are the characters far more concerned with finding food and shelter, and with fighting for various forms of social change than with language or culture, but also the story takes place as much on the ramparts of a palace in Argos, in the mountains of Bolivia, and up Dunsinane hill as on the slopes of Mount Royal.

Read in the light of oversights which Simon finds in prevailing accounts of modernity ("Espaces" 41-42), the "elsewhere" of the characters' struggles and identifications is significant. Majzels's novel brings to the writing of modernity an engagement with discourses of revolution in areas of the developing world such as Latin America and China, and with discourses of prayer among Quebec's First Nations. In effect, *City of Forgetting* begins the process of thinking "un cosmopolitanisme qui englobe le Tiers monde" (Simon, "Espaces" 42). Insofar as the novel situates homelessness "at home" in Montreal and makes it relatively unappealing, little exotic, the novel limits modernity's tendency to idealize otherness. The characters live the legacy of modernity's (and their own) failed ideals. Focusing almost exclusively on the relations among marginal characters, *City of Forgetting* troubles the tidy Self-Other distinction of exile; there is no coherent norm against which to imagine oneself marginal or fashionably "other." The characters, who are marginal in diverse ways and to varying degrees, form a loosely-woven, mobile community which disbands and reconstitutes itself as needed in order to resist and survive. In this way, the novel marks a certain departure from "la vision de la marginalité comme une position purement individuelle," a vision which Simon suggests is typical of prevailing versions of modernity (42).

At the same time that it resists taking comfort in the figure of the Other, *City of Forgetting* is also very much a text of modernity. The novel focuses not so much on what characterizes a community and who represents it as on the radical or hybrid elements within it, on affiliations that move beyond it, and on its porous interface with other communities. A character such as Clytæmnestra, for example, figures disruptive elements within the narratives of Ancient Greece; her brief reign marks a hiccup in the passage of power from the rule of the Gods to the rule of men (112). Guevara's conviction that "[t]he revolution has no geographic borders. The battlefield should be wherever there is imperialism," cited in Gonzalez and Salazar (191) and paraphrased in Majzels's text (93), emphasizes his multiple affiliations beyond national, cultural and geographical borders. In *City of Forgetting*, the interface between different cultural, intellectual or political traditions is often presented in terms of intercalated texts: Le Corbusier modifies his unit of measure on the basis of Suzy's reading of American pulp fiction (101-103); the conditions of Macbeth's demise – Great Birnham Wood to high Dunsinane hill –

translate the conditions of marxist revolution (120); and a *Chicago Tribune* article condemning Valentino as excessive and effeminate finds an echo in Guevara's guerrilla morality (133).

Juxtaposing fragments of texts drawn from different discursive fields, *City of Forgetting* explores yet another form of homelessness: intertextuality. Intertextuality insists upon the "interaction of the different codes, discourses or voices traversing the text" (Godard, "Intertextuality" 568). It not only unties the text from a single source or origin but also understands subjects – writers and characters – as "intertextual sites" (569), something which makes them difficult to construe as self-consistent representatives of a single community. The intercalation of texts mentioned above is an example of the radical possibilities of intertextuality: the reader confronts texts that would not conventionally fall within the pages of the same book. Such unexpected adjacencies, facilitated by the conjunction of characters from different cultural traditions and different historical moments, remind us that intertextual relations admit of curious anachronisms.

Making historical characters present in the city of Montreal asks readers to attend to forgotten histories and, at the same time, to grapple with the actuality, the contemporaneity of the conflicts in which the characters are embroiled. The juxtaposition of Mohawk phrases and prayer with the story of de Maisonneuve's "passion," for example, recreates a moment when both discourses had currency, when both might be heard. With a certain irony, it recreates a moment when the Founder of Montreal could not get the words of a *prior* settlement, a prior civilization, out of his mind. At the beginning of Montreal's history, then, there is a Mohawk prayer: "A whispering prayer, almost inaudible, but somehow drowning out his own prayers to the Virgin. *Kontírio, Otsi'tén':'a, Ohonte'hshon:'a, Okwire'shon:'a. The animals, the birds, the green plants that heal and feed us, and the trees of the forest*" (74). But the prayer stands not just at the beginning of Montreal's history. The conflict of discourses is *ongoing* within the present tense of the narration, ongoing in the mind of de Maisonneuve and ongoing in Montreal today, as the writer's acknowledgements to the Mohawk Language Curriculum Centre remind us (5).

The Mohawks are not the only figures adjacent to de Maisonneuve. The latter shares his makeshift shelter, a trench in an abandoned archaeological dig in the Old Port, with Le Corbusier, leader of the international modern movement in architecture. Finding these two in an abandoned dig is significant in several ways. Not only does the novel dig them up from the past, it also confounds the layers, the strata, in which one would expect to find them. An archaeological model of the cultural past is here abandoned in favour of a model of history which can conjure de Maisonneuve (1612-1662) alongside Le Corbusier (1887-1965). This intertextual model of history, fundamentally anachronistic, can explore the relationship between different moments in the "building" of Western culture, different instances of the colonization of peoples and spaces. It can also play with the ironies of de Maisonneuve "eyeing Le Corbusier's drafting table, which would make a perfect wall against the water" (39) which is gradually seeping into the trench. In other words, Le Corbusier's many plans for inhabitable modern cities and for low-cost concrete-block housing have come to this: the need to use his drafting table to shore up the temporary shelter in which he lives. Le Corbusier is, in this sense, a vivid figure of the bankruptcy of his own grand designs.

Measuring up: universal standards and cultural difference

The adjacencies of *City of Forgetting* allow for conversations among figures who could not (or would not) have spoken to one another historically. Such a conversation follows a long trek by several characters up Mount Royal. The topic is Le Corbusier's universal unit of measure, "Modulor," the unit upon which he claims the proportions of several architectural landmarks of the ancient world are based. Le Corbusier believes that international acceptance of Modulor as the standard unit of measure will allow standardization of building materials, mass housing on a global scale and, hence, a social revolution. Importantly, Modulor is no fiction: much of Le Corbusier's dialogue defending it, much of his totalizing theory, is directly quoted from his writings on the subject. The larger point of the conversation – and of another exchange discussed later in this section – is to tease out the mechanisms by which universalizing discourses give the appearance of all-inclusiveness at the same time that they write out entire communities.

In the terms of Le Corbusier, Modulor begins with the height of an average man with his arm raised above his head. When Suzy steps forward to demonstrate, Le Corbusier rejects her; as the narrator explains, "she is clearly neither man nor average" (100). In the ensuing debate about the height of the average man, Guevara suggests that Le Corbusier has based the measure on the height of the average Frenchman; Lady Macbeth affirms that "'the French are a short people'" (100); Clytæmnestra reminds everyone that "'[t]he African Zulu measures something over two metres'" (100); and Suzy proposes they use Rudy to size up Modulor: "'I mean, shit, ain't he the King of Romance, the Prince of Sex Appeal, the Screen's Greatest Lover, the Sheik of Araby?'" (100-101). When Le Corbusier insists that he seeks the *norm* "'not some larger-than-life fiction'," Guevara wonders why the "universal measurement" should be based on "less than exemplary men" and proposes the new socialist man, expected to measure at least six feet (101). Recognizing that they have reached an impasse, Suzy looks for new data in the books in the librarian's bag – a pocket romance, a detective novel and a script of *The Sheik* – and in each case finds the desired norm for the male hero to be six feet. She also points out that for Rockefeller, whose financial support Le Corbusier is trying to secure, "'the average man is an American'" (101). Le Corbusier begins to see that Modulor must grow. When he asks the height of an average American, Guevara answers that Malcolm X stood well over six feet before they shot him, and Rudy mentions the current popularity of basketball players.

I recount this scene at length not only to capture a sense of the way conflicting discourses coexist but also to illustrate the strategies the text uses to destabilize categories such as "universal measurement," "average man" and "American." Measurement is usually seen as a way of quantifying objectively yet, as *City of Forgetting* shows, measurement is ultimately contingent upon those who determine the unit of measure. In this case, the universal measurement is based on an exclusively masculine model, on something as variable as height, and on a European or, more specifically, a French conceptual grid. (None of the characters acknowledge that Le Corbusier was born not in France but in the adjoining Switzerland.) In spite of Le Corbusier's protest against Rudy's larger-than-life stature, *fiction* is precisely the ground of the precious Modulor. The fact that Le Corbusier is willing to "adjust" the universal measurement in the interests of wooing American capital confirms Guevara's observation that "'power . . . determines the standards of measurement'" (99). Not that the average height of an American is easy to ascertain: who, the text asks, qualifies as an average American and who decides? The figures the text's characters are able to imagine – Malcolm X, basketball players, Rudolph Valentino – are not conventionally understood as "average"; unlikely candidates, they highlight the fact that the prevailing representation of the average American is white and, most often, northern European in origin.

The kind of productive disturbance generated by juxtaposing "average American" and "Malcolm X" occurs again later in the novel, in a scene with Clytæmnestra and an African-American family at the lookout atop Mount Royal. Clytæmnestra is described striding past the family "without a glance" and taking "her central position on the ramparts" (121). Clytæmnestra, who rules during the absence of her husband Agamemnon, watches for his return from the Trojan War and waits to avenge his sacrifice of their daughter Iphigeneia. As she scans the horizon, the family beside her jostles for a turn at the binoculars. Dusk falls and Eschylus, the writer of Clytæmnestra's story, begins to fall asleep. This momentary lapse gives Clytæmnestra the chance to dream her way out of his trilogy, out of a narrative which sees her kill Agamemnon and then sees her killed by her son Orestes in a gesture which restores the rule of men. She dreams of women from many countries dancing, writing, loving and, as she dreams, she dances or spins. There is one person at the lookout who watches Clytæmnestra as she spins and eventually falls to the ground, still muttering the names of women: a small girl from the family of African-American tourists. When the girl approaches the fallen Clytæmnestra and touches her cheek, Clytæmnestra opens an eye and says "Iphigeneia," the name of the daughter she has lost. The family, at first concerned about their little girl bending over the stranger, soon moves to help Clytæmnestra to her feet and onto a park bench where the latter sits "surrounded by her family" (123).

This scene atop the mountain, like the scenes from Gail Scott's novel *Heroine*[4] which inspire it, draws attention to technologies of seeing, to the relation between seeing and not seeing. Initially Clytæmnestra does not see anyone; she is preoccupied by her own vision. The girl watches her, sees her fall and comes to help. Clytæmnestra sees the girl and recognizes her as her daughter. There are a number of ways of reading this scene and, especially, Clytæmnestra's naming of the girl "Iphigeneia." Is it a case of mistaken identity, the delusion of an old woman? Is it an extension of Clytæmnestra's dream, a gesture of solidarity between women across generations and across race? Is it a white woman recognizing in a black woman a figure of sacrifice by the privileged white father? What does it mean for Clytæmnestra to imagine the girl as sacrificed, especially when Clytæmnestra herself has overlooked her? Is it a black woman coming to the rescue of a white woman? Is it an oblique indicator of Clytæmnestra's own blackness, of her own difference from herself, of what she does not see about herself? Is it an alternative way of conceptualizing a family, that is, as an internally heterogeneous grouping? Each of these questions opens onto other questions. Part of the point of the scene, I would suggest, is to unsettle the systemic ways of seeing and not seeing difference.

Another part of the point is that Clytæmnestra's feminist dreaming and the litany of names of women across East-West frontiers are of little significance if she remains oblivious to those standing with her at the lookout, if she is unable to see the differences that constitute her visionary City of Women. Just as the discussion of Modulor exposes the specificity, contingency and interestedness of universal standards of measurement, this scene problematizes any totalizing feminist vision. As the disparate feminisms of Clytæmnestra, Lady Macbeth and Suzy show, such a vision is as untenable as de Maisonneuve's mission to convert the Iroquois, Le Corbusier's sense of a well-planned city, or Guevara's conception of socialist *man*.

Valentino: radical sheik

If adjacencies work to foreground differences *within* communities, they also allow Majzels's novel to reframe characters, to intervene in the way those characters were able to constitute themselves historically. Consider the example of Rudolph Valentino. The "Rudy" of *City of Forgetting* is a composite of Rodolpho Guglielmi, the Italian immigrant who arrived in the US with a dollar in his pocket; Rodolpho Di Valentina, the New York gigolo; Rudolph Valentino, the Hollywood star dressed up as gaucho or sheik; and the man who, in spite of several failed marriages, became known as the King of Romance. Valentino's series of names is symptomatic of contradictions that structured early-century American attitudes toward cultural difference, contradictions that required him to alter his modes of self-presentation repeatedly. As a professional dancer and ladies' escort, Valentino was valued for what biographer Irving Shulman describes as his "Continental appearance" (103), "foreign accent, sensual eyes, good manners and grace on the dance floor" (104). Encouraged to construct himself as a gentleman, a European gentleman, "Di Valentina" observed wealthy Americans and imitated their postures and mannerisms in front of a mirror (108). Ironically, belonging in America for Valentino meant becoming a Count. In Hollywood, he found that if he wanted to avoid "being cast as a slick foreigner" (124), that is, as a seducer and villain, he had to Americanize himself; he had to control his accent, pluck his brows and show restraint in his gestures and facial expressions (140-42). Metro, the studio with which Valentino made his first successful film, doubted if Mary Pickford could "fall in love with a Latin" (143) and refused him a permanent contract. Yet American women fell in love en masse with "the Sheik," a figure for which Valentino was apparently perfectly cast.

Valentino's is an identity built, dismantled and rebuilt on the barricades. Continually refashioning himself and playing heroes from various backgrounds (rarely Italian), his identity is mobile both on screen and off. Anything that might be called Valentino's "immigrant identity," the text suggests, is caught in the refracted light of Valentino imitating Hollywood imitating cultural difference. Through the figure of Valentino, Majzels's novel explores the interface between cultural, sexual and gender identities and, particularly, the mechanisms by which each comes to figure the other. As Miriam Hansen has demonstrated, the spectatorial relations of Hollywood cinema through which Valentino was constructed as both scandalously other and wholesomely familiar, hyper-masculine and vaguely feminine, are an important site for this exploration.

The most vivid staging of such spectatorial relations in *City of Forgetting* is a scene in which Rudy, often referred to as the "Italian gaucho," dresses up as a sheik in a men's washroom at the summit of Mount Royal. This scene is all the more significant for its location; the Montreal mountain is historically an important meeting place for gay men. The scene begins with Rudy's desire "To shed this skin. To be reborn. A hero. Riding across the sand, untamed, the fearless lover" (132). For Rudy, becoming a hero, a fearless lover, involves stripping off his gaucho costume and "remaking himself in clean white cotton robes, stringed beads, headgear, until finally, there, standing like a dark mystery in the mirror above the sink: the figure of the Sheik" (132). Interestingly, the very process of becoming a masculine hero – dressing up and applying make-up, preparing himself to be looked at and looking at himself – sexualizes and feminizes him.

Both Miriam Hansen and Marjorie Garber have commented at length on the ambivalence within the cinematic persona of Rudolph Valentino, Hansen in the context of a discussion of female spectatorship and Garber in the context of a study of transvestism. Garber hypothesizes that entertainers such as Valentino use transvestism "to signal their cross-gender identities" and that this "quality of crossing" is "fundamentally related to other kinds of boundary-crossing in their performances" (354). The bisexuality in Valentino's self-presentation, she argues, is "emphasized, if not in fact made possible, by the Arab dress he wore in his most famous film" (360). Although Garber does not elaborate this point, the implication is that the Arab dress, a figure of otherness, speaks of the oscillation between feminine and masculine which structures Valentino's experience of another boundary crossing, that of coming to the United States as an Italian immigrant. The close-ups which Rudy tests in the washroom mirror, "the lover's gaze, the savage leer, the regal pose, the slow blink of innocent charm, [and] the glance of a stranger across the room" (133), are those of the Hollywood figure of the "Latin Lover," a man who is both alluring (vaguely feminine) and threatening (hyper-masculine). The description of the close-ups as "flawless, wordless silence speaking volumes" (133) refers simultaneously to the silent pictures, to immigrant experience and to the ways in which the picture industry commodifies signs of cultural difference.

Hansen suggests that "Valentino's appeal depends, to a large degree, on the manner in which he combines masculine control of the look with the feminine quality of 'to-be-looked-at-ness'" (12). His films heighten the latter quality, she points out, by privileging him as object of the close-up (12) and "by casting him as a performer (torero, dancer) or by situating him in a historically removed or exotic mise-en scene" (13). In this sense, Valentino's performance of cultural difference raises his value as "erotic commodity" (15). Even more interesting for my discussion is Hansen's argument that Valentino's films both thematize and contain the scandal of his actual difference, his roots in southern Europe (24). Just as the "discourse of exoticism – the Arab sheik, the Indian rajah, the Latin-American gaucho – allow[s] the female spectator to indulge in the fantasy at a safe distance" (24), unexpected turns of plot such as the one which reveals the sheik to be of Scottish descent ultimately legitimize the desires of American women (17, 24).

In *City of Forgetting*, Guevara is the spectator at the scene in the washroom; "half surprise[d], half disgust[ed]" (133) by what he sees, Guevara reprimands Rudy for what he calls the latter's inappropriate "moral conduct," lack of "self-control" and "excess[es]" (133). Majzels's text uses the washroom scene both to give representation to the homoeroticism which underwrites Valentino's relationships in films (Garber 311) – and in daily life (Walker 110-23) – and to expose the terms of the anxiety, even panic, provoked by a man who likes to dress up and perform. The most vivid historical instance of such panic in response to Valentino is an editorial entitled "Pink Powder Puffs" printed in a 1926 *Chicago Sunday Tribune*. As I mentioned earlier, Majzels's text intercuts excerpts from the editorial with the conversation between Rudy and Guevara. Parallels in the discourse of Guevara and the editorial suggest, rather ironically, that Guevara's ideal guerrilla fighter resembles the *Tribune*'s ideal of American masculinity. Guevara has difficulty understanding Rudy's revolutionary statement "[i]t so happens I am sick of being a man" (133) and his revolutionary act of ripping a hand dryer out of the wall, heaving it into a cubicle, "exploding the porcelain urn and releasing a geyser of turbid water" (134). In fact, his way of making sense of figures such as Rudy is to translate their gender and sexual difference into political difference. When Suzy first introduces Guevara to

Rudy, for example, Guevara "eyes the elaborate gaucho outfit doubtfully" and asks "Is he Peronista?" (96). Baffled by the question, Rudy immediately reads it as an insult to his manhood. Following the "explosion" in the washroom, the local newspapers interpret Rudy's dress more literally; the headlines read "Chalet Toilets Destroyed in Suicide Bombing. Arab Terrorists Suspected" (141). Here, Rudy's Arab dress is taken to be a mark of cultural affiliation. Once again, the radical implications of gender ambivalence and homoeroticism are denied. *City of Forgetting*, insofar as it reads the Arab dress as a signifier of various kinds of overlapping boundary crossings, points to the limitations of readings which can only fix the dress to a single cultural or political identity.

Rudy, himself, is in a constant state of panic about his masculinity and, like the historical figure of Valentino, expends considerable energy trying to prove himself. In one scene in the streets of Montreal, Rudy responds to the "Pretty boy" taunts of a pimp by baring his chest and challenging "Come, we'll see who is the real man" (85). When Suzy steps up and hears "Look at this, now he's hiding behind a dyke. Get out of the way, sawed-off hairless cunt," she lunges at the pimp screaming the words "Cunt. Hairless cunt" (86) over and over again. Suzy's echolalic response is the more effective of the two. Everyone, including Rudy, freezes. Both Rudy and Suzy are up against a fear of women, a fear of the feminine. But rather than claim masculinity as Rudy does, Suzy forces the pimp — and Rudy — to confront their fear of her. By placing Rudy on Suzy's arm, Majzels's novel not only obliges Rudy to confront desires and practices that might be construed as feminine, but also taps into the creative possibilities made available by Valentino's historical relationship with his wives, "women who were reputed to be lesbians" (Garber 360). Suzy, who constructs herself as a boy as well as a girl, opens the possibility for Rudy to do the same. A line like "It so happens I am sick of being a man" (133) becomes thinkable and Rudy's funeral, which historically turned into a riot, becomes a kind of gay pride parade.

Through the character of Valentino or "Rudy," *City of Forgetting* examines the extent to which cultural identity is performed and its performance understood in gendered (and sexual) terms. Like Suzy, Rudy is constantly in the process of reconstructing himself. Rudy reconstructs, refashions, because he needs to in order to survive financially but also *because he likes to*. To be ever between identities is not only Rudy's problem, what gives him a great deal of anguish, but also a tactic for resisting being type-cast. More than combatting contradictory attitudes within American culture toward cultural difference, the Rudy of Majzels's text mobilizes them. The possibilities of self-construction that Majzels's novel opens for a character such as Rudy require that a sense of identity and belonging can shift, that Rudy can be variously, even simultaneously, an Italian, a gaucho, an American, a failed husband, a lover, a gentleman, a low-life, a sheik, a man who likes to dress up, and "the Prince of Sex Appeal." Of course, it kills him. But as Suzy shows, perhaps it does not have to.

Majzels's *City of Forgetting* brings together different discursive fields, different social and political struggles, different historical moments, different mountain-top sites and different literary traditions. These unexpected adjacencies dramatize the differences which structure any collectivity, creating a cosmopolitan space of relationships between and beyond cultural communities. The conjunction of different, even conflicting, elements facilitates an analysis of intertextuality, of the extent to which subjects and texts derive not from stable sources but from intersecting and overlapping codes, discourses and voices. Perhaps the most vivid instance of such intertextuality is the Mohawk prayer of de Maisonneuve as he carries his cross toward Mount Royal. In making the Mohawk language heard in the streets of Montreal, Majzels's text unsettles the priority of de Maisonneuve, his status as Founder of Montreal or, from the perspective of Pilote, his status as "the First One" (135). What is more, that Mohawk systems of belief haunt de Maisonneuve in *contemporary* Montreal suggests that the latter systems of belief come before and continue after the moment of European settlement on the island. Assembling characters who could not have interacted with one another – because of constraints of time, space or fictional frame – has the effect of opening new spaces and new modes of self-representation. As I argue in the third section, a character such as Rudy is transformed by his adjacency to Suzy. But whether he is on Suzy's arm or dressing up in a washroom on the mountain, Rudy is always "beside himself"; far from self-consistent or self-same, Rudy is a kind of serial performance, a performance which leaves him very vulnerable to charges of effeminacy. Guevara's response to Rudy's self-fashioning, insofar as it resembles that of the *Chicago Tribune*, reminds us that similarities in adjacent discourses can be as telling as differences. Parallels in Guevara's and the American newspaper's attitudes toward masculinity, like parallels in Clytæmnestra's and Le Corbusier's senses of the norm as white and northern European, emphasize the mechanisms by which racism, sexism and homophobia are reproduced at various historical moments and across very different discursive fields.

Throughout my discussion of Majzels's text, I have tried not to offer an overarching narrative; in this I am guided by the text itself. An account such as Le Corbusier's of the "average man," the text suggests, not only universalizes a single case and effaces differences within groups, but also claims the legitimacy of official, scientific discourse while ensuring that entire communities do not figure in the calculation. Similarly, Clytæmnestra's oversight on the mountaintop demonstrates the weakness of any totalizing critique and the need for temporary, tactical alliances which recognize their internal differences. *City of Forgetting* combines scepticism toward overarching narratives of history, identity and cultural belonging with a keen analysis of the power relations and discursive mechanisms which ensure that difference is simultaneously valued and demonized, written in and written off, both by prevailing narratives such as colonization, modernism or the American Dream and by revolutionary narratives such as marxism and feminism. Because the characters' struggles and identifications are not only, or even primarily, cultural, Majzels's text does not at first glance seem to speak to the problematic of minority writing. Yet, the novel stages intertextual encounters which de-idealize modernity's tropes of homelessness and otherness, foreground processes of colonization and hybridization, expose the lie of universals, highlight the whiteness of Western feminism, mark the borders that Guevara's socialism will and will not cross, and map the intersections between cultural, sexual and gender differences. A novel of modernity, with all of the attendant suspicions, *City of Forgetting* is nevertheless preoccupied with questions of identity, especially with constructions of the self which allow for fluid becoming and, at the same time, enable collective resistance.

NOTES

I would like to thank Nancy Roussy for her research assistance and her insightful comments about my reading of Suzy and Rudy. I gratefully acknowledge the funding which enabled this research: the Fonds pour la Formation de Chercheurs et d'Aide à la Recherche, Québec (FCAR) and the Social Sciences and Humanities Research Council of Canada (SSHRC).

1. I use the term "culture" to refer to the set of identifications, practices, institutions, modes of self-performance and relations to time and place through which a subject negotiates a sense of belonging to a community, a community which is itself hybrid. Although I often use "culture" to refer to a national, geographic or religious affiliation, the discourse of my text cannot contain the term and fosters a certain interference with the broader field of life-practices.

2. See Majzels's "Anglophones, Francophones, Barbarophones" and Gail Scott's "Miroirs inconstants"; Moyes's Postscript to the dossier "Écrire en anglais au Québec" which includes the French version of Majzels's text. For earlier discussion of Deleuze and Guattari's *Kafka: Toward a Minor Literature*, see Caccia and D'Alfonso's *Quêtes* and "Dix-huit auteurs italo-québécois"; Caccia's introduction to *Sous le signe du phénix*; Simon's "The Language of Difference" and "Espaces incertains de la culture"; Godard's "Comments," "The Discourse of the Other" and "Writing from the Border"; and L'Hérault's "Pour une cartographie de l'hétérogène."

3. For further discussion of homelessness, including the relation between homelessness and Jewishness, see the interview with Majzels ("This Could Be What a Conversation Is" 19-21).

4. In the opening scene of *Heroine* and repeatedly throughout the novel, the narrative consciousness turns to focus on the figure of a "Black tourist" who stands at the lookout in front of the Chalet atop Mount Royal. In the first scene, the tourist encounters a québécois security guard inside the Chalet who tells him in accented English to put "no foreign objects nor foreign monee" in the coffee vending-machine (9). At the same time that the guard's enunciation blurs the border between the foreign and the familiar, the category of race enters the scene to complicate any binary analysis of the relations between French and English.

WORKS CITED

Caccia, Fulvio, ed. Introduction. *Sous le signe du phénix: Entretiens avec 15 créateurs italo-québécois*. Montreal: Guernica, 1985. 7-22.

Caccia, Fulvio, and Antonio D'Alfonso. "Dix-huit auteurs italo-québécois." Interview with Robert Désaulniers. *Vice-Versa* 1.4 (Feb./Mar. 1984): 22-23.

——. and Antonio D'Alfonso, eds. *Quêtes: Textes d'auteurs italo-québécois*. Montreal: Guernica, 1983.

Deleuze, Gilles, and Félix Guattari. "What is a Minor Literature?" *Kafka: Toward a Minor Literature*. Trans. Dana Polan. Minneapolis: U of Minnesota P, 1986. 16-27.

Garber, Marjorie. *Vested Interests: Cross-Dressing & Cultural Anxiety*. New York: Routledge, 1992.

Greenstein, Michael. *Third Solitudes: Tradition and Discontinuity in Jewish-Canadian Literature*. Kingston: McGill-Queen's UP, 1989.

Godard, Barbara. "Comments." *A/PART: Papers from the 1984 Ottawa Conference on Language, Culture and Literary Identity in Canada*. Ed. J. M. Bumsted. *Canadian Literature* Supplement 1 (May 1987): 130-37.

——. "The Discourse of the Other: Canadian Literature and the Question of Ethnicity." *The Massachussetts Review* 31.1-2 (1990): 153-84.

——. "Intertextuality." *Encyclopedia of Contemporary Literary Theory: Approaches, Scholars, Terms*. Ed. Irena R. Makaryk. Toronto: U of Toronto P, 1993. 568-72.

——. "Writing from the Border." *Trois* 11.1-2 (1996): 167-180.

Gonzalez, Luis J., and Gustavo A. Sanchez Salazar. *The Great Rebel: Che Guevara in Bolivia*. Trans. Helen R. Lane. New York: Grove, 1969.

Hansen, Miriam. "Pleasure, Ambivalence, Identification: Valentino and Female Spectatorship." *Cinema Journal* 25.4 (Summer 1986): 6-32.

L'Hérault, Pierre. "Pour une cartographie de l'hétérogène: Dérives identitaires des années 1980." *Fictions de l'identitaire au Québec*. Ed. Sherry Simon et al. Montreal: XYZ, 1991. 55- 114.

Majzels, Robert. "Anglophones, Francophones, Barbarophones: Écrire dans une langue rompue." In dossier "Écrire en anglais au Québec: un devenir minoritaire?" Ed. Lianne Moyes. *Quebec Studies* 26 (Fall 1998/Winter 1999): 17-22.

——. "Anglophones, Francophones, Barbarophones: Writing in a Broken Language." *Matrix* 49 (1997): 58-59.

——. *City of Forgetting*. Toronto: Mercury, 1997.

——. *Hellman's Scrapbook*. Dunvegan, ON: Cormorant, 1992.

——. Introduction. *The Moosehead Anthology: Forbidden Fiction*. Ed. The Montreal Fiction Collective. Montreal: DC, 1994. 6-7.

——. "This Could Be What a Conversation Is—Simply the Outline of a Becoming: Robert Majzels in Conversation with Lianne Moyes." *Matrix* 52 (1998): 16-25.

Moyes, Lianne. Postscript. "Écrire en anglais au Québec: un devenir minoritaire?" *Quebec Studies* 26 (Fall 1998/Winter 1999): 26-37.

Scott, Gail. *Heroine*. Toronto: Coach House, 1987. (Now published by Talonbooks, Vancouver).

——. "Miroirs inconstants." In dossier "Écrire en anglais au Québec: un devenir minoritaire?" Ed. Lianne Moyes. *Quebec Studies* 26 (Fall 1998/Winter 1999): 23-25.

Shulman, Irving. *Valentino*. New York: Trident, 1967.

Simon, Sherry. "Espaces incertains de la culture." *Fictions de l'identitaire au Québec*. Ed. Simon et al. Montreal: XYZ, 1991. 15-52.

——. "The Language of Difference: Minority Writers in Quebec." *A/PART: Papers from the 1984 Ottawa Conference on Language, Culture and Literary Identity in Canada*. Ed. J. M. Bumsted. *Canadian Literature* Supplement 1 (May 1987): 119-28.

——. *Le Trafic des langues: Traduction et culture dans la littérature québécoise*. Montreal: Boréal, 1994.

Walker, Alexander. *Rudolph Valentino*. London: Elm Tree-Hamish Hamilton, 1976.

The Third Solitude

*Francophone Writing
in the Canadian West*

Pamela V. Sing

Community: Reinvention and Repression

With the emergence of a "Québécois" culture during the Quiet Revolution, the term "French-Canadian" became old-fashioned and, therefore, pejorative. While its obsolescence may have stimulated the birth of nationalist feeling for French-speaking people living in Quebec, it deprived all ex-Quebeckers and descendants of Quebeckers living elsewhere in Canada of their membership in a certain sociopolitical and cultural entity. Faced with the need to redefine themselves, these groups have twice assumed a new name. In the early years, they referred to themselves as "French Canadians outside Quebec." As this emphasized their exclusion, they have since adopted a linguistic-geographic designation, identifying themselves as regional, hyphenated Francophones, such as Franco-Columbians/Albertans/Manitobans, etc. If, as Michel Morin points out, the designation "Québécois" signifies not only an ideological break with a past deemed humiliating and a desire to start afresh, but also the "forgetting" of a certain sense of history, and consequently, of continuity, then what are we to make of the designations conceived in reaction to (or rather against) the term "Québécois?" "French Canadians outside Quebec" indicated a desire to belong to a social group that, while problematically split in two, was nevertheless still a community. Admittedly, the Quebec diaspora did indeed live "in Canada," and not "in Quebec," but maintained, or seemed to maintain, a connection among themselves as well as with their Quebec ancestors and relatives, thanks to their common "French"-ness. By contrast, the current designations have the advantage of repressing the rupture with Quebec and the latter's indifference to its "exiles," but do not at all prevent such exiles from experiencing their isolation as a catastrophe (Harvey). Each Francophone community claims a specific identity, and yet (though unable or unwilling to admit it) still wants to be recognized, legitimized, supported by Quebec. Naturally, the smaller the Francophone community, the more likely it is to lack its own cultural institutions and the greater its distress. Where can it look for that gesture which would make it visible to the world, rescue it from non-existence?

No Salvation Outside Quebec

As early as 1962, Jacques Ferron expressed a certain indifference to the Quebec diaspora. In the story "La Vache morte au canyon," François Laterrière leaves Quebec to "become a habitant" (Ferron 77) in the Far West – more precisely, Alberta. Living in a Quebec-style house in an "absurd and unlikely" (98) canyon near Calgary, his destiny is represented by his companion, a cow, symbol of the good life of his ancestors. By the end of the story the cow is dead, yet manages to survive. Its eyes bulging out of its head, which pokes through the skylight, it moos nostalgically in the direction of its former village back in Quebec. For Ferron, Calgary and Edmonton are hardly better than the canyon. In the novel, *Le Ciel de Québec*, both cities offer at most one or two taverns where one can occasionally speak French.

This caricature is representative of the Quebec vision of the life of a "Francophone outside Quebec." It recalls René Lévesque, for whom, in the 1970s, Francophones in the Canadian West were "dead ducks," or Yves Beauchemin, for whom they were "corpses not yet cold," or Pierre Bourgault, who in 1977 spoke of the need to "forget the French minorities in the other provinces, except for those in Ontario and New Brunswick" (13). Certainly, these disparaging remarks reveal more about their authors' ignorance of the vitality of Francophone culture in minority situations than they do about any sociocultural reality. Still, however hardy these hyphenated Francophone communities may be, their invisibility has serious consequences for the issue of identity. Since the turn of the century, the two official cultures have been expecting the Quebec diaspora to become assimilated by its Anglophone environment, but this has failed to happen (Aunger). Even in the westernmost regions, where the Francophone community is most fragmented, cultural production continues to evolve and grow. And yet, how many people have heard of Francophone Alberta?

A Unique No-Man's Land

This non-existence is nowhere more striking than in the cultural sector of literary production. The Francophone minority writer observes a Canada interested in the works of Michael Ondaatje, Wayson Choy, Joy Kogawa and Rohinton Mistry, but not in the works of Canadians writing in French. They might take consolation by invoking the language problem, but that would only reveal a fact even more difficult to accept: Quebec takes an interest in the works of authors such as Serge Kokis, Ying Chen, Fulvio Caccia and Anne-Marie Alonzo, but not in the works of its own diaspora. This is precisely why the situation of minority Francophones is unique in Canada. They live in a country that recognizes two official languages, English and French. They were raised in both these languages, grew up with them and use them still. Yet they are recognized neither by English Canada, nor by Quebec.

Moreover, if writers are living in a province with no institutions devoted to literature of French expression, their situation is doubly desperate. In the Canadian West, for example, the Francophone community is found in its most fragmented form. The result of this is not only a troubled sense of belonging, but also a political impotence.[1] Up until the 1970s, one consequence of this was the injunction against teaching all subjects in French. Although average Franco-Albertans of an older generation speak French at home and in social settings such as church, they cannot write French easily. And the oral nature of this culture has had important effects in the literary domain. On the one hand, Franco-Albertans are more interested in promoting theatre and music written and performed by one of their own than in literature written by one of their own. But if this literature is not read even by Franco-Albertans, who will do so? On the other hand, a whole generation of Franco-Albertan writers writes in English, unless they have had access to higher education.[2] Furthermore, the lack of a literary infrastructure, indispensable to the development of a culturally specific literature, means that those who write have the impression that they are acting in a void. Francophone Saskatchewan has the small publishing house, Nouvelle Plume. The subsidies it receives are, naturally, minimal. This is also the situation of the Ronsdale Press in British Columbia, which publishes bilingual books (in English, and in Chinese, Japanese, French, etc.). Alberta is home to Éditions Duval but, apart from three works of fiction,[3] the firm publishes only pedagogical documents in

French. This situation means that whenever a Franco-Albertan writer overcomes his or her inferiority complex about being published, he or she must rely on a publisher located in *another* Francophone community. If the publisher belongs to another minority Franco-Canadian community, the Franco-Albertan writer cannot but tend to feel that the priority of that publisher will necessarily be "his or her own" community, and books written by "one of his or her own." As for vehicles of literary criticism, a telling case is that of *La Revue littéraire de l'Alberta*, founded in Calgary by the Société littéraire francophone de l'Alberta, which published four issues between 1982 and 1986, before dissolving. While at one time *Le Franco,* the only Franco-Albertan weekly, regularly published a column devoted to Francophone literature of the West, this practice has become sporadic since the beginning of the present decade. Apart from this, the journals *Cahiers franco-canadiens de l'Ouest* and *Francophonies d'Amérique* are virtually the only other publications in a position to feature a topic on Franco-Albertan literature, invest it with some importance, and interest readers in the subject.

An additional dimension of the angst felt by Franco-Canadian writers in the West is the unique character of the no-man's land they occupy. On the one hand, it consists of their exclusion from the two official Canadian cultures in which they feel a simultaneous membership and, on the other hand, of their invisibility to members of their own community. In another study (Sing), I confirmed the persistence of the village-experience theme in Quebec literature through three historical periods: traditional, modern and postmodern. I concluded that the village, a poeticization of the perceived necessity of collective sociocultural expression, was closely connected to the issue of survival of the Quebec Francophone community in the midst of the Anglophone majority on the

North American continent. This leads us to hypothesize that writers with roots in Quebec, practising their art in extreme solitude – sociocultural, geographic, psychic and linguistic solitude – must be writing works that are singularly different, perhaps innovative, and strikingly postmodern.

I will test this hypothesis by examining the case of a Franco-Albertan writer, Marguerite-A. Primeau. Author of five books, she was awarded the Prix Champlain in 1986 for her third, *Sauvage-Sauvageon*. This prize honours the best North American work published in French "outside Quebec." In spite of this, Primeau remains unknown among both Anglophones and Francophones in Alberta, not to mention in the other provinces, including Quebec. Writing for nearly a half-century, she has inscribed a territory in the Canadian literary landscape that, in spite of partaking of each of Hugh MacLennan's officially consecrated "two solitudes," is unknown in both of them.

The Third Solitude

When Primeau was still a student at the University of Alberta in the 1940s, her creative writing professor warned her that it would be much more difficult to break into the market if she wrote in French rather than English. Although able to write in both languages, she chose to write in French. The prediction of her former professor proved correct. Nonetheless, Primeau, who has lived in Vancouver for nearly forty-five years, and almost exclusively in English for the last twenty, completed her sixth French manuscript in the winter of 1998.[4] Whom could she send it to? Who would want to publish it? Who would read it? For she had not forgotten that the manuscript of her previous collection of short stories,

published in 1996, had been subjected to considerable
rewriting in certain passages, rendering her voice almost
unrecognizable. The question was not only who would
publish her manuscript, but who would market it? Remembering, perhaps, the scant publicity accorded the four
books that she published in Saint-Boniface, notably
Sauvage-Sauvageon, she sent her manuscript to Éditions
Prise de Parole in Sudbury. It was the beginning of a long
and agonizing, though not entirely pessimistic, waiting
period. Meanwhile, in the summer of 1998, she was ap-
proached about an English translation of the novel that
had earned her the Prix Champlain, but Primeau was
sceptical, even though the Canada Council seemed to
have agreed to subsidize the publication. Yet, in February
1999, just as Éditions Ekstasis in Vancouver was on the
verge of printing the translation of *Sauvage-Sauvageon*,
the Canadian Embassy invited Primeau to launch it at
the Paris book event of the year, the *Salon du livre de
Paris*. Very flattered by the invitation and by the media
attention suddenly focused on her, she nevertheless observed that the original version had never received as
much "limelight," and it was in the euphoria of preparing for Paris that she received her rejection letter from
Sudbury. Knowing that Quebec was the guest country of
honour for the 1999 *Salon*, Primeau remarked wryly that
she might have the privilege of rubbing elbows there with
representatives of certain "*Québécois*" publishing houses.[5]
Anyone who knows her would have detected in her tone
of voice the ironic expression of vain hope that any Quebec publisher might be interested in her.

The case of Primeau raises a number of questions on
the subject of minority Francophone writing in Canada,
and in many ways, the subject of ethnic minority writing in general. For example, how do authors write about
their socio-psychic position as the invisible, marginalized
spokespersons for a culture that is itself invisible and

marginalized? A culture that neither knows nor supports the literary artists who, through their writing, speak to them and about them? What is this Canadian writing in French as practised in the West, a writing inevitably decentred vis-à-vis its counterpart in Quebec? How does this writing – created in a period fascinated with multiple voices and intercultural diversity, yet a period apparently indifferent to the intracultural marginalization this produces – reconfigure issues of identity and community? And finally, what does the indifference to this writing tell us about the kind of linguistic-cultural openness apparently espoused by certain cultural centres? These are the questions that will inform our examination of the work of one of the rare Francophone writers native to the Canadian West.

Origins and Connections

Born in Saint-Paul-des-Métis (now called St. Paul), a French-Canadian village in the north of Alberta, of Quebec-born parents, Marguerite-A. Primeau received her elementary and secondary education in her village, and at the Académie Assomption in Edmonton. Having obtained her teaching certificate at the Normal School, she taught for ten years in small rural schools in Alberta. Well-liked by her students, she nevertheless felt herself ill-adapted to this environment, and decided to pursue her bachelor's and master's degrees at the University of Alberta. At the end of her studies, Primeau received a scholarship from the French government, which allowed her to enroll at the Sorbonne. But after a year her financial situation obliged her to take a job as teaching assistant at the *Collège moderne des jeunes filles* in Nice. The following year, she returned to Alberta, where she taught secondary school for two years and at the University of Alberta for one year. The university was able to offer her nothing better than a position teaching conversational French courses for war veterans.

In 1954, the University of British Columbia offered her a contract to teach French in its Department of Romance languages and Primeau moved to Vancouver. Today we can only imagine the status, at that time, of a French Canadian without a doctorate, who came not from Quebec but from a Francophone community in the backwoods of Alberta – a place inconceivable to British Columbians. Primeau's efforts to stimulate interest in French-speaking culture on the Canadian West Coast brought her little recognition from her colleagues. No one in UBC's Romance languages department paid any attention to the radio programs in which she presented, in the form of lectures or scenarios, the works of a number of contemporary French authors, and few of her colleagues cared to read her first novel, *Dans le muskeg,* published in 1960 by Fides of Montreal.[6] Apart from articles of literary criticism and short creative texts based on the work of writers such as St-Exupéry, Primeau would not write again until her retirement in 1979. Between 1983 and 1996, however, when the author was increasingly living in English and felt that her mother tongue was slipping away from her, she wrote four books, three of them published by Les Éditions des Plaines in Saint-Boniface: *Maurice Dufault, sous-directeur* (1983), *Sauvage-Sauvageon* (1984), *Le Totem* (1988). The last, *Ol' Man, ol' Dog et l'enfant et autres nouvelles* (1996), was published by Les Éditions du Blé in Saint-Boniface. Les Éditions des Plaines had refused the manuscript of her last book, supposedly because of its brevity, and suggested to Primeau that her books did not sell!

Whether this last remark was intentional or not, it explains Primeau's sense that she is writing against all odds. It also reveals a key element in the issue of identity for a Francophone writer in the West. Whereas Quebec or Acadian, or even Franco-Manitoban and Franco-Ontarian

writers, belong to a community and a territory, Primeau
has the feeling of belonging to the French-speaking world,
but not to a particular French-speaking community. Her
memories, those from which she creates the world of her
characters, inevitably bring her back to Alberta, but she does
not consider herself a "Franco-Albertan" – not only because she felt herself to be out of place in rural Alberta
when she was younger, but also, no doubt, because of the
humiliating circumstances that, in 1939, obliged the
Primeau family to leave the village where Marguerite was
born. Based on autobiographical elements in the short story
"La maison d'autrefois," from the collection entitled *Le
Totem*, we believe that during the Depression of the 1930s,
Primeau's father, who owned a business, allowed his cus-
tomers to buy on credit. When his general store was subsequently unable to pay its own debts because farmers had
not paid their bills – a fact he kept quiet out of naïve kind-
ness and modesty – the father thought that he would be
protected by his reputation for honesty and supported by
his friends, who had benefited from his generosity. But this
was not the case. The whole affair ended with a bankruptcy, accusations of fraud, a trial and claims filed by credi-
tors. The father had to leave the village to start his life over
elsewhere, and it was only three or four years later that his
family was able to join him. Thus, for Primeau, the (imaginary) hometown village is a highly ambiguous source of
inspiration. Moreover, although she has spent more than
half her life in Vancouver and although the British-
Columbian Francophone community considers her as one
of its own, Primeau does not call herself a Franco-
Columbian: she harbours the sentiment that the community has done little to recognize her work. She likes to call
herself a "Francophone of the West," as she admitted in
1995, even though the Francophone West seems little interested in her and her work. Thus, she must draw her feelings of Francophone identity from an affective and

imaginary space that has no firm roots, and which is, above all, ambiguous.

Failure, Madness and Genius

This uncertainty of identity suggests a vacillation between the pole of self-affirmation and that of disappearance and death. On that point, paradoxically, Primeau, who claims to feel more French than ever having to live exclusively in English,[7] incarnates the Francophone community of the West. According to Claude Bertrand and Michel Morin, the creator is precisely a "deviant," "a person defective in relation to the norm," and the defect manifest in the creator is that of the society to which he or she belongs:

> Cette défaillance est le lieu de sa folie, de la folie de sa société. C'est aussi le lieu du génie qui n'est ainsi que l'envers de cette défaillance, c'est-à-dire son expression positive ou son dépassement dans une œuvre . . . [L]'expression créatrice, loin d'être portée par une quelconque normalité ou maturité politique, met en question le lien social lui-même et a fortiori toute forme de contrat social. Le créateur est d'abord celui par qui tout contrat se trouve brisé. Ce dont découle paradoxalement la singularité du rapport au contrat social d'une société donnée. Le créateur met à l'épreuve la société à laquelle il appartient, et de la capacité à soutenir cette épreuve sortiront à la fois la véritable force et la véritable singularité de cette société. (10-11)

In light of this dynamic, it is not surprising to see in Primeau a tendency to favour marginal characters, right from her first novel, begun in 1953. She persisted in this, despite a certain Franco-Albertan discourse (Dubé, "L'Espace conflictuel") that, until quite recently, conceived of the struggle for survival, if not in terms of "contamination" by other Francophone or Francophile cultures, then at least in terms of the preservation of a fixed, defensive identity, an "authentic" core.

Dans le Muskeg recounts the founding of the village of Avenir in northern Alberta. A young Quebec teacher, Joseph Lormier, arriving in the West in 1919, seeks to preserve at any cost the homogeneous French character of the village. His nationalism drives him to marry, not the blonde Francophile Métisse he loves, but an "old stock Quebecker" (Québécoise pure laine) with whom he will share a loveless marriage. Their first child is a daughter. Their second, the son so eagerly hoped for by the teacher, dies at birth because there is no doctor in town when his wife goes into labour. Lormier has recently forced the doctor out of the village because he is an Anglophone. The Depression arrives, and an Irish Anglophone merchant saves the village. Moreover, he has a son with whom Lormier's daughter falls in love. They marry and the novel ends on the day after the wedding, with the new couple leaving for their honeymoon.

Until recently, critics discussing this novel have focused on "the first seeds of an innocent and happy bilingual identity" (Dubé, "Je est un autre" 88) or on the absence from the world of the novel of "a beautiful, attractive, sensual, balanced woman, who is neither bitter, stupid or devious" (Tessier 195). But they have neglected the textualization of the blonde Métisse, a secondary character, yet influential and disruptive, not only in relation to the emotions of the protagonist, but also in relation to the story and the structure of the novel. We will limit our comments here to pointing out that the marginal figure of the Métisse injects a surreptitious force of dissent into the work, disturbing the "Canadian" vision of the world that the novel explicitly upholds. The positive representation of a member of an oppressed group, one not usually represented at all, subverts the "official" system that ignores both the feminine and Francophone differences of the Canadian West, and this suggests a new order, one that advocates "the free circulation of differences" (Van Schendel 119). At the end of the story, the teacher, imbued with a purist nationalism that history has relegated to obsolescence, represents the patriarch who, had he been flexible and willing to negotiate, might have made contact with the profound unity of the prairies through a hybrid union.

In Primeau's subsequent texts, all written since the author has retired, the main characters continue to live at the margins of the society to which they would like to belong. These are Francophones or Francophiles who are not only of Aboriginal, Polish, Vietnamese or Jewish origin, but who are also old, poor, eccentric, physically deformed or intellectually handicapped. They are often women, though not always, all fiercely independent, and most of them have a special relationship with language.

For example, in the title story from the collection *Ol' Man, ol' Dog et l'enfant et autres nouvelles* (1-24) – the only story in the book not set in Alberta – a university professor who has been forced to resign from his post takes refuge on an island in the Pacific Ocean. The old man, whom the children call "Traîne-le-patte" (Slowpoke), has become a misanthropist. His only companion is his dog, until the day he meets a young boy with eyes "shaped like almonds" and an "enormous" head. Paul White, whom his schoolmates call "Grosse binette" or "Blockhead," stutters in "half sentences" that are "broken, garbled" (4). But this brings the old man out of his usual grouchy silence. A friendship forms between them and the ex-professor finds in this a sensory experience, as the "visual, almost tactile" (22) character of the boy's language carries him back in time to the *great beginnings* associated with the myths and legends he loves so dearly. The alliance of these two "abnormal" beings humanizes, and even renews, the universe, giving rise to a certain measured optimism.

Two other texts in the collection recount similar experiences of communion between two marginalized individuals. In "Mon petit ami 'de' juif," a grandmother recalls the forbidden friendship she had, at the age of nine, with a young Jewish boy who shared with her an irreverent attitude to the French language. The friendship between "Nanette" and "Jaky," the children's secret names for each other, evolves in the context of a certain attitude to authority, accompanied by the complicity of mischievous laughter and whispered sceptical remarks. The novice, who is having difficulty with French grammar, asks "why not 'le lune' and 'la soleil,' why 'la maison,' and never *it* as in English" (*Ol' Man* 26). The questioning amounts to a protest against the arbitrary laws that draw borders between masculine and feminine, and surely, by extension, between what is socially acceptable and unacceptable. This boy, different by his accent, skin colour and eyes, is teased, though without malice, by the other children of the village, but the girl is in love with these differences in her friend, even "practising" in secret his way of "rolling his R's in the back of his throat" (26), as if she sought a personal experience of contact between two cultures, languages or codes. Admitting that she did not understand, at the time of the story, the anguish that can result from the impossible desire to "belong, to be at last like the others" (26), the narrator proceeds to tell about discovering a word for an intimate Jewish cultural practice, symbolic of "belonging to the chosen people" (34). The custom is mocked by the other children in the village and misunderstood by Nanette, leading to the boy's shame, self-imposed isolation, and ultimately, departure. At the end of the story, the narrator expresses the need for intercultural exchange:

> Et je me suis demandé pourquoi on ne nous avait jamais rien expliqué à nous, enfants chrétiens, que le premier janvier célébrait la circoncision de l'enfant Jésus. Pourquoi nous fêtions le Jour de l'An sans savoir que c'était un rappel de la religion hébraïque. (34)

She hopes that the boy's destiny has led him to a peaceful kibbutz somewhere, and not to a Nazi concentration camp. Though barely mentioned, this reference to the most extreme and atrocious form of marginalization of the twentieth century is enough to end the story almost directly under the sign of death.

In a similar vein, the story "Une Veille de Noël" describes how a friendship begins between two solitary patients: the narrator, an old Franco-Albertan woman losing her memory, whom everyone calls "Frenchy," thinking she is a Quebecker, and a Vietnamese woman with a deformed back, who is apparently mute. One day, however, the latter demonstrates that not only can she indeed speak, but also, that she can do so in French – although, as the Franco-Albertan woman remarks, it is a "different" French. We then learn about her horrible and tragic story of loss. As with the image of the holocaust, that of the violence and horror of the Vietnamese experience are readily understood, and both serve as metaphors for the marginalization of the Franco-Albertan character.

One striking aspect can be detected in Primeau's entire body of work: the indirect delimitation of a space bordering death. It expresses the difficulty and anguish of inhabiting a third solitude: to be a French-speaking Canadian without being a Quebecker is the equivalent of not being anything. Speaking French and English without an accent, the ethnic difference of Franco-Albertans is physically "invisible" and they can pass among Anglo-Albertans as one of their own. If they re-

veal their French identity, they are considered Quebeckers. For Quebeckers, however, they are an assimilated
people or on the way to assimilation. Yet even if, in linguistic terms, they were to assimilate, what would they
become in cultural terms? For those who have been raised
and educated in French, would living in English not mean
ignoring an aspect of themselves, repressing a part of
their past and of their being? Besides, can one really be
"culturally bilingual?" Or does one rather, by turns, send
into exile aspects of each cultural "self," so as to be constantly the same and different, not only for others, but
for oneself? As suggested above, sharing this self-con-
tained otherness with other Franco-Albertans like oneself may sometimes give the impression of easing the
sense of ruptured identity; but what sort of alienation
must Primeau experience, no longer able to identify with
any concrete Francophone community and feeling, moreover, that her art has not succeeded in creating a literary,
spiritual or intellectual community? Part of the answer
lies in the themes of her works. While voicing a certain
"optimistic" awareness of sharing a similar extreme
marginalization that can result in the formation of limited, and probably transitory, communities, her themes
nevertheless reflect a rather fragile sense of life, if not an
illusion of life, a sort of death in life. Primeau's protagonists tend to become friends with new Canadians
who are real exiles, in that they come from another country, while the protagonists themselves are exiles in their
own land.

Writing the Third Solitude

If, on the one hand, Primeau's writing demonstrates a
rare mastery of the French language, [9] on the other
hand, it is to be expected that the experience of extreme

decentering demands, or results in, a particular kind of writing – all the more so since, as the author herself admits, living in English has somewhat dispossessed her of her mother tongue. In the words of Lise Gauvin, for the Francophone writer:

> la langue d'écriture est un espace à inventer et à conquérir à partir des multiples possibles que lui offre la proximité d'autres langues, dont certaines . . . font partie de son propre patrimoine langagier. (111)

In the case of the minority Francophone writer, the proximity, or rather omnipresence, of the dominant language is oppressive, even overwhelming. Consequently, in Primeau, the writing language, French, or what could more precisely be called her minority practice of French, constitutes a "deterritorialization" (Deleuze and Guattari), a "degrammaticalization" or an "agrammaticalization" (Cixous) of language that may be considered either a faulty, impoverished French or a repossession of the language that dismantles it, re-assembling from its parts a counter-discourse, a symbol of minority experience and membership. As a type of sociolect, this French redefines and renews the idea of linguistic community, and consequently leads us to think about the relativity of "language" and the contingency of "culture." To write in "her" French, Primeau constantly tries to reconquer it, to express "in French" an experience that is taking place in English, or has taken place in French, but is remembered in snatches in a non-linguistic language. In both cases, it is necessary to untangle the languages, decide which words best translate the images or the memories. Increasingly, Primeau practises what Sherry Simon calls a "poetics of translation":

> un procédé de création interlinguale qui a pour résultat la manifestation 'd'effets de traduction' dans le texte,

d'éléments d'interférence qui créent une certaine ouverture ou 'faiblesse' sur le plan de la maîtrise linguistique et du tissu de références auxquelles s'affilie le texte . . . Par son vocabulaire disparate, sa syntaxe inhabituelle, par un dénuement 'déterritorialisant,' mais plus souvent par une circulation intense de références culturelles hétéroclites, le texte se distancie du langage *heimlich* et chaudement sécurisant du terreau communautaire. (*Le Trafic des langues*, 27)

The practice described by Simon in relation to migrant writing in Quebec is different from that applied in minority Franco-Canadian writing, however. The Quebec writing, nourished by a plurality of sources, is lacking in what George Steiner calls a "local force," "the assertion of a specific identity."[10] But in the Franco-Albertan context, writing practised as translation, as a re-enunciation in which a speaker "says things in his or her own particular way,"[11] is the only possible means of expressing and asserting a specific identity. As a poetics of "the sidelines and of the state of separation, articulating the exile of the writer who lives outside language communities," Franco-Albertan writing transgresses accepted, entrenched linguistic codes and is imbued with a disconcerting "strangeness." This strangeness calls for dialogue, exchanges, and a renewed way of looking, but uninitiated readers, seized by the urge to preserve their language as they know it, often see in this language not a "poetics of the sidelines," but a poetics to be sidelined, to be stricken from the ranks of books available on the market. This kind of intolerance is reminiscent of the relationship between the "beautiful big village above" and the squalid "little village below," as depicted in *Le Ciel de Québec* by Jacques Ferron, which I have analyzed in the Bakhtinian context of the carnavalesque (Sing 81-147): the incursion by a disruptive element, considered inferior, into the sphere of the "beautiful" destabilizes the status quo. The act of accepting such disruption is a way of renounc-

ing one's smug inertia and engaging in a dialectical relationship that leads to the renewal of the world, ensuring
individual and communal creativity. In Ferron's novel,
this is the condition, sine qua non, of modernity.

The case of *Le Totem*, a collection of short stories
published in 1988, is typical of the reaction that
deterritorialized writing can elicit. The minority Franco-
Canadian critics all appeared to be sensitive to the "nervous, quivering narrative" (Joubert 227) or the "simple,
supple" (Gaubau 15) narration of these stories of the
different ways in which marginal characters assert themselves as they (re)invent their membership in a benevolent community. These critics' familiarity with the
difficulty of surviving in French in the West seemed to
dispose them favourably to the ontological motive of
the stories, assigned to the subtext characteristic of the
two types of narrative unit that Barthes identifies as the
"catalyses" and the "indices" (15-16). None of them
had the impression that "nothing happens in the stories." By contrast, the great majority of Quebec critics
generally considered the collection unworthy of comment. One exception was Diane-Monique Daviau, writing in the magazine *Lettres québécoises*.

Daviau, visibly outraged by the nonconformist character of the stories, did not hesitate to rail against a
writing that, in her view, was in need of a "grammati-
cal, stylistic cleanup, at the very least, an orthographic
one" (Daviau 37). Nor did she refrain from insisting
that readers could believe neither the "stories" (which
they are not, according to her), nor "the importance
that the memories could possibly have had in the lives
of the characters of the narrative." If errors of spelling
and gender are inexcusable, and mainly due to the neg-
ligence of the publishers, it remains that the style, grammar and images in these stories are, in my view, a sign of
the renewal that comes with the blurring of cultural and

linguistic barriers, as indicated by Simon. According to Daviau, however, the "depths of boredom" that pass for stories in Primeau's book accumulate "lame and tortured syntactical constructions," anglicisms, "over-wrought" or "outrightly disconcerting" images and "completely incongruous amalgams of popular expressions and unlikely over-refined language" (37). Finding nothing convincing except the "boredom" and "emptiness" of the lives of the characters, the critic concludes, "I dived into this abyss of boredom and bored myself to death reading these texts that cannot be called stories. Not good ones, at any rate." Acerbic and hardly subtle, Daviau's text reveals more about a certain attitude to be found in a culture that dreams of hegemony than it constitutes an evaluation of the collection of stories at hand.

Quite another opinion is voiced in a piece written by Pierre Hébert for the journal *Littérature canadienne*, reviewing an anthology of short stories by authors from the Canadian West. Primeau's story, "La Maison d'autrefois," included in this anthology, was the emblematic story from *Le Totem* so detested by Daviau. In Hébert's view:

> Il est certes exigeant, dans un court récit, d'amener le texte à un niveau de haute densité; à cet égard, le plus intéressant de tous, le plus long d'ailleurs, est celui de Marguerite-A. Primeau, "La Maison d'autrefois," qui raconte l'histoire d'un vieillard qui veut retourner dans son village d'antan. Marguerite-A. Primeau narre avec justesse l'effet du temps qui embellit trop souvent le passé. Si plusieurs des nouvelles du recueil se contentent de raconter, celle de Marguerite-A. Primeau évoque, fait réfléchir et engendre une certaine rêverie. (136)

Daviau fails to notice a particular syntactic ambiguity that appears at the end of this same story (a thoroughly autobiographical story, in my view) and which expresses the inexpressible – in this case, a life lived on the margins, that is hardly a life at all.

The octogenarian protagonist of "La Maison d'autrefois," Paul Deschamps, decides to attend, uninvited, the seventy-fifth anniversary celebrations of "his" Franco-Albertan village, a village he helped to found. His daughter, with whom he lives in British Columbia, tries to discourage him, predicting that he will be disappointed. Did not this village betray him and then send him into exile? She evokes the bitter memories of "the bankruptcy, the trial, her mother's death, Lucien's cowardly desertion" (it was he, her lover in those days, who gave her the nickname "Cathy," and she has never forgotten him) (*Le Totem* 67) and the "disaster" (64): the family fled the village, never to return again, at least until now, when Paul Deschamps expresses his desire to go see his deceased wife's grave as well as his old house with the lilacs. Arriving in the community that bears no trace of his former life, Deschamps does indeed experience a series of disappointments – his friends are gone, the war monument does not bear the name of the son who died in Italy, the names of the streets have all changed, and his old house has apparently been converted into condominiums. Determined to see his old house again, however, he wanders through the strangely named streets, having lost not only his sense of direction, but also his sense of identity. The text accordingly situates the character on the threshold of (psychological) non-existence with the following sentence: "The old man, deathly sad, put one foot in front of the other, slowly, desperately" (84). But suddenly, he finds himself in front of his old house, and immediately loses himself in the most joyful reverie, an intense communion with his past life in the village. This revitalizes him, and when he comes out of his trance, he wants only one thing: to take some lilacs to his wife's grave. And so, one after the other, he strips the two bushes of their lilacs. Suddenly the wife of the owner of the house catches him in the act. Screaming with rage, she draws the attention of her husband, Cathy's former lover, but he denies ever having known a Paul Deschamps, a friend of his father, Félix, nor a "Cathy," and instead, he calls a policeman. Paralyzed, the old man is unable to say the words appropriate to the circumstances, such that even the simplest questions pertaining to his name, his occupation, his papers, etc. have the effect of depriving him of his identity and his place in society. He then loses his power of speech, his hands start to shake, whereupon, inwardly talking to himself, seeing only the lilacs he is holding, which are starting to wilt, he withdraws completely from the situation. Finally, the policeman takes one hundred and twenty dollars from the old man's wallet, which the couple counts rapaciously, and tells him, in disrespectful terms, to go away. Humiliated, alienated, dispossessed, Deschamps has come as close to death as is possible without slipping into the next world. Nevertheless, miraculously and mysteriously, he finds the energy and courage to continue his fight to survive. This is the textualization of his reaction:

> Le vieillard se redressa de toute sa taille . . . Les épaules droites et la tête haute, il prit le chemin du cimetière. Sans remarquer les petites fleurs au bleu terni qu'il semait à chaque pas, en mourant comme étaient morts son village, sa femme, et sa vieille maison. (98)

A careful reading reveals the ambiguity of the final fragment, where the subject of the verb "dying" is both the flowers and the man. Here the writing seeks to express the tenuous character of the new life in death that the marginal character finds each time he has suffered a defeat.

Deschamps becomes acquainted with an extreme form of solitude and alienation in his very own village –

a place which, of all places, should have provided him
with a heightened sense of his identity, his personal worth
and his membership in the Franco-Albertan community.
We may ask, therefore, whether his crime did not consist
in trying to re-live his Francophone culture as an experience of the centre, whereas he had spent more than half
his life living it as an experience of the margins. This
interpretation seems to be confirmed by the closing of
the story. "Forgotten" by a representative of his past,
now a member of the new elite, rudely dismissed by a
representative of the law, Paul Deschamps must turn
away from the village that is no longer the hometown
of his memories. Rather, the site of his Franco-Albertan
identity lies elsewhere. Thus, the old man walks to the
outskirts of the village. There, he will find, behind the
church that he helped to build so long ago, the cemetery
where his late wife lies. In the good old days, the church,
the presbytery and the cemetery formed the centre of the
French-Canadian village. In the postmodern Canadian
West, however, the spiritual heart of the Francophone
community has been displaced to the confines of an unrecognizable space.

Breaches of Language and Challenges to Authority

The Francophone literary space of the Canadian West is
a site of resistance, a place of possibilities. Located outside the two "official" Canadian solitudes, yet at the
same time partaking of them both, it occupies a unique
third position. A fusion of multiple "foreign" identities,
its expression (a product of the intersection of two languages and two cultures), its subjectivity and its voice
are all concerned with de-identification. Challenging the
authority of the dominant discourse, it proposes a col-

lective counter-discourse. Because it presents a strangeness that textualizes and materializes the cultural difference of one of the several cultural zones that constitute the *Pan*-Canadian Francophone world, it invites us into a dialogue and into what Sherry Simon calls "new pacts of translation" (184). The works of the Franco-Albertan author, Marguerite-A. Primeau, extend just such an invitation. As a triply marginalized author in terms of her sex, her minority Francophone status (whose survival depends on her biculturalism and bilingualism) and her place at the margins of the French-speaking world, Primeau practises a transgressive, innovative and potentially renewing form of writing. We have drawn attention here, in some of her works, to a hybrid quality at the textual, linguistic and cultural levels that is characteristic of the otherness pervading and defining the Franco-Albertan literary text. It is an otherness that we could allow to lapse into oblivion and silence, preferring "othernesses" that are deemed more interesting. Or we could welcome it, decipher it and appreciate it in order to establish new social relationships and tap their riches. Today there is talk of loosening certain boundaries of language, cultural and identity. Should we not accept, and even wish, that this loosening be extended as far as . . . the Far West?

NOTES

1. Compare the Franco-Manitobans who, with a smaller population, but one which is concentrated in Saint-Boniface, form an electoral riding, which gives them a basis of political power and official visibility. Among their institutions are two publishing houses and the head office of the Centre d'études franco-canadiennes de l'Ouest.

2. Notably Marie Moser, author of *Counterpoint* (Irwin Publishing, 1987), translated into French by Gisèle Villeneuve (*Courtepointe*, Québec-Amérique, 1991) and Jacqueline Dumas, author of *Madeleine and the Angel* (Fifth House, 1989), not yet published in French translation. On the subject of these authors, see Pamela Sing, "Memory, Sexuality and Patriarchy: Emancipatory Strategies in Contemporary Franco-Albertan Women's Writing" in Paula Ruth Gilbert and Roseanna Dufault (ed.), *Doing Gender: Franco-Canadian Women Writers of the 1990s* (Fairleigh Dickinson UP, 2001) 310-334. This is not a permanent situation, certainly, as the school system is currently educating readers and future writers for whom French is not an anomaly.

3. These are: *Anecdotes du vécu* and *Religieux et religieuses* by Guy Lacombe, published in 1993, and *Mon grand livre d'images* by France Levasseur-Ouimet, published in 1994.
4. A short excerpt from this manuscript has been published under the title "Et dansent les hirondelles" in the *Revue éloizes, La revue acadienne de création* 26 (1998): 75-76.
5. During a telephone conversation, March 8, 1999.
6. This edition is now out of print. In the winter of 1998, I wrote to the director of Fides to ask if they would be interested in re-issuing the novel, but my letter has remained unanswered.
7. During a personal conversation at her home in April, 1998.
8. I would refer anyone interested in further discussion of this point to Pamela Sing, "La voix métisse dans le roman de l'infidélité," *Francophonies d'Amérique* 8 (1998): 23-37.
9. In the article referred to above, Jules Tessier writes: "Among the writers currently working in the territory of French-speaking America, there are few who express themselves in a language as refined, polished and disciplined as Marguerite Primeau" (Tessier 202).
10. Steiner (4), quoted by Simon (20).
11. Folkart (14), quoted by Simon (21).

WORKS CITED

Aunger, Edmond A. "Les Communautés francophones de l'Ouest: la survivance d'une minorité dispersée." *Francophonies minoritaires au Canada: l'état des lieux.* Ed. J. Yvon Thériault. Moncton, NB: Éditions d'Acadie, 1999. 273-294.

Barthes, Roland. "Introduction à l'analyse structurale des récits." *Communications* 8, *L'Analyse structurale du récit.* Coll. "Points Littérature." Paris: Seuil, 1981. 7-33.

Bertrand, Claude, and Michel Morin. "Imaginer le territoire." *Vice versa. Culture politique: la parole et le geste* 17 (1986-87): 10-12.

Bourgault, Pierre. "Le Québec face au Canada français," *Langue, littérature, culture au Canada français. Cahiers du C.R.C.C.F.* Ed. Robert Vigneault. Ottawa: Les Éditions de l'Université d'Ottawa, 1997. 13-19.

Cixous, Hélène. Personal interview by telephone and by correspondance with Kathleen O'Grady of Cambridge University. March 7, 1996.

Daviau, Diane-Monique. "De deux sortes de vertige." *Lettres québécoises* 52 (hiver 1988): 36-37.

Deleuze, Gilles, and Félix Guattari. *Kafka. Pour une littérature mineure.* Paris: Minuit, 1975.

Dubé, Paul. "L'Espace conflictuel de la culture franco-albertaine." "La Perception de l'Autre et la francophonie: hier, aujourd'hui et demain." Conference paper. Colloque du CEFCO à la Faculté St-Jean, Edmonton. October 24, 1998.

———. "Je est un autre: et l'autre est moi." *La Question identitaire au Canada francophone. Récits, parcours, enjeux, hors-lieux.* Ed. Jocelyn Létourneau, Sainte-Foy, QC: Presses de l'Université Laval, 1994. 79-99.

Ferron, Jacques. "La Vache morte au canyon." *Contes. Édition intégrale. Contes anglais, contes du pays incertain, contes inédits.* Montréal: HMH, 1968. 74-98.

Folkart, Barbara. *Le Conflit des énonciations.* Candiac: Éditions Balzac, 1992.

Gaubau, Marie J. "Six nouvelles où le passé confirme le présent." *Liaison* (janvier 1989): 15.

Gauvin, Lise. "Littératures visibles et invisibles. Introduction." *Études françaises* 33.1 (1997): 111-113.

Harvey, Fernand. "Le Québec et le Canada français: histoire d'une déchirure." *Identité et cultures nationales. L'Amérique française en mutation.* Ed. Simon Langlois. Sainte-Foy, QC: Presses de l'Université Laval, 1995. 49-64.

Hébert, Pierre. "Plus ou moins." *Littérature canadienne* 117 (été 1998): 136.

Joubert, Ingrid. "L'Ouest canadien." *Littérature canadienne* 129 (été 1991): 226-228.

Morin, Michel. "L'Autre Amérique." *Vice Versa. Nonobstant la langue* (décembre 1989): 7-11.

Primeau, Marguerite-A. *Dans le muskeg*. Montréal: Fides, 1960.

——. *Maurice Dufault, sous-directeur*. Saint-Boniface: Les Éditions des Plaines, 1983.

——. *Ol' Man, ol' Dog et l'enfant et autres nouvelles*. Saint-Boniface: Les Éditions du Blé, 1996.

——. *Sauvage-Sauvageon*. Saint-Boniface: Les Éditions des Plaines, 1984.

——. *Le Totem*. Saint-Boniface: Les Éditions des Plaines, 1988.

Simon, Sherry. *Le Trafic des langues. Traduction et culture dans la littérature québécoise*. Montréal: Boréal, 1994.

Sing, Pamela V. *Villages imaginaires. Édouard Montpetit, Jacques Ferron et Jacques Poulin*. Montréal: Fides, 1995.

Steiner, George. *After Babel*. Toronto: Oxford UP, 1975.

Tessier, Jules. "La Dialectique du conservatisme et de l'innovation dans l'œuvre de Marguerite Primeau." *Les Outils de la francophonie*. Vancouver/Winnipeg: Centre d'études franco-canadiennes de l'Ouest, 1988. 186-204.

Van Schendel, Nicolas. "L'Identité métisse ou l'histoire oubliée de la canadianité." *La Question identitaire au Canada francophone. Récits, parcours, enjeux, horslieux*. Ed. Jocelyn Létourneau. Sainte-Foy, QC: Presses de l'Université Laval, 1994. 101-121.

Ethnic Heterotopias

The Construction of "Place" in Italian-Canadian Writing

Domenic A. Beneventi

The recent proliferation of writing by minorities in Canada has engendered a reformulation of the country's social and cultural imaginary; in fact, it has changed the way in which we think about ourselves as a collectivity. Demographic shifts in the ethnic makeup of the country have elicited corresponding shifts in the terms of debate about national identity and culture and, if the furore over multiculturalism is any indication, of the desire to grapple with the social and cultural implications of such changes. Paradigms for thinking the nation have shifted in recent years from an essentially bicultural, bilingual country with "folkloristic colourings" to a more realistic recognition of the plurality that inscribes itself on our everyday social, linguistic and cultural practices. The problems raised by putting the official policy of multiculturalism into practice have been much debated, yet, questions of ethnic assimilation, ghettoization and acculturation have yet to be resolved.

While critical studies of minority literatures in Canada have raised a number of important issues, including questions relating to cultural memory, acculturation, difference, language, racism and the place of ethnic writing within the broader sphere of Canadian literature, very little work has been done on the experience and representation of "place" from a minority perspective, on the ways in which ethnic communities and individuals construct spatial imaginaries which reflect their own senses of identity and belonging.[1] A large body of early literary criticism in Canada focused on the country's vast landscape, on the topographical metaphors which were seen to reflect the immediate concerns of settling a harsh natural world. Atwood's "survival theme," Moss's "isolation," and Frye's "garrison mentality" were spatial metaphors which served as interpretive models of a uniquely Canadian temperament. Similarly, the Quebecois "roman du terroir" of the first half of this century was seen to reflect the French-Canadian *"petit peuple,"* while the newly modernized Québec space of the second half of the twentieth century was figured as the site for the nascent political consciousness of its people. While these strong links between identity and territory have historically occupied a central role in the literary and nationalist discourses of English and French Canada, very little critical work has been done specifically on urban themes in Canadian literature, and even less so from a minority perspective. The diversification of Canadian literature would suggest the need to revisit the intersections between "place" and Canadian cultural identities, the need to look at the ways in which articulations of space in the literary production of minority communities reframes and destabilizes the traditional (dual) territorial models of Canada.

This article will address the ambiguous relationship between territory and identity in one such ethnic community through a reading of the work of Antonio D'Alfonso, Mary di Michele and Gianna Patriarca so as to understand how the fictionalization of space operates in ethnic "self-fashioning." I propose that references to Canadian and Italian spaces in these texts are attempts at working out a sense of cultural specificity and hybridity in relation to the codes, practices and ideologies of place – a way of appropriating and making familiar Canadian space but, also, one of maintaining ties, however tenuous they may be, to the country of origin.

The recent interest in critical theory, literary studies, and in the humanities, in general, with space and its social, political and imaginary construction has emanated in part from feminist, postcolonial and postmodern explorations of marginal social positions, liminal cultural spaces and territorial agency. This articulation of the spatial in contemporary theory has produced important discourses in a variety of disciplines which examine the relationships between spaces (both real and imagined) and the identities, social roles and cultural practices which are shaped by those spaces. The renewed saliency of spatial metaphors in describing today's social and cultural phenomena is attributable to several broad realities of contemporary life, such as the radical delegitimation of national and cultural boundaries as a result of a decolonizing and increasingly globalizing world, the identity politics of feminist, diasporic and ethnic subjects and, finally, the rampant effects of global capitalism which simultaneously emphasizes cultural difference while homogenizing it for easier market commodification. Michel Foucault has recognized that while the nineteenth century was marked with a concern with temporality, with the "accumulation" of history through a linear unfolding of its social processes, the present century has mostly generated discourses about space:

> The present epoch will perhaps be above all the epoch of space. We are in the epoch of simultaneity, we are in the epoch of juxtaposition, the epoch of the near and the far, of the side-by-side, of the dispersed. We are at a moment, I believe, when our experience of the world is less that of a long life developing through time than that of a network that connects points and intersects with its own skein. (22)

Frederic Jameson has also argued that the present postmodern era can be differentiated from the preceding modern one through its logic of spatial rather than temporal organization: "I think it is at least empirically arguable that our daily life, our psychic experience, our cultural languages, are today dominated by categories of space rather than categories of time, as in the preceding period of high modernism" (16). Jameson articulates these ideas through the notion of *cognitive mapping,* a representational aesthetic with the aim to "enable a situational representation on the part of the individual subject to that vaster and properly unrepresentable totality which is the ensemble of society's structures as a whole" (51). Cognitive mapping enables the positioning of self in relation to the socio-spatial environment through the imaginary representation of space, a strategy of "making meaningful" the complexities and ambiguities of place. I would suggest that a similar form of cognitive mapping occurs for immigrant/ethnic communities, where individuals must re-present or re-situate themselves in relation to new spatial and cultural environments.

The inscription of spaces as having "dual" or multiple meanings has been theorized in relation to Canadian ethnicity and postcoloniality. In "Decolonizing the Map" Graham Huggan identifies several rhetorical strategies in contemporary Canadian and Australian literatures which problematize the notion of territorial integrity and homogeneity in postcolonial settler societies. Huggan argues that the ironic or parodic use of maps by certain Canadian writers represent resistance to the cartographic enclosure and "containment" of British colonial and nationalist discourses. He further argues that the resignification of colonial/postcolonial Canadian space not only contests the framing of settler societies by the colonial power, but that the internal inconsistencies of place, that is, the writing of or about other places and cultures *within* settler societies, also present problems for reductionist discourses about national boundaries, spaces and territory:

> In the case of contemporary Canadian and Australian litera-
> tures, these (postcolonial) territories correspond to a series
> of new or revised rhetorical spaces occupied by feminism,
> regionalism, and ethnicity, where each of these items is un-
> derstood primarily as a set of counter-discursive strategies
> which challenge the claims of or avoid the circumscription
> within one or other form of cultural centrism. (410)

Insofar as Italian-Canadian and other minority literatures fictionalize "different" spaces and cultural realities
within Canada's boundaries, they highlight the inconsistencies of equating a single national territory with a
homogeneous idea of culture. The ethnic ghetto within
the Canadian metropolis is a striking illustration of this,
for it provides possibilities of reading place as resistance,
disjunction and slippage in relation to the cartographic
representationality and homogeneity of a national space.
The ethnic ghetto is in this sense akin to Foucault's heterotopia, a space which generates meanings beyond itself, one which paradoxically refers to other, absent
spaces.[2] In the context of Canadian ethnicity, Francesco
Loriggio writes:

> The Little Italies or the Chinatowns of North America are
> forward-moving (they are not Italy or China), but they are
> distinct from their surroundings because they are also past-
> oriented, refer to an elsewhere, and because of the effort
> that goes into retaining, into re-presenting that past or that
> elsewhere . . . Little Italies can be studied as instances of the
> precarious pluridimensionality of the nation in the twenti-
> eth century. If they move beyond the origin, immigrant en-
> claves also resist the location, the structure hosting them.
> (11-21)

The emerging and often contestatory articulations of
space put forth by ethnic and other minority communi-

ties undermine what Keith and Pile call the "myth of spatial immanence," that is, the assumption that there is a definitive or objective understanding of place, "a *singular*, true reading of any specific landscape involved in the meditation of identity" (6). This "radical openness" of space enables its appropriation and construction by subjects who are positioned outside of dominant discourses, and enables them to rewrite the significations attached to places from their own minority perspectives. Finding himself or herself in an ambiguous position "between" cultures, the ethnic subject in Canada generates meanings and readings of space that are a consequence of locatedness and cultural specificity, readings that construct place differently and sometimes in opposition to the mainstream or majority culture:

> It may be argued that simultaneously present in any landscape are multiple enunciations of distant forms of space – and these may be reconnected to the process of re-visioning and remembering spatialities of counter-hegemonic cultural practices. We may now use the term 'spatiality' to capture the ways in which the social and spatial are inextricably realized one in the other; to conjure up the circumstances in which society and space are simultaneously realized by thinking, feeling, doing individuals and also to conjure up the many different conditions in which such realizations are experienced by thinking, feeling, doing subjects. (Keith and Pile 6)

Thus space as a category of human experience is subject to the gaze of the individual who appropriates, utilizes or writes that space, and is intimately tied up with differing conceptions of community, identity and cultural specificity. How then do these considerations of spatiality relate to ethnicity and cultural identity in Canada? The immigrant/ethnic experience enables a heterogeneous articulation of imaginary space – both the spaces that are physically inhabited and those that are absent traces or memories of the past. Both these "types" of space are involved in ethnic meditations on and constructions of identity. By figuring identity as a function of memory and topology, the Italian-Canadian writer embraces both the Canadian present and the "absent" Italian past within the same discursive and poetic space, one that is "essentially a hyperspace, a hermeneutical nowhere and everywhere in which the ethnic subject floats between two worlds, two cultural models" (Boelhower 232). In this manner, the Italian-Canadian writer situates himself or herself at the crossroads between old culture and new, as so strikingly illustrated by Mary di Michele: "With one bare foot in a village in Abruzzo / the other laced into English shoes in Toronto / she strides the Atlantic legs / stretched / like a Colossus" (*Stranger in You* 5).

The distinction must be made between the ethnic's experience of the Canadian city, in which he or she intersects with the cultural mainstream, and the experience of the place of origin, often idealized or rendered mythic by virtue of its spatial and temporal distance. In Italian-Canadian writing, Italian space, like the Italian language, is often equated to a desire for and pursuit of an "authentic" self that has somehow become lost in the transition to Canada: "The distant shore becomes rhetoricized and so evokes connotations of heritage, cultural identity, authenticity, and origin" (Federici 66). Canadian space, on the other hand, is experienced as a difficult cultural terrain that must be understood, negotiated and eventually appropriated through a network of meanings, associations and strategies employed in the aim of finding a space in Canadian society. This involves not only such things as learning the common language and customs of the country in question, but also the physical, cultural and imaginary appropriation, use and fictionalization of its spaces. Nicholas Harney writes:

The presence, in polyethnic states, of diverse immigrant communities that maintain ties across state borders requires that we rethink the connections between how spatial arrangements influence the imagining of complex forms of identity and culture . . . This remapping of identity onto new spaces is integrated into the global imagining of Italianness by those in the transnational networks. Reterritorialized communities actively create sites for the elaboration of cultural practices. (8)

The elaboration of such culture-specific sites in Canadian society puts into question the traditional spatial models of the country. Whether "real" or imaginary, space becomes an essential aspect of individual and collective memory for ethnic communities, for within it, cultural practices, codes and traditions are made meaningful. Because it resides in an unretrievable past, Italian space must be resignified through memory, language and through the writing process itself. The first step in crossing the chasm between the old world and the new involves reinscribing the self within a genealogical and historical continuum, often in the context of the "return journey."[3] For instance, Mary di Michele details, in a catalogue fashion, the historical register of her Italian place of origin:

> Born in the fifth house
> under the sign of Leo
> on the sixth of August
> four years after Hiroshima
> Born Maria Luisa Di Michele,
> baptized at Santa Lucia
> in an ancient town, Lanciano. (1)

This introductory poem in di Michele's collection grounds personal identity within specific historical and temporal contexts, and situates the narrative voice within the Italian landscapes of birth and childhood. The narrator conflates important historical events, people and places

with her own personal narrative, highlighting the centrality of her own perspective upon the surrounding
world, creating "a great spiralling mélange of history,
geography, astrology, and myth . . . at once absurd in its
localization and profound in its defiance of conventional
ascriptions of importance" (Holmes 183). Memories
which transpired in Italian are located in a constant *elsewhere* that must be recalled into the present, and the
personal voice moves toward a synthesis of memory and
historical contingency.[4] Di Michele is concerned with
translation – be it the translation of personal experience
into language, or the translation of Italian memory into
English text. Her narrators' senses of identity are negotiated through the interplay of territory, language and signification: "They say that landscape and language / the
ampersand, are imprinted on our minds / in the same
way geese / fix on the first moving sign as Mother . . . /
Original" (62). The language and landscapes of childhood are imprinted on the mind of the Italian child, and
later function as mnemonic devices for the adult writer,
as points of entry into a past that is seen as being somehow more authentic. Acculturation to the English world
eventually brings about the effacement or displacement
of that "original" Italian idiom. Italian landscape becomes indelibly imprinted upon the mind, where it dis-
turbs the smooth surface of an English-Canadian up-
bringing: "Twenty years and my Canadian feet formed
of Prairie wheat / can still find their own way, can run
ahead / while my thoughts seem to resist and find / the
pomegranate, the fig, and the olive" (6). The "resistence"
of thought is contrasted to the facility with which the
body negotiates the Italian terrain. The old world is figured as the ground of instinct, memory and corporeality,
while the new world is related to the language of the
rational, to the need for translation, and to economic
necessity. As Joseph Pivato writes, "In di Michele's dream

the rational English-Canadian mind meets the emotional Italian soul" (170).

Di Michele re-evaluates her "Italianness," her performance of ethnicity within the spaces of the Canadian city. Markers of ethnicity (figured through references to da Vinci, red wine, olive skin, Italian food, and so on) occupy a precarious existence in her poetry, for they are at once authentic, undeniable aspects of Italian-Canadian identity but, also, inauthentic in that they quickly become empty stereotypes and ethnic excess. For this reason, these markers function as simulacra of Italian-Canadian ethnicity, as silent performance of difference never neatly translatable to a mainstream Canadian public. A subtle irony emerges between the narrator and explorations of her own ethnicity, for the otherness which is marked upon the body becomes something to be consumed, a "feast for your eyes" (4). As the lengthy and ironic title of one poem suggests ("Life is Theatre or O to be Italian Drinking Cappuccino on Bloor Street at Bersani's & Carnevale's"), ethnicity is a performance on the part of the narrator and an imposed "othering" on the part of her non-Italian lover: *You're so melodramatic*, he said, *Marriage to you would be like living in an Italian opera*" (42). There is a dual movement toward and away from markers of ethnicity, a desire to "translate" her otherness so that it will be meaningful to the English majority but, also, a desire to move beyond ethnic masks and theatrics. The "Italian-ness" of Italian-Canadians may be a liberating source of cultural self-discovery and belonging, but it may also trap them in that very difference, as Nicholas Harney notes:

> The charm of Mediterranean exotica in "Little Italies" around the city creates opportunities for Italian Canadians to reap financial rewards by marketing their "Italian" authenticity, their "practical knowledge," and their "cultural vitality" to the Canadian public, but it also limits and restricts

those who wish to break out into different fields and new
directions" (173).

Like di Michele, Gianna Patriarca is concerned with
"grounding" personal identity within the social, historical and spatial context of Italy and, in one poem, the
link is made between the narrator's sense of identity and
the countryside in which she grew up: "I come to you /
from peasant stock / from gardens of large rocks / where
thirsty flowers / lie unphotographed" (*Italian Women* 12).
The narrator affirms her rural beginnings and identifies
with the landscapes of childhood which remain
"unphotographed," for they are unrecorded and forever
lost to emigration. Patriarca cultivates a sense of her own
past through the spatial metaphors she employs, strategies of textual juxtaposition in which Italian and Canadian territory are intermingled, creating constant shifts
in narrative perspective between old country and new: "I
sometimes wonder / where we will be years from now /
were we there already?" and "they can never seem to
figure out / the difference in time from here / to Italy"
(60). In one poem titled "College Street, Toronto," she
traces the immigrant odyssey from the difficult first steps
in a new country to the succeeding generation's acceptance of the duality which they have inherited. The modern Canadian city is "remapped" from an immigrant
perspective as Patriarca describes the trajectory of an immigrant family through different sections of working-
class Toronto: "I have come back to this street / to begin
a new chapter of my inheritance / my Canadian odyssey" (28). Leaving his family behind in the old world,
her father arrives with other Italian labourers described
as "homeless, immigrant dreamers / *bordanti*" (28). They
establish a small space for themselves within this foreign
city where they "cooked their pasta, drank bad red wine
and argued the politics of / the country they left behind

/ avoiding always the new politics" (28). They are soon joined by their families, who travel inward across a vast Canadian territory, moving "slowly / to Halifax / To Union Station / to College Street" (29). Patriarca creates the image of immigrant populations traversing the vast Canadian landscape, inscribing their various personal stories and experiences upon its surface.

Walking about in Toronto's Little Italy involves Patriarca in a process of remembering and reconstructing her immigrant history. The ethnic ghetto functions as an "open space" which allows for a variety of interpretations and histories, like those of the immigrant labourers seeking out economic prosperity in a new country. It is telling that these voiceless labourers occupy a confined, subterranean space in the city, for the basement apartments to which they are confined signals their social status as well as their cultural isolation. Eventually, economic prosperity brings the possibility of moving outside of the ghetto and into the more prosperous suburbs of the city: "the Italians are almost all gone / to new neighbourhoods / modern towns" (*Italian Women* 30). Negotiating the difficult terrain between Italian and Canadian value systems, Patriarca comes to a precarious balance in which she is able to appropriate the urban spaces which were once solely the domain of men without completely effacing her own ethnicity:

> My father is gone
> Bar Italia has a new clientele
> women come here now
> I come here
> I drink espresso and smoke cigarettes . . .
> How strange this city
> sometimes it seems so much smaller
> than those towns
> we came from. (30)

As the first wave of Italian immigrants move out to the

suburbs of the city, the ghetto as a semiotic site shifts in meaning, and Italian ethnicity becomes a trace of what it once was, a sort of performance of Italian-ness in what remains of the shops, restaurants, and cafés.

Like Patriarca, Antonio D'Alfonso seeks to reinscribe himself within the spatial frame of Italy, seeks to find the linkages between his personal history as an ethnic Canadian and the Italian diaspora of the 1950s. In his poetry and prose works, D'Alfonso creates topographic narratives which reflect the desire to transform a space that is merely inhabited into one that conjures up senses of community and belonging. His narrator in *The Other Shore* is a *flâneur* who strolls along the winding paths and empty squares of Guglionesi, the small Italian village of his ancestry, seeking a renewed sense of his cultural heritage. The figure of the *flâneur* finds aesthetic pleasure in his or her experience of place; idle strolling is more than just strolling but, also, an active construction of space, a way of domesticating the foreign and "making meaningful" the spaces of the city.[5] It soon becomes clear that meandering along Guglionesi's streets and squares is a metaphor for writing itself, for the slow coming-to-consciousness of an Italian sense of identity and of the "curiosity of knowing the other shore. The feasts across the borders . . ." (13).

Just as the Benjaminian *flâneur* of the last century constructs an urban imaginary which reflects the modernist self caught in the optic of capitalist production, so too the ethnic *flâneur* fashions a heterogeneous spatial imaginary which reflects his or her ambiguous position and duality with respect to two distinct cultural locations. As the ethnic subject "reads" and creates the significations attached to a particular space, he or she is also engaged in a discourse about identity in relation to that place: "Flânerie" can, after Baudelaire, be understood as the activity of the sovereign spectator going about the city in order to find the things which will occupy his gaze and *thus complete his otherwise incomplete identity; satisfy his otherwise dissatisfied existence* (Tester 7; emphasis added). Ethnic self-interrogation involves this dissatisfaction on the part of D'Alfonso's *flâneur*, stemming from the unease with his cultural duality. Circulating in the Italian village elicits a particular form of desire – a desire to *know* place, to pluck from it the truths it contains – but also the desire to inscribe onto it his own meanings. *Flânerie* becomes a way of reappropriating that part of Italian identity which has been lost to emigration, and the black and white photos of Guglionesi's empty streets and squares dispersed throughout the text signal the importance of these sites in the construction of a personal narrative, a spatial aesthetic that rejoins the visual and the literal. The appropriation of space through its "visual consumption" (Shields 75) is at the core of D'Alfonso's ethnic self-fashioning, for the images provide an opportunity for a meditation on the contingencies of history that have brought him, full circle, back to this small Italian village. It is the difference between one historical outcome and another that fuels the obsessions of the narrator – his desire, as well as his inability, to completely "cross over" to the other shore, that is, to straddle the space of years and experiences that have made him an outsider and foreigner to Italy. The narrator becomes painfully aware that "there is no return, only a coming to, a coming towards. No linearity in experience or identity, only an awareness" (*The Other Shore* 64).

The *flâneur* uses his freedom of circulation to define the meanings around him, and it is in the Canadian city that the narrator of D'Alfonso's novel *Fabrizio's Passion* appropriates, circumscribes and rewrites urban space in his own fashion, as an extension of his own ethnic sensibilities. The ethnic subject's fictionalization of Canadian space represents a displacement of the historical, social and personal meanings already attached to that territory, creating a palimpsest in which diverse readings of place are juxtaposed one atop the other. The novel describes the intellectual and aesthetic development of writer and film-maker Fabrizio Notte, tracing his ethnic experience from the old world of his Italian parents through to their immigration to Canada and their new lives in working-class Montreal. What is of particular interest in the novel is the manner in which the young Fabrizio is intensely aware of the culturally complex territory which he and his immigrant family inhabit. The domestic space of the immigrant household represents both a haven from an alien outside world and a prison of ignorance of the Canadian and Quebecois reality. When the young Fabrizio first ventures out into the street of this new habitat, he is aware of the linguistic and cultural barriers between himself and the francophone children he encounters. The street becomes a place in which identity is negotiated and performed: "To walk out and then step into the real world we create for ourselves without our parents. A world which will change our contradictions into complex entities. Our identity is a game, a pastime, but never a source of confrontation . . . to free oneself of one's origins in the street . . . a neutral playground" (54).

The novel includes extracts from *L'Histoire économique de Montréal*, and the geographical place-names, roads, population densities, and so on, serve as a backdrop to the individual stories and subjective experiences which transpire within that space. The incongruity between the official records and the lived experience of place described in the novel attest to the elisions and disjunctions inherent in any representational scheme of space.

The novel presents Montreal as a rich textual and

textural fabric, and Fabrizio's pronunciation of its name divulges his ethnic, cultural, and linguistic experience of the city: "The city I call my native city was called *Monreale*. It had no accent on the *e* nor a *t* for the cross on Mont Royale, yet the term gained a glorious *e* at the end which acted as a constant reminder of my origins" (212). Within this short phrase D'Alfonso manages to relate the social, cultural, and linguistic complexity of the city while highlighting the centrality of his ethnic perspective upon it. The "glorious *e*" of Monreale, spoken in the heavy accent of the city's Italian neighbourhoods, effectively raises questions about the significations attached to place, questions about who names the city, who interprets it, and who fictionalizes it. As Lianne Moyes has pointed out, "Conceptualizing the city as a system of signs more than a symbolic landscape of the mind, makes it possible to rewrite or remap the city, to give it an alternative reality" (11). Indeed, in the plurilinguistic and pluricultural matrix of signs and significations of D'Alfonso's narrator, the ability to conceive of a different Montreal or *Monreale* or Montréal is, in fact, a rewriting of that urban landscape from a minority perspective, a displacement of expected meanings.

While space is socially constructed, categorized and determined by the discourses which occupy it, that space can also be contested, rewritten or imagined otherwise. Places do not have single or essential identities and are therefore a function of historical, social and cultural contexts. As Doreen Massey notes, "People's routes through place, their favourite haunts within it, the connections they make (physically or in memory and imagination) between here and the rest of the world vary enormously. If it is now recognized that people have multiple identities then the same point can be made in relation to places" (238). In other words, place "takes significance" because it is signified by the subject who experiences it.

The minority subject occupies a liminal space within which identity is constantly being negotiated, rewritten and performed, that is, refashioned in an endless articulation of self in relation to two spatial and cultural polarities (the here and now of Canada vs. the there and past of Italy). All subjective enunciations and narratives, both oral and literary, are already marked with assumptions about spatiality, positionality and location, and these articulations of place and identity play against one another in a "jeu of ambivalence" (Boelhower 232) which shapes ethnic discourses on identity. There is a level at which a writer's awareness of positionality constitutes an important aspect of identity construction (i.e., D'Alfonso's or di Michele's understanding and generation of self as "in between," as "exiled," as "dual," etc.) and a level at which specific characters and events in the novels or poetry are intricately affected and shaped by the subjective experience of place. This creates an effect of spatial confusion, refraction, doubling, and conflation. It is for these reasons that place is central to the construction of ethnic identity, for it grounds personal history and immigrant experience within the sites of ethnic articulation. Paradoxically, place is at the same moment inimical to ethnic self-definition, since place presents constant shifts in meaning, perspective and signification, rendering difficult the construction of a "stable" ethnic identity. The Italian-Canadian writer's concern with personal and familial history, with the absent homeland, and with the difficulties of adaptation to a new territory represents an ongoing "fashioning" of an identity caught up in the memories and tradition of the old world but, also, to the narratives and meanings attached to Canadian space.

NOTES

1. Some work has been done on ethnic minorities in the Canadian city. See, for instance, Simon Harel, "La parole orpheline de l'écrivain migrant," *Montréal Imaginaire: Ville et littérature*, ed. Pierre Nepveu and Gilles Marcotte (Montreal: Fides, 1992) 373-418. A recent article by Christl Verduyn suggests the idea of "disjunction" between place, cultural memory, and identity in minority literatures; see "Disjunctions: Place, Identity and Nation in 'Minority' Literatures in Canada," *Canadian Issues* 20 (1998): 138-52.

2. Michel Foucault writes that "the heterotopia is capable of juxtaposing in a single real space several spaces, several sites that are in themselves incompatible. Thus it is that the theatre brings onto the rectangle of the stage, one after the other, a whole series of places that are foreign to one another; thus it is that the cinema is a very odd rectangular room, at the end of which, on a two-dimensional screen, one sees the projection of a three-dimensional space" (25). I would argue that the ethnic ghetto works in a similar fashion by juxtaposing dissimilar social and cultural contexts onto a singular site of transaction and display. See Foucault.

3. For a discussion of the importance of the "return journey" in Italian-Canadian literature, see Joseph Pivato.

4. In an interview with Nathalie Cooke, di Michele describes her poetry as a "synthesis" that "grows out of and moves beyond personal experiences" (44).

5. In his seminal study of the Paris of the nineteenth century, Walter Benjamin explores the figure of the *flâneur* in the poetry of Baudelaire and examines the ways in which he (for it was always a male figure) appropriates the spaces of the city for his own aesthetic and sensual pleasure: "The street becomes a dwelling for the flâneur; he is as much at home among the façades of houses as a citizen is in his four walls. To him the shiny, enamelled signs of businesses are at least as good a wall ornament as an oil painting is to the bourgeois in his salon. The walls are the desk against which he presses his notebooks; news-stands are his libraries and the terraces of cafés are the balconies from which he looks down on his household after his work is done" (37).

WORKS CITED

Bachelard, Gaston. *The Poetics of Space*. 1958. Trans. Maria Jolas. New York: Orion, 1964.

Benjamin, Walter. "The Paris of the Second Empire in Baudelaire." *Charles Baudelaire: A Lyric Poet in the Era of High Capitalism*. London: NLB, 1983. 11-106.

Bhabha, H. "Postcolonial Authority and Postmodern Guilt." *Cultural Studies*. Ed. L. Grossberg, C. Nelson and P. Treichler. London: Routledge, 1992. 55-66.

Boelhower, William. "Italo-Canadian Poetry and Ethnic Semiosis in the Postmodern Context." *Arrangiarsi: The Italian Immigration Experience in Canada*. Ed. Roberto Perin and Franc Sturino. Montreal: Guernica, 1992. 229-244.

D'Alfonso, Antonio. *Fabrizio's Passion*. Toronto: Guernica, 1995.

——. *The Other Shore*. Montreal: Guernica, 1986.

Di Cicco, Pier Giorgio, ed. *Roman Candles*. Toronto: Hounslow, 1978.

Di Michele, Mary. "Mary di Michele: On the Integrity of Speech and Silence." Interview with Nathalie Cooke. *Canadian Poetry* 26 (Spring 1990): 43-53.

——. *Stranger in You: Selected Poems and New*. Toronto: Oxford UP, 1995.

Federici, Corrado. "The 'Other Shore' Isotope in Italian-Canadian Poetry." *Rivista di Studi Italiani* (December 1992): 64-73.

Foucault, Michel. "Of Other Spaces." *Diacritics* 16.1 (Spring 1986): 22-27.

Harney, Nicholas deMaria. *Eh, Paesan! Being Italian in Toronto*. Toronto: U of Toronto P, 1998.

Holmes, M. "Mary di Michele." *Canadian Writers and Their Works*. Poetry Series.

Ed. Robert Lecker, Jack David and Ellen Quigley. Vol. 7. Toronto: ECW, 1995. 158-223.

Huggan, Graham. "Decolonizing the Map." *The Post-Colonial Studies Reader*. Ed. Bill Ashcroft, Gareth Griffiths, and Helen Tiffin. New York: Routledge, 1995. 407-411.

Keith, Michael, and Steve Pile. *Place and the Politics of Identity*. New York: Routledge, 1993.

Jameson, Frederic. *Postmodernism, or the Cultural Logic of Late Capitalism*. Durham, NC: Duke UP, 1991.

Loriggio, Francesco. Introduction. *Social Pluralism and Literary History: The Literature of the Italian Emigration*. Toronto: Guernica, 1996. 7-28.

Massey, Doreen. "A Global Sense of Place." *Studying Culture: An Introductory Reader*. Ed. Ann Gray and Jim McGuigan. London: Edward Arnold, 1993. 232-240.

Moyes, Lianne. "Cities Built From the Dreams of Women." *Tessera* 16 (Summer 1994): 6-12.

Patriarca, Gianna. *Italian Women and Other Tragedies*. Guernica, Toronto:1996.

Pitkin, Donald S. "Italian Urbanscape: Intersection of Private and Public." *The Cultural Meaning of Urban Space*. Ed. R. Rotenberg and G. McDonogh. London: Bergin, 1993.

Pivato, Joseph. "The Return Journey in Italian-Canadian Literature." *Canadian Literature* 106 (Fall 1985): 169-176.

Shields, Rob. *Fancy Footwork: Walter Benjamin's Notes on Flânerie. The Flâneur*. Ed. Keith Tester. New York: Routledge, 1994. 61-80.

Tamburri, Anthony. "Gianna Patriarca's 'Tragic' Thoughts: *Italian Women and Other Tragedies*." *Canadian Journal of Italian Studies* 19 (1996): 184-200.

Tester, Keith. Introduction. *The Flâneur*. Ed. Tester. New York: Routledge, 1994. 1-39.

Thompson, Dawn. "Technologies of Ethnicity." *Essays on Canadian Writing* 57 (Winter 1995): 51-69.

Tuzi, Marino. *The Power of Allegiances*. Toronto: Guernica, 1997.

One Hybrid Discourse of Doukhobor Identity

The Freedomite Diary from Agassiz Prison

Julie Rak

For many writers who belong to minority groups, autobiography has not come to operate as a genre, but as a discourse for identity negotiation. In this discourse, ethnic minority writers or speakers can address issues about the relationship of a minority subjectivity to the ideas of nation-state which exclude minority histories, minority identities and minority rhetorics. Anne Goldman's call in *Take My Word* "for a wider autobiographical field [so that] we describe a wider spectrum of the ways and means by which people in the twentieth century speak themselves into existence" (ix) recognizes that if there is a link between identity formation and autobiographical discourse, then those writers and speakers who could be considered "bad subjects"[1] do not forsake autobiography altogether when they decide to work out what their positions are within a nation-state discourse which does not acknowledge them. Instead, autobiography criticism needs to examine when and why "bad subjects" enter and exit autobiographical discourse and how that discourse alters when it "encounters" subjectivities which exceed the canonized parameters of a singular, unique self that is already established as a discursive fact before the narrative even begins.

To do this, I will look at a prison diary written by a group of radical Doukhobors from a group of Sons of

Freedom or Freedomite[2] protestors from British Columbia who were incarcerated for nude protest, arson and
(in a few cases) bombing between 1962 and about 1970
at the fireproof Agassiz prison camp built for them in
the Fraser Valley east of Chilliwack, British Columbia.
My examination will show how one aspect of autobiographical discourse (in this case, the discourse of individual subjectivity assumed in diary forms) can be
marshalled by writers who are not part of Western narratives of subjectivity that presuppose a white, singular,
propertied, literate subject who can easily enter – and
affect – history. The result in this case is a hybrid diary
form which troubles distinctions made between a private, diary-writing subjectivity and a plural, public subjectivity so that the writers can transmit their story to
non-Freedomites while retaining their own terms for
identity. These terms do not easily fit into the liberal
discourse of Canadian multiculturalism with its emphases
on cultural difference as essentialized, non-hybrid and
politically neutral. Moreover, the diary form operates as
a site where the space of Agassiz and what happens there
is the subject around which the identities of the writers
orient themselves, as opposed to the more mainstream
orientation in autobiography discourse of tropes connected to growth, personality or discovery. This marks
the Agassiz diary as, in Caren Kaplan's words, an "out-
law genre" which remains in contact with autobiography as it resists some of its terms. This resistance and
acceptance is political in its refusal of singularity and
its shift in focus from self-development to plural testimony which rewrites what was thought to have happened:

> These emerging out-law genres require more collaborative
> procedures that are more closely attuned to the power dif-
> ferences among participants in the process of producing the

text. Thus, instead of a discourse of individual authorship, we find a discourse of situation, a 'politics of location.' (Kaplan 119)

The resulting decision of the writers of the Agassiz diary to retain some aspects of autobiography's power to admit personal testimony while refusing other paradigms attached to this shows how these writers may operate in a rhetorical public sphere where they are not usually admitted as subjects capable of representing their concerns.

Therefore, the identities generated in this text are not "other" to a presupposed unconscious, but in their problematizing of the proper name necessary to autobiographical discourse, they reinscribe Lejeune's autobiographical "pact" as a performance of plural identities which the reader must acknowledge as material, rather than the linking of identity and signature which stresses that autobiography is a text made by only one person that is made *for a market* (Lejeune 44). In the marketplace of autobiographical identities, the authors of the Agassiz prison diary enter themselves and their concerns under a sign of difference and tell their readers to read that difference as part of their politics.

The Doukobors, the Freedomite Doukhobors and Autobiography

This revision of what autobiography is "supposed" to be occurs in the Agassiz prison diary because the Doukhobors generally – and Freedomites, specifically – have had, at different times, to turn to alternate strategies to retell their own histories, orally and in writing, against the grain of the sensationalist image of Doukhobors propagated by government commissions and by the Canadian media. The Agassiz prison diary represents one appropriation of some aspects of Western autobiographical discourse which blurs distinctions between autobiography as a discourse of a single subject made for mass consumption with autobiography as testament and testimony, a form of alternative memory for an entire people. This means that the plural subjectivity expressed within a form which usually features a private, individual subjectivity signifies a hybridizing of both the form of autobiography and the identities generated within its changed form. Autobiography in this sense becomes a technology of alternative identities, as indicated in Hertha Dawn Wong's work on pre-contact and post-contact autobiographical discourses by Native Americans, which includes the pictographs of the captured Fort Wayne Chipewan Indians; in Genaro Padilla's study of Chicano/Chicana autobiography after the American conquest of northern Mexico, which the *compañeros* use so that they can resist assimilation and construct a Mexican-American identity; and in Anne Goldman's study of ethnic working-class women in America and the alternative autobiographical strategies, such as the writing of "ethnic" cookbooks, they employ.

The Doukhobors generally, and the Freedomite Doukhobors in particular, engage in similar strategies which use autobiographical discourse in hybrid forms where "autobiography" has not previously been thought to be found because, like other groups whose ethnic identities fall outside those prescribed by emerging nationalisms, they use autobiographical discourse as a way to gain visibility as subjects without subjecting themselves to assimilative paradigms that would take their language, their traditions and their plural subjectivities away from them in order to make them docile (individual) subjects in a liberal democratic state. Before looking specifically at the strategies Freedomites have used in the Agassiz diary, I will provide some contextual background about

the Doukhobors and the Freedomite Doukhobors to indicate how they have fallen outside liberal democratic
discourses which mark Canadian citizenship.

As a Russian sectarian migrant group that arrived in
Canada in 1899, the Doukhobors refused all offers of
assimilation proffered by federal and provincial governments as soon as they arrived, from language instruc-
tion to voting rights, at every level of the migration
process and, in some cases, for several generations after-
wards. They did this because as Doukhobors they were
adherents of an orally based religion which rejected all
institutions, individual ownership of property, military
service and citizenship of any nation or empire except
what they termed a mystical belonging to the Kingdom
of God.[3] These beliefs and practices, combined with a
history of conflict with secular and church authorities
and a conviction that they were destined to be exiles
and wanderers until a prophesied return to Russia, meant
that Doukhobor identity was grounded in beliefs that at
key points ran counter to the coalescing discourses of
imperialist, and then nationalist, English-Canadian identity.

Some of these key points included a belief held by
many Doukhobors that schooling in English would be
in effect schooling in patriotism and militarism, so that
many devout Doukhobors from about 1905 to the 1970s
either refused to send their children to school or pulled
them out when conflict with the federal or provincial
governments increased. Their beliefs also included (and
still include) pacifism, which meant that they felt marriages, births and deaths did not need to be registered,
since registration indicated that an authority other than
God's was evoked, and that registration might be a first
step to military service. Doukhobor beliefs also included
a strong commitment to communal living, communal
ownership of property, and shared work. Eventually,

Doukhobor differences in these areas and their refusals to conform to developing English-Canadian institutional expectations about citizenship, the use of the English language, the separation of church and state, and what became the "sanctity" of private property meant that federal and provincial authorities thought that the Doukhobors constituted a serious threat to an idea of Canada as a nation within the British Commonwealth because no efforts at assimilation seemed to work.[4]

For this reason, the Doukhobors twice lost their lands: once in Saskatchewan in 1907 when the Doukhobors refused to swear an oath of allegiance to the Queen and to register their lands individually and, once again, in 1939 after they had established a large collective enterprise in British Columbia. The difficulties in 1939 were particularly severe since it was government inaction – in response to public pressure – which probably spelled the end of the Doukhobor communal enterprise, the CCUB (Community of Christian Universal Brotherhood), when an insurance company was allowed to foreclose and sell off the commune's considerable assets (Woodcock 239). This caused much unrest in the already-shaken Doukhobor communities. Many Doukhobors joined the Freedomites and began to protest against what they saw as the latest non-Doukhobor attempt to assimilate Doukhobors, and against what they interpreted as the resulting "selling-out" of other Doukhobors to materialism, private property ownership and schooling in the English language as Doukhobors attempted to adapt to the loss of communal living in British Columbia.

It may seem unlikely that members of the Freedomites would produce any autobiographical work at all, since most of these Doukhobors until the 1970s did not subscribe to those discourses of self that autobiography privileges. Of the three major Doukhobor groups – the others are the Independents and the Community/Orthodox Doukhobors – the Freedomites have most strenuously rejected the marks of Canadian citizenship. Such refusals first occurred in 1902 when more than one thousand Sons of God, as they were known at the time, marched south across the Saskatchewan prairie hoping to reach a land "nearer the sun," while they threw away their money and any goods made from animal skins to emphasize their rejection of what they described as Canadian materialism. Forms of protest such as stripping, burning farm equipment and marches begun by the earlier Sons of God resurfaced during periods of nude protest and arson beginning in the late 1920s, and were used by Freedomites until the end of large-scale protest in the late 1960s. At these times, many Freedomites connected what they termed "true" Doukhobor identity to group affiliation, a rejection of materialism, enthusiast religious protests which came to have political consequences and a messianic belief, based on Doukhobor prophecies and psalms, that the Doukhobors would return to Russia after they had endured much suffering.[5]

Judging from the long prison sentences Freedomites received for nudity and arson (from three to twelve years), as well as the fact that in 1962 the RCMP brought against the Freedomite Fraternal Council the rather unlikely charge of "intimidating the Parliament of Canada" (Woodcock 352), Freedomite depredations apparently represented more than vandalism to the authorities and to the Canadian public. They appeared to strike at cherished ideas of citizenship, the ownership and care of property, and state-sanctioned control of the nude body as a private, rather than a public and politicized entity. Although Freedomites often publicly said during the 1950s and 1960s that they committed depredations in order to critique Canadian institutional control and materialism and, also, so that they could be allowed to migrate either back to Russia or somewhere else, little attempt was made by provincial or federal bodies to address these concerns.[6] The public applauded the BC provincial government's bid to assimilate Freedomite children by rounding them up in a series of night raids beginning in 1953 and teaching them in English at a fenced-in dormitory for up to six years. To publicize their plan to assimilate Freedomite children, the Dormitory even released photos of the children with hockey sticks in their hands or playing in the snow as happy recipients of institutionalized Canadian forms. These photographs were clearly propagandist and did not reflect the unhappy situation of these Freedomite children, whose parents were only allowed to visit them every two weeks and who, even then, only saw them behind a chain-link fence.

Therefore, the fact that Freedomites have written more autobiographies than other Doukhobor groups means that Freedomites must have had different reasons for writing autobiography than autobiographers who are interpellated by and respond to at least some of the features of master-narratives of identity, because the non-Doukhobor reaction to Freedomite protest – and the subsequent decision of non-Doukhobors to identify *all* Doukhobors as other in the same ways – so fiercely protected many of the markers of identity which are the same ones that underwrite much mainstream autobiography. These models depend on forms of identity that involve a high level of literacy and depend on the idea of a unique, pre-existing self marked off from all others or, at least, on a critique of that self by a writer who is part of that discourse. As a communally oriented group with an oral mystical and historic tradition, and with a low literacy rate due to a refusal to send their children to English-speaking schools, the Freedomites' constructions of identity did not depend on the Western split between self and life mirrored by a subject/object split that guarantees self-reflexivity and a regrounding of the narrated self in configurations that allow it to be packaged and "sold" to a reading public as narrative. In *Subjectivity, Identity, and the Body*, Sidonie Smith remarks that this version of selfhood and autobiography constitutes a reinforcing discourse which allows self to be "discovered" in narrative repeatedly because narrative is the mechanism for "healing" the split. Mainstream autobiography depends on tropes of privilege in order to be

> a mimetic medium for self-representation that guaranteed the epistemological correspondence between narrative and lived life, a self-consciousness capable of discovering, uncovering, recapturing that hard core at the center . . . [S]elfhood and autobiography mutually implied one another . . . and so, autobiography consolidated its status as one of the West's master discourses, a discourse that has served to power and define centers, margins, boundaries, and grounds of action in the West. (18-19)

But these barriers did not prevent autobiographical writing: they encouraged it.[7] This happened due to the performative aspects of autobiographical discourse which some Freedomite writers, already accustomed to pamphlet-writing and other forms of public awareness-raising, appropriated so that their identity formations could be performed in public spaces in recognizable configurations, but without all the trappings of Western subjectivity's dependence on a dialectics of a singular self and other within a discourse of interiority. To clarify how this happens, I will suggest here how performativity can be reread as a trope of visibility within difference.

Performativity, Exteriority and Migrating Figures

According to Sidonie Smith in "Performativity, Autobiographical Practice, Resistance," performativity in autobiography "constitutes interiority" and that interiority is an *effect* of autobiographical narrative as opposed to its originating centre (18). Smith assigns agency to the act of narration and othering to the rhetoric produced in the narration, much as Judith Butler in *Excitable Speech* assigns agency, and historicity, to the act of language performing *itself* rather than to a subject who speaks or uses it because "the 'agency' of language is not only the theme of the formulation, but its very action" (Butler 7). As an effect of language, performativity for Smith also constructs dis/continuous subjects within the "space" of interiority where identity becomes identification, a flexible dialectic of temporary correspondences that can unfix attempted identifications ("Performativity" 21).

While Smith's and Butler's descriptions of performativity seek to retain agency within linguistic acts and so restore the possibility of political activity as part of decentred subjectivities, both of these versions of performativity rely on an idea of subjectivity that owes something to the primal scenes of the psychoanalysis of language and identity acquisition in some versions of psychoanalysis, even if the linkage is eventually shown to be hallucinatory. For example, in *Excitable Speech*, Butler's discussion of performativity and censorship turns on the Lacanian idea of "entrance" into language which "produces[s] an unspeakability as the condition of subject formation" (135). This entrance, Butler suggests, is politicized because it does not simply occur as part of the primal scene of subject formation in infancy, but as rules which constrain the intelligibility of the subject as they structure subjectivity *throughout* the life of the subject (36). What Butler has done here is to extend the primal scene to the moment of iteration for a subject where the moment of iteration is also a moment of danger to the integrity of the subject. This means that the conditions for speech, which guarantee the survival of subjects, in fact, contributes to the dissolution of subjectivity. Politics, as Butler says, can then be seen as a "production of discourse" because confession of any kind must turn on the paradoxical relationship between the discourse which structures subjective intelligibility and the subject who *must* speak against that very intelligibility (137). The subject cannot do anything but negotiate that caesura constructed by discourse which is always other to it. In this sense, autobiographical performativity is an "effect" of language which is constituted by the call of autobiographical discourse. There are no possible ways to surmount what Butler calls the Lacanian "bar" (135) of interiority and exteriority which makes language other to the others who use it.

But for those marked as "other" within discourses of Western subjectivity which, in this case, includes J. S. Woodsworth's figure of the stranger within "our" gates, the migrant who cannot and will not be assimilated, who cannot learn the language of "our" institutions and, yet, who cannot leave either (197), the primal scene does not ever occur. The migrant, especially in Canada at the turn of the last century, is the mirror self, the double-negative in the "primal" scene of nation. Interiority and agency – if the migrant possesses them – are already marked as a fiction or a reflection and, in the case of the Freedomites, interpreted by the RCMP, the media and the public of British Columbia as insanity and criminality since the Freedomites insisted on remaining migrants in a spiritual sense and refused to assimilate. The question of agency in language is crucial here. For those autobiographers whose memories and collective histories have been treated as fictional, *as not being worthy of interiority* but, perhaps, worthy of ethnographic curiosity, the "rules" of autobiography discourse do not always apply. Models of self/other and of individuation may not assume primacy for these writers and speakers, and performativity may not just be an effect of language which decentres the subject, but a strategy of a subject who has never been centred. As Genaro Padilla observes, it is possible for autobiographers outside of dominant discourses of subjectivity to use alternate forms of autobiography "owned neither by Western culture nor by writing" (8).

Once thought this way, performativity can operate as exteriority, as a communication of identity issues which does not tell the self to the self or heal the split between the lonely points of enunciation and utterance so much as recover the fractured memories of a community, or operate as a means of telling the community's story to itself and to other communities. Mikhail Bakhtin in "Forms of Time and Chronotope in the Novel" describes such a situation when he writes of the original chronotope of autobiography as a set of ritual praises in the Athenian public square. These life narratives took place as a dialogic activity between the speaker and the listeners and, for Bakhtin, this constituted consciousness. This "individual" consciousness, in turn, became part of the public consciousness only when it was spoken. The negotiation of self/other had not yet begun. People were "completely *on the surface*, in the most literal sense of the word" (133).

Instead of the Lacanian mirror, where the child *sees* himself or herself and recognizes the "I" at the moment s/he sees his or her reflection as "not I" (Lacan 4) and, at that moment, renders the *cogito* a mirage because language, with its split between signified and signifier, encodes the resulting split (165), the orator speaks a citizen's life into the *ears* of the community members, who hear and respond to this life with affirmation (Bakhtin 133). To praise oneself was to praise the community, and to return that praise to the community whole, since Bakhtin holds that there is no inside to hold any part of "bio" away from "graphe": "[t]o be exterior meant to be for others, for the collective, for one's own people" (135). Before the self/other split, then, there is no dialogic contestation between others, but a meeting-ground of others, where self belongs to the community and does not struggle to permeate or monologize discourses of the other. Bakhtin's image of exteriority is particularly useful when discussing Freedomite writings such as the Agassiz diary because the diary itself is not written by one person, but is *signed* under the proper name of one person so that the proper name, and its connection to the location of imprisonment, operates as a kind of public square where plural subjectivities can be performed *as exteriorities* which do not violate the collectivity of Doukhobor subjectivity. In fact, the residue of a diary form serves to focus these plural identities, not around a narrative of a single subject, but around a place: Agassiz. This is what makes the Agassiz diary a hybrid form – between diary and witness narrative – and this is what makes the subject produced from this combination of two separate discourses hybrid also – between the tradition of Freedomite protest with its insistence on shared, collective and oral experiences, and the tradition of the witness narrative which records and thematizes events under the sign of a single proper name so that outsiders will know what happened *to that person in terms of what s/he saw*.

The Agassiz Diary: the Sign of Difference

Mike Chernenkoff's diary, for example, uses the form of a diary as day-to-day witness record with its flexible use of subject-positions that change over time. However, its author on the front page does not appear as Mike

Chernenkoff, but "Mike Chernenkoff and Friends," although listings of it in English bibliographies tend to name Chernenkoff as the only author. The assumption originally discussed by Felicity Nussbaum in "Towards Conceptualizing Diary" that diary discourse is private and singular, and that it is produced by a private and singular subject, does not apply here (128). Instead, the preface of the diary and the subsequent "entries" use the diary form's features of immediacy and location while combining this form with aspects of memoir and witness narratives. As a witness narrative, the diary also contains historical passages, copied letters, photographs, lists of prisoners' names, a recipe for borscht made by the prisoners, psalms and poems composed in prison by various people, and a variety of narratives, sometimes by other people and sometimes simply called "Dormitory 4," "Dormitory 2," or "Dormitory 3." These narratives describe key problems such as the force-feeding of the vegetarian prisoners with boiling meat broth while they were on a hunger strike (which happened at Agassiz while prison authorities had placed Chernenkoff in solitary confinement in another prison), or the death of Paul Podmoroff from pneumonia, brought on by force-feeding during a Freedomite fast (which, again, Chernenkoff did not personally witness because he was in another dormitory).

Authorship in the Agassiz diary also serves the requirements of a plural witness narrative more than those of a private diary. At one point an anonymous author from Dormitory 4 says that *his* diary – it is not clear whether he means Chernenkoff's manuscript or some other one – has been seized by the authorities, and it becomes uncertain as to when he (or others) eventually pieced the narrative together. He writes, "For me to continue further in connection with this will be more difficulty, but all the same, I will try to do everything I can"

(49). Constructing the narrative at other points becomes a collective enterprise, as the first-person of Chernenkoff is sometimes replaced by collective arrangers who say, for instance, that "we are placing here" (50) an account from other prisoners as a witness narrative. As part diary, part witness narrative, and even as a "biography of Mountain Prison," which is what Chernenkoff has called the book in a personal letter to me, this prison narrative operates as a hybrid text which straddles several life narrative forms while it produces a hybrid subject that is singular and plural at different points to fit the requirements of its message as a witness document. Therefore, Freedomite subjectivity appears fluid in this diary, operating much as Anne Goldman describes autobiographical identity formation in autobiographies by ethnic working-class women. According to Goldman, this kind of autobiography resists dominant identity constructions because it can be read on a continuum along the trajectories of "I" and "we" rather than as a synecdoche of a culture in the first-person singular or a metonym for a collective in the third-person plural (xxiv).

This diary's plurality, then, can be read as a strategy that, at times, stresses the collectivity of the imprisoned Freedomites as they experience hardship occurring under the sign (and power) of one name. The witness narrative form of the diary links together the identities and stories of individual prisoners or anonymous inhabitants of dormitories as a displaced people who must suffer within the space of the prison. This situation links them symbolically to their nineteenth-century imprisoned forbearers in Russia. For example, although the narrative ultimately is collected under Chernenkoff's name and a large photograph of Chernenkoff appears as the frontispiece, the preface, which was written by Joe Ogloff rather than Chernenkoff, presents the diary as a public manifesto about a collective conflict. This conflict is linked to a one-thousand-year struggle against the evils of institutions of church and state. The diary, then, is intended to be a witness narrative which will encapsulate the whole Sons of Freedom struggle, as well as a collective testament gathered under the sign of one person's proper name. Therefore, the text's collective purpose overshadows the author's writing of it. At first, authors are not even mentioned, as Ogloff writes, "this diary was written with the intention that if [it] got safely to the world, and if sometime in the future or the present people are led by fate to read it, they then will be able to appreciate fully the great trouble of the Doukhobor 'Sons of Freedom' in Canada" (ii).

In this passage, Ogloff appears to be writing about Freedomite history. But he goes on to introduce Chernenkoff as the diary's author in a moment which indicates his awareness of the power of a diary to record and witness events. Ogloff first mentions Chernenkoff as an autodidact who lacks formal education, saying that he "did not go to Russian school and he taught himself Russian reading and writing" (ii). He switches to a discussion of the location and purpose of Mountain Prison at Agassiz, where the diary was written, and concludes with an apology for his own and others' illiteracy while he indicates that the diary was a collective effort and had a material existence. In doing so, Ogloff constructs a non-Doukhobor idea about diary writing and about who is "qualified" to do that writing so that these Freedomite writers may enter that discourse with an awareness of the *techne* which such a discourse requires:

> As for me, I also must say that I am self-taught. And although I helped a lot to improve this diary so the reader could understand it, however, there are many shortcomings, for which I earlier asked the reader to divorce himself from our inexperience. This diary covers the time period from 1962-1972 and it was written on paper taken from jars of canned goods and on yellow paper in which they wrap things bought in stores. (ii)

Here, Ogloff discusses the "unworthiness" of the Freedomites in terms of entering a discourse closely connected
to literacy, but he recognizes that in the diary form, in
the assumption of literacy, there is visibility. He accesses
the power of recognition inherent in the Western diary
discourse even in his discussion of his different creden-
tials because he appeals to the reader to forget what he
causes the reader to remember: we are to recall Freedomite
inexperience and illiteracy bracketed by the scene of writing (literally, the prison) and the materiality of writing
under duress. In this way, the Freedomite writers of this
diary can construct their versions of events within the
parameters of a discourse of recognition while asking for
the reader to "divorce himself," that is, recognize
Freedomite difference, in order to inscribe their position
as writing subjects in terms of difference.

Chernenkoff's dedication features a similar "apology" for difference by means of literacy level. This apology validates a narrative style which moves from a
singular to a collective version of Freedomite history. It
can do this because it is not "professionally" produced.
Chernenkoff's dedication, for example, moves from dedi-
cating the diary to his own family and other Freedomites,
to telling the story of the sufferings of his wife, Lukeriya,
while he was in prison. It turns to an account of Paul
Podmoroff's death by force-feeding, a topic which occupies much of the diary. Then Chernenkoff apologizes
for illiteracy on behalf of the group: "who would have
thought the diary would come out in book form," he
writes, "for we were all so uneducated, illiterate. . ."
(iv). The first sentence of the first paragraph of the diary, however, begins with his sense of his own literacy
level, combined with an awareness of collectivity and
mission: "I am fully aware and conscious of my own
lack of ability and illiteracy [sic] to do this business, to

describe the events surrounding our experience in a prison specially built for one goal, to keep Doukhobors" (1).

The Agassiz prison diary, then, is not only a collection of historic materials commemorating a sojourn in prison but also a *performance field* where the diary's principal and secondary authors can negotiate, under the sign of difference, collective and individual identities as Freedomite Doukhobors for others to read. In this sense, they engage in a type of identity performance which alters the trope of performativity as it makes use of it. Performativity here is not a trope of radical interiority of the subject where the object is language, but a trope signifying *exterior* identity negotiation with others. Bakhtin's image of simultaneous praise evokes an external type of performativity that relies on the visibility of the community members to each other rather than on the hidden split between subject and object. The Agassiz diary functions in this way as a field where the self/other dichotomy is not so much disrupted as it is elided, and where a discourse of private selfhood found in the diary form is appropriated to gain visibility for Freedomite subjects under the hybrid signs of plurality and difference. In this way, the Agassiz diary is a non-assimilative text which refuses the interpellative call to docile subjectivity extended by the trope of the Canadian multiculturalist mosaic. The writers of this diary are subjects who refuse to stay in the places prescribed for them within that trope, and who decide to rewrite an aspect of Canadian historic narrative on terms which multiculturalism, with its stress on non-politicized forms of inclusion, does not readily accommodate. A hybridized performativity of autobiographical identities forms the basis of a "publicity" where Mike Chernenkoff and friends work out these terms, for each other and for a wider readership.

NOTES

I would like to acknowledge the support of the Social Science and Humanities Research Council which made the early stages of writing and research possible. I also wish to thank Mike Chernenkoff, Steve Lapshinoff and Jack MacIntosh of Special Collections at the UBC Library for their generosity and assistance.

1. I refer to Althusser's description of "the 'bad subjects' who on occasion provoke the intervention of one of the detachments of the (repressive) State apparatus" (127).

2. The use of the term "Sons of Freedom" may seem patriarchal in English. In fact, there were many female leaders, informal and formal, in the Freedomite groups. Doukhobors traditionally considered women to be spiritually superior to men because they "model" Mary, the mother of Jesus, on earth. In practical terms, this meant that in the *sobranie* or Doukhobor decision-meetings, prophetic statements by Doukhobor women, especially on religious matters, carried considerable weight in the community as a whole. To offset this, I will refer to the Sons of Freedom by the literal translation of their name *svobodnikii* as "Freedomites."

3. For more detailed studies of Doukhobor beliefs and history, see George Woodcock and Ivan Avakumovic; Koozma Tarasoff.

4. The government couched its demands in terms that directly linked questions of private property and ownership to Canadian identity discourses based on liberalism and individualism because the reports of colonization agents stressed that communal living was unhealthy, "childlike" and unnationalistic. See Janzen (46-48) for a detailed discussion of these reports.

5. These beliefs were held generally by Community Doukhobors as well as by Freedomites. For example, Marie Maloff's 1997 letter to the centrist Doukhobor publication *Iskra* indicates that a general belief in a return to Russia was widespread and is still current: "My dad used to often sing ("Krai moi krai rodnoi") ["Land, my homeland"]. Throughout all of our years in Canada most people expected to move away – there was a longing in their hearts, and ours. They used to say Lushechka [Lukeriia Kalmakova, a nineteenth-century Doukhobor leader] prophesied this and that, and what was said, the people believed, and expected it to come to pass . . . They also believed in a 40 year stay in Canada and then an exile to somewhere else. It did not work out that way, but some people are still expecting something. It is good to have hope, expecting something good" (27).
The difference was that more radical Freedomites believed committing depredations would hasten deportation from Canada, and that the deportation would fulfil Lushechka's prophecy of a return to Russia. For more information about common Freedomite interpretations of exile and return, see Fred Davidoff's account (Holt 229-230).

6. One notable exception is the 1952 Hawthorn Report from the U of British Columbia called *The Doukhobors of British Columbia*, which did attempt to address these concerns in some detail. Some recommendations, such as the repeal of legislation to limit Doukhobor voting rights, were followed but most recommendations regarding treatment of Freedomites were not.

7. To date, I have located two Freedomite prison diaries, the privately published Agassiz diary about the 1960s protests that I examine in this paper, and another by Alex Efanow from the 1930s or 1940s; the autobiography of Peter N. Maloff, produced as part of his requested statement for a 1952 commission about Freedomite activity; and two autobiographies by former Freedomite extremist Fred N. Davidoff. One of Davidoff's autobiographies appears as a chapter titled "Autobiography of a Fanatic" in Simma Holt's book, and one is handwritten and unpublished.

WORKS CITED

Althusser, Louis. "Ideology and Ideological State Apparatuses: Notes Toward an Investigation." *Lenin and Philosophy and Other Essays*. New York: Monthly Review, 1971. 127-87.

Bakhtin, M. M. "Forms of Time and Chronotope in the Novel." *The Dialogic Imagination*. Ed. Michael Holquist. Trans. Caryl Emerson and Holquist. Austin, TX: U of Texas P, 1981. 84-258.

Butler, Judith. *Excitable Speech: A Politics of the Performative*. New York/London: Routledge, 1997.

Chernenkoff, Mikhail i drugie [Mike E. Chernenkoff and Friends]. *Tyuremni Dnevnik; sobuitie i perezhivanie v Gornoi Tyurmye Agassiz, BC 1962-1969 [Prison Diary: Events and Experiences in Mountain Prison, Agassiz, BC 1962-1969]*. Crescent Valley, BC: Steve Lapshinoff, 1993.

Goldman, Anne E. *Take My Word: Autobiographical Innovations of Ethnic American Working Women*. Berkeley/Los Angeles: U of California P, 1996.

Hawthorne, Harry B., ed. *The Doukhobors of British Columbia*. Vancouver: UBC-Dent, 1955.

Holt, Simma. *Terror in the Name of God: The Story of the Sons of Freedom Doukhobors*. Toronto/Montreal: McClelland, 1964.

Janzen, William. *Limits on Liberty: The Experience of Mennonite, Hutterite and Doukhobor Communities in Canada*. Toronto: U of Toronto P, 1990.

Kaplan, Caren. "Resisting Autobiography: Out-Law Genres and Transnational Feminist Subjects." *De/Colonizing the Subject: The Politics of Gender in Women's Autobiography*. Ed. Sidonie Smith and Julia Watson. Minneapolis: Minnesota UP, 1992. 115-38.

Lacan, Jacques. *Écrits: A Selection*. Trans. Alan Sheridan. New York/London: Norton, 1977.

Lejeune, Philippe. *On Autobiography*. Ed. Paul John Eakin. Trans. Katherine Leary. Minneapolis: U of Minnesota P, 1989.

Maloff, Marie. Letter to the Editor. *Iskra* 1831 (March 1997): 27.

Nussbaum, Felicity. "Towards Conceptualizing Diary." Ed. James Olney. *Studies in Autobiography*. New York: Oxford UP, 1988. 128-40.

Padilla, Genaro. *My History, Not Yours: The Formation of Mexican American Autobiography*. Milwaukee, WI: U of Wisconsin P, 1993.

Smith, Sidonie. "Performativity, Autobiographical Practice, Resistance." *a/b: Auto/Biography Studies* 10.1 (Spring 1995): 17-33.

——. *Subjectivity, Identity, and the Body: Women's Autobiographical Practices in the Twentieth Century*. Bloomington/Indianapolis: Indiana UP, 1993.

Tarasoff, Koozma. *Plakun Trava: The Doukhobors*. Grand Forks, BC: Mir Pub. Soc., 1982.

Wong, Hertha Dawn. *Sending My Heart Back Across the Years: Tradition and Innovation in Native American Autobiography*. New York/Oxford: Oxford UP, 1992.

Woodcock, George, and Ivan Avakumovic. *The Doukhobors*. Toronto: McClelland, 1977.

Woodsworth, J. S. *Strangers Within Our Gates*. 1st ed. Toronto: U of Toronto P, 1909.

Biographies

Domenic A. Beneventi is currently completing a Ph.D. in Comparative Literature at the Université de Montréal. His thesis examines the construction of a symbolic urban landscape through the figure of the contemporary *flâneur*. His main research interests include urban representation, minority/ethnic writing, Canadian and Québécois literatures, and contemporary Italian literature.

Licia Canton has a Ph.D. in Canadian literature from Université de Montréal. Her articles on Italian-Canadian writing have appeared in *The Toronto Review of Contemporary Writing*, *Pillars of Lace: The Anthology of Italian-Canadian Women Writers* and *La Comunità*. She is editor of *The Dynamics of Cultural Exchange* (Cusmano, 2002) and *Antonio D'Alfonso: Essays on His Works* (Guernica, 2004). She has served on the executive of the Association of Italian-Canadian Writers as newsletter co-editor (1998-2000) and vice-president (2000-2002). She is currently working on a collection of short stories and a book on the Italian-Canadian novel.

Amaryll Chanady is Professor of comparative literature and departmental chair at the Université de Montréal. She has published mainly on marginalization, the construction of collective identity, multiculturalism, postcolonialism and Latin American literature and culture. Her publications include *Magical Realism and the Fantastic: Resolved versus Unresolved Antinomy* (NY and London: Garland), *Entre inclusion et exclusion: la symbolisation de l'Autre dans les Amériques* (Paris: Champion) and (as editor) *Latin American Identity and Constructions of Difference*.

Heike Harting obtained her doctoral degree in English from the University of Victoria. She holds a SSHRCC postdoctoral fellowship (and teaches) at the University of Western Ontario. Her present research examines narratives of ethnic civil war in the context of globalization theories and postcolonial studies. She is currently working on a book manuscript entitled "Unruly Metaphor: Nation, Body, and Performativity in Contemporary Diasporic Writing." Her essays on postcolonial fiction and drama have been published in a number of anthologies and in such journals as *Ariel* and *Third Text*.

Lucie Lequin is Associate Professor in the Département d'études françaises at Concordia University. Her articles and critical reviews have appeared in numerous periodicals and journals as well as in the *Dictionnaire des oeuvres littéraires du Québec*. With Maïr Verthuy she has published *Multi-culture, multi-écriture: la voix migrante au féminin en France et au Canada* (Paris: L'Harmattan, 1996). She has also collaborated on an anthology of migrant women authors, which will shortly be published by Nota Bene, as well as on a book titled *La francophonie sans frontière: une nouvelle cartographie de l'imaginaire au féminin*. She is currently working on a book on the issue of migrant women authors in Quebec. Her other areas of research are: the "francophonie," multiculture and history of women, literary essays as they relate to ethics and literature. She is a member of l'Association internationale des études québécoises. She is also director of her department.

Lianne Moyes is Associate Professor of English at Université de Montréal. She works on various forms of cross-border writing including fiction theory, bilingual writing, franco-Ontarian and anglo-Quebec writing. She also works on intertextual models of feminist literary history, and on contemporary feminist appropriations of the baroque. She is editor of *Gail Scott: Essays on Her Works* (Guernica, 2002) and since 1993 has been co-editor of the feminist periodical *Tessera*.

Daisy Neijmann received her Ph.D. from the Vrije Universiteit in Amsterdam. Her research interests are in the areas of cultural identity construction and transplantation, and nationalism/ethnicity and literature. From 1994 until 1999 she held the position in Icelandic-Canadian Studies at the Department of Icelandic at the University of Manitoba, and she is currently the Halldór Laxness Lecturer in Modern Icelandic at University College London. She has published widely in the area of Icelandic-Canadian literature, including a book on the contribution of Icelandic-Canadian writers to Canadian literature, and is presently editing a history of Icelandic literature and contributing to an anthology of Nordic Women Writers.

Julie Rak is an Assistant Professor of English at the University of Alberta. She has published work in *Textual Studies in Canada, biography: an interdisciplinary quarterly,* and *Canadian Poetry*. She is currently working on a manuscript about Doukhobor identity and autobiography.

Don Randall is an Assistant Professor of English Literature at Bilkent University in Ankara, Turkey. He has also held the SSHRCC Postdoctoral Fellowship in the Department of English, Queen's University at Kingston, and the Visiting Postdoctoral Fellowship of the Humanities Institute at the University of Calgary. His principal research is in Victorian and postcolonial literature and culture. He is the author of several articles in his field, including a paper in *Journal of Commonwealth and Postcolonial Studies*, which reads Ondaatje's *The English Patient* in relation to Kipling's *Kim*. Most recently, he has published his first book, *Kipling's Imperial Boy: Adolescence and Cultural Hybridity* (Palgrave, 2000).

Sherry Simon teaches in the Département d'études françaises at Concordia University. She is the author of *Le Trafic des langues* (Boréal, 1994), *Gender in Translation* (Routledge, 1996) and *Hybridité culturelle* (Ile de la tortue, 1999) and has most recently co-edited with Paul St-Pierre *Changing the Terms: Translating in the Postcolonial Era* (University of Ottawa Press, 2000).

Pamela Sing is Associate Professor at the Faculté St-Jean of the University of Alberta. She teaches French, Québécois, and Franco-Canadian literatures. Her publications include *Villages Imaginaires. Edouard Montpetit, Jacques Ferron et Jacques Poulin* (Montréal: Fides, 1995), and several articles, such as: "Jouissance et écriture ou la différence au féminin" (1997), "La voix métisse dans le roman de l'infidélité. Jacques Ferron, Marguerite Primeau et Nancy Huston" (1998), "Divinités, diables et autres bric-à-brac dans *Le Lys de Sang* de Georges Bugnet" (1999), and "L'Ouest et ses sauvagesses: écriture et prairie" (2001).

Christl Verduyn teaches Canadian literature, Canadian Studies, and Women's Studies at Wilfrid Laurier University, Waterloo. Her research interests include Canadian and Quebecois women's writing and criticism, multiculturalism, life writing and interdisciplinary approaches to literature. Her books include *Margaret Laurence: An Appreciation* (1988), *Dear Marian, Dear Hugh: The MacLennan-Engel Correspondence* (1995), *Lifelines: Marian Engel's Writing* (1995), *Literary Pluralities* (1998), *Marian Engel's Notebooks* (1999), *Aritha van Herk: Essays on Her Works* (2001) and *Silt* (2002). Before joining the faculty at Laurier in 2000, Christl Verduyn taught at Trent University, where she was founding chair of Women's Studies (1987-90), and chair of Canadian Studies (1993-99). She was president of the national Association for Canadian Studies (2000-2002).

Samara Walbohm is a Fourth Year Doctoral candidate at the University of Toronto. Her main literary interests include twentieth-century Canadian Fiction. Her projected thesis is entitled "Writing and Clubbing: Toronto women writers between the wars."